Scripture on the Silver Screen

Other books by Adele Reinhartz
from Westminster John Knox Press

Women's Bible Commentary, Expanded Edition (contributor)
Jesus, Judaism, and Christian Anti-Judaism: Reading the New Testament after the Holocaust (with Paula Fredriksen)

Scripture on the Silver Screen

Adele Reinhartz

Westminster John Knox Press
LOUISVILLE • LONDON

Scripture quotations, unless otherwise indicated, are from the New Revised Standard Version of the Bible, copyright © 1989 by the Division of Christian Education of the National Council of the Churches of Christ in the U.S.A., and used by permission.

Book design by Sharon Adams
Cover design © 2003 designpointinc.com

First edition
Published by Westminster John Knox Press
Louisville, Kentucky

This book is printed on acid-free paper that meets the American National Standards Institute Z39.48 standard. ⊗

PRINTED IN THE UNITED STATES OF AMERICA

03 04 05 06 07 08 09 10 11 12 — 10 9 8 7 6 5 4 3 2 1

Library of Congress Cataloging-in-Publication Data is on file at the Library of Congress, Washington, D.C.

ISBN 0-664-22359-1

To my students

"For our teachers, and their students, and all the students of their students, and for all those who engage in the study of Torah, whether in this place or in any other place. May they and you have great peace, grace, kindness, and mercy, long life, ample nourishment, and salvation from their Parent in heaven and earth, and let us say, Amen."

—"The Teachers' Kaddish," *Siddur Chaveirim Kol Yisrael*

Scripture on the Silver Screen

Acknowledgments

My thanks go out to many people:

To the students, friends, and relations who read portions of this book and helped out at various stages: Janet Bannister, Richard Corneil, Erich Engler, Paul Gallagher, Jennifer Nettleton, Carey Newman, Craig Perfect, Mikal Radford, Jan Willem van Henten, Miriam-Simma Walfish, Mordechai Walfish, and Benjamin Wright; to Dora Fischer for her keen proofreader's eye;

To Carey Newman, formerly of Westminster John Knox Press, and now of Baylor University, for suggesting this book, and to Gregory Glover, Julie Tonini, and their team at Westminster John Knox, for seeing it through;

To McMaster University and the Social Sciences and Humanities Research Council of Canada for their generous support of this project;

To my entire family of all generations, not only for their ever-present love and support but for their readiness to watch movies and talk about them with me. As always, a special thanks to my husband Barry, and my children Miriam-Simma, Mordechai, Shoshana, and Simcha, for whose presence in my life I give thanks daily.

Finally, to those who studied Bible and film with me formally—in Religious Studies 2YY3 at McMaster University—and to the many who have heard me lecture on this subject in Canada, the United States, Israel, and Europe, for their interest in this subject, their many insightful comments, and their excellent movie recommendations. It is to all of you that I dedicate this book.

Introduction

There was a time in our household when Cecil B. DeMille's *The Ten Commandments* (1956) was the hands-down favorite of the under-ten set, who viewed all 220 minutes of it several times a week. Even now, they can describe each scene in detail. They were enthralled with the grand vistas, the raw emotion, and the beautiful actors, but, above all, with how the film gave life to a story that they had heard told and retold since birth.

With the passing of the epic film genre, there have been relatively few feature films that explicitly set out to retell biblical narratives.[1] But the Bible has by no means disappeared from the cinema. In fact, every year sees growth in the inventory of mainstream commercial films in which the Bible appears, in roles great and small.

In some films, the Bible appears as a "prop" on the screen. In the 1993 comedy *Coneheads*, for example, an alien couple, newly arrived on Earth, explores the various items they find in their motel room. While the male Conehead, Beldar, samples the soup and toilet paper in the bathroom, his spouse, Prymaat, leafs through the Gideon's Bible she has found on the nightstand and laughs uproariously—not the response we might expect to a book that we commonly associate with solemn religious piety. By contrast, the main character in the 1996 drama *Sling Blade*, a so-called "retarded man" newly released from the state prison hospital, carries his Bible with him everywhere and treasures it not just for its contents but for its material presence in his life. On his release from the prison hospital, he meets a young boy named Frank. To Frank he gives his Bible, along with the rest of his small book collection, at the end of the film. In giving Frank his Bible, he gives him a part of himself, in order that Frank might continue to remember him and feel connected with him even after they must separate.

1

Just as explicit as the physical presence of a Bible on the screen is the use of direct biblical quotation. Spider Man's adoptive mother (*Spider Man*, 2002) recites Psalm 23 when she fears death at the hands of the Green Goblin. In *Liar, Liar,* Fletcher Reid, a smooth-talking lawyer, proclaims, "The Truth shall set you free" (John 8:32); in doing so, he pledges to stop lying for twenty-four hours in answer to his young son's fervent birthday wish.

Even more prevalent than biblical quotations are biblical allusions. Often these are verbal allusions to biblical phrases, people, and places. *The Matrix* (1999) has several prominent allusions: the holy city is called Zion, a biblical synonym for Jerusalem; the rebel space ship is the Nebuchadnezzar, the powerful Babylonian king whose armies conquered the Kingdom of Judah and destroyed Solomon's temple in 586 B.C.E. Another film rich in biblical allusion is *Deep Impact* (1998), in which the President of the United States launches Operation Noah's Ark to save the world from a deadly comet, an act accomplished by Space Mission Messiah.

Many films feature main characters who are explicitly modeled on one biblical character or another. Sister Agnes, the lead character in the 1985 film *Agnes of God*, is a Virgin Mary figure in her insistence that her baby, born in the convent, had no human father. The sexual behavior of Bess McNeill, the protagonist of the 1996 drama *Breaking the Waves*, initially recalls the traditional images associated with Mary Magdalene; by the end of the film, she is portrayed in Christ-like terms as she sacrifices herself to save her husband.

Biblical stories often form the basis of film narratives that on the surface are entirely unconnected to the Bible. This is true of at least some of the movies already mentioned; for example, *Deep Impact* has obvious affinities with the biblical flood story (Genesis 7), and *Agnes of God* with the Jesus' infancy narratives (Luke 1; Matthew 1). The classic horror film *Frankenstein* (1931) evokes (or subverts) the Genesis creation narratives in its focus on a scientist who hopes to usurp the divine role in the creation of human life. The animated film *The Lion King* (1994) features a Moses-like hero who flees the land of his birth, wanders in the desert, begins life anew in a foreign land, and is persuaded to return as leader after experiencing a theophany. Most prevalent, however, is the use of the Jesus story in stories of salvation and redemption, such as *Cool Hand Luke* (1967), *The Green Mile* (1999), as well as most of the films we have already mentioned (*Sling Blade, The Matrix, Deep Impact, Breaking the Waves*), all of which feature heroes who sacrifice themselves for the sake of others.

My interest in the movies is entirely amateur, in both senses of the term: I am an amateur in my pure and often uncritical enjoyment of movies, which are one of my favorite forms of entertainment (neck in neck with reading novels); and I am an amateur in the sense of professing no professional training or expertise. I am not a film critic, a professional student of film, or a scholar in film studies, nor am I a film maven who can rattle off actors, directors, and film plots by the dozen. Rather, I am a Bible scholar who has become particularly attuned to the frequent appearance of scripture on the silver screen. But only in recent years has it occurred to me to make some use of this fortuitous conjunction between my professional interests and my leisure-time pursuits. The impetus for doing so was initially circumstantial. In an effort to increase undergraduate enrollment in religious studies courses, the Department of Religious Studies in which I was teaching (at McMaster University) was encouraged to develop courses that would appeal to a broad range of students. Like many of my colleagues, I had already been using the occasional film in courses to good effect. Why not, I thought, structure an introductory Bible course systematically around film?

Beyond these pragmatic concerns, I soon saw strong pedagogical potential in a course like this. In particular, Hollywood provided obvious and welcome support for my ongoing campaign on behalf of biblical literacy. Surely the extensive and broad-ranging use of the Bible in popular films demonstrates how important it is that everyone know something about the Bible, or at least acquire some basic familiarity with its contents. As sacred canon, the Bible has an important and special role for many of us, both as individuals and as participants in Jewish and Christian communities. But for all of us, no matter our religious affiliations (or lack thereof), the Bible is a foundational document whose impact on Western history, culture, and society cannot be overestimated. Knowledge of the Bible is important not only for understanding the masterpieces of Western civilization; looking at Hollywood films through the lens of the Bible also reveals the importance of scripture for our ability to appreciate popular culture.

One of the biggest challenges in creating the course was not a dearth of films—in fact there is an embarrassment of riches—but the relative lack of secondary reading materials that focus specifically on the explicit use of the Bible in popular film. I learned much from the books that explore other, more subtle aspects of the interplay between the Bible and film, such as the work of Larry Kreitzer, who has studied the interconnections between biblical texts, selected works of Western literature, and the cinematic adaptations of those literary works[2]; Robert Jewett, who discusses and critiques a number of popular films from the point of view of Pauline theology[3]; and, most recently, the fascinating collection entitled *Screening Scripture: Intertextual Connections Between Scripture and Film*, edited by George Aichele and Richard Walsh.[4] Also useful were the articles in the on-line *Journal of Religion and Film* (www.unomaha.edu/~wwwjrf/), as well as the corpus of writings in religion and film more generally.[5] While all of these works contained discussions that were directly relevant to the material I was studying with my classes, I longed for a book that would focus specifically on the explicit role of the Bible—as distinct from biblical or religious themes—in popular film. Finally I decided to write my own.

For this book I chose twelve films that draw explicitly on a variety of biblical texts. The discussions are arranged according to the order in which the texts appear in the Christian canon. Given that most of these films draw on several biblical sources, I begin each chapter by citing a reference that provides an important entry point to the film as a whole. All biblical quotations in the superscriptions as well as in the body of the chapters are from the New Revised Standard Version, unless otherwise noted. Quoting from the films proved to be more complicated. For some films, there is a published shooting script, from which one could theoretically quote in the usual style used for print materials, were it not for the fact that the dialogue and even the order of the scenes in the film itself almost always diverge from the shooting script. The useful website "Screenplays for You" (http://sfy.iv.ru/) also provides shooting scripts, but these too are not identical to the films themselves. Unless otherwise noted, quotations from the films are taken from my own transcriptions.

A brief introduction to each chapter discusses the focal Bible passage and places it in its literary and historical context. This discussion is followed by a summary of the film and also, in some cases, a brief treatment of the film's main themes, to the extent that these are essential for comprehending the ways in which the film draws on the Bible. This summary provides the basis for a description and analysis of the film's use of the Bible. Despite the difficulty in teasing apart the many elements of any film (plot[s], themes, characters, dialogue, camera angle, etc.), I have divided this discussion of the film's use of the Bible into two sections (Plot and Character, and Themes). These sections will pay some attention to film techniques and devices but only where they seem essential to the discussion. Brief concluding remarks round off each chapter.

I have attempted to write these chapters accessibly, both for those who have seen the film and for those who have not, though it is my hope that readers will be encouraged both to view the films and to read the biblical books to which they refer. The analyses in each chapter present my own reading of the films, occasionally aided by reviews and other secondary materials where such exist. They do not, however, exhaust the topic, nor do they represent the only way that the film and its biblical components can be read. Rather, they are intended to pique the reader's interest and to provide a starting point for reflection and discussion, whether by individual readers, students in formal university or college courses, or participants in less formal youth and adult education settings. Above all, I hope that this book will serve as an argument in favor of biblical literacy. Though the Coneheads and the sling-blade-swinging Karl should not be our role models, we would do well to follow their example in one regard, to open up our Bibles and read.

1

The Truman Show and the Great Escape from Paradise (Genesis)

And the LORD God planted a garden in Eden, in the east; and there he put the man whom he had formed.

Genesis 2:8

INTRODUCTION

In North American urban society, leaving home is seen as an inevitable or even desirable event in the lives of families. Whether for educational or professional opportunities, for marriage, or for sheer adventure, young people part from their parents and strike out on their own. Parents, in turn, greet this development with a variety of emotions—acceptance, trepidation, relief. Some parents encourage or even force their children out of the house; others resist their departure with all the means at their disposal.

But leave-taking is not a feature of modern life alone. The Bible presents so many examples of this theme that such departures must surely have been a feature of ancient Israelite society as well. Genesis 3 is the quintessential biblical story of leaving home. In this story, Adam and Eve, offspring of God—if not God's children in the human biological sense—leave the garden of Eden, their home and haven since their creation. But their departure is not of their own volition. Rather, it is God who expels them, for they have disobeyed. In leaving the garden, Adam and Eve enter the realm of responsibility, just as young people today do when they leave home. For the primordial couple, their departure from the garden requires them to labor for their food and to bring children into the world.

The expulsion story does not stand alone; it follows two biblical accounts of the world's creation. In the first story, Genesis 1:1–2:4a,[1] God creates the world and all living species, including humankind, in the space of six days. First he[2] creates the physical world: the heavens and the earth—light, day, sky, earth, and seas. He then populates the earth, the heavens, and the seas by creating vegetation, stars, sun, moon, birds, fish, and animals. Finally, "God created humankind in his image, in the image of God he created them; male and female he created them"; he blessed them, ordered them to "be fruitful and multiply," and gave them dominion over the other creatures (Gen. 1:27–28). On the seventh day he rested.

This account is not a story at all but the description of a process. We never learn what, if anything, happened in this apparently static world, for this description of creation is immediately followed by a second account (Gen. 2:4b–3:24) in which God first creates the earth and heavens, and then a male human being. God plants the garden "in the east" (2:8), causes the trees to grow and the rivers to flow, and places the man in the garden so that he might tend it. God then creates the animal species and, finally, a woman, from the body of the man.

After the woman appears on the scene, the story moves inexorably forward to its end point, their departure from the garden. God allows his human creatures free access to everything in the garden except for one thing, the fruit of the tree of knowledge of good and evil (2:17). In Eden, ignorance truly is bliss. Surely this restriction is a small price to pay for the privilege and luxury of living in Eden. But apparently not. When the wily serpent comes along and tempts the woman to eat the luscious fruit, she does not hesitate. She eats it and offers some to the man, who eats as well. The consequences of disobedience are not long in coming. The serpent is reduced to crawling on his belly and eating dust; he is despised by the woman, and, forever, by all of humankind (3:14–15). The man is saddled with the labor of tilling the soil; the woman, with the labor of giving birth.[3] From the point of view of Adam and Eve, as they are now called,[4] the departure from the garden is not a welcome development. On the other hand, what kind of a story can there be without conflict, pain, and death? By populating the world and fending for themselves, Adam and Eve also create the opportunity for the multiple and complex relationships and situations that are the stuff of story and of life itself.

Modern source critics see the presence of two different creation stories as key evidence that the book of Genesis and indeed the Pentateuch as a whole are derived from different sources that stem from different periods of time, represent different political and religious interests, and employ different vocabularies.[5] But ancient readers saw the stories as being of a piece and accounted for their differences in a variety of ways.[6]

Similarly, artistic works that draw on the Genesis accounts will use one, the other, or both. Indeed, the creation accounts have been represented and interpreted in every art form, including film. The apple, taken popularly to be the fruit of the forbidden tree,[7] is a ubiquitous symbol of temptation.[8] Many films, from *Frankenstein* (1931) to *Blade Runner* (1997), meditate on the creation of the human species; they draw on the creation accounts to reflect on the essence of humanity and what it is that distinguishes human beings from other created beings, whether biological or mechanical. In this chapter, we will look at a film that not only uses particular images from both creation stories but, more fundamentally, adopts and adapts the narrative structure of the second creation narrative for its own purposes.

FILM SUMMARY

The Truman Show, directed by Peter Weir, is a movie about a television show (also called *The Truman Show*), its star (Truman, played by Jim Carrey), its creator (Christof, played by Ed Harris), and its viewers (millions of people the world over). *The Truman Show* series is the world's "longest running documentary soap opera," a hybrid genre that capitalizes on the ongoing popularity of soap operas as well as on the current trend towards "reality TV."[9] Broadcasting live, seven days a week, twenty-four hours a day, *The Truman Show* depicts the daily life of Truman Burbank as he gets up in the morning, clowns around in front of the bathroom mirror, sets off for work, and engages in all the ordinary tasks of day-to-day life. The show has a huge and faithful following that watches Truman continuously, even obsessively, in private from their living rooms, kitchens, and bathrooms; and in public, from specialty bars and restaurants.

The Truman Show differs from other television programming not only in its 24/7 coverage, but also in the fact that Truman is oblivious to his television role. Nor does he realize that his home, Seahaven Island, is not a "real" place but rather an elaborate made-for-TV set, a television town built on a giant parcel of land in Burbank, California, and outfitted with five-thousand concealed mini-cameras that capture and broadcast Truman's activities in every nook and cranny.[10] The entire set is covered over by a great dome. Christof and his crew sit in a giant "moon" in this "sky." From his broadcast satellite, Christof masterminds every aspect of Seahaven and micromanages every detail of Truman's life. Truman's "parents," his "wife," and his "best friend" are all actors who presumably have real lives—including real friends, lovers, spouses, and children—off set. They come Truman's way not by virtue of the natural processes of human affection and connection that we in our culture consider to be the basis of these bonds, but rather through the choices made by Christof and his team.[11] The television show requires that all the participants, from Truman's "family" and "friends" to the dozens of technicians behind the scenes, collude in keeping Truman ignorant of the fundamental facts of his own existence. The population of Seahaven, actors all, has concealed the truth from Truman for almost thirty years, from his birth and adoption by the OmniCam Corporation, through a difficult childhood torn by his father's drowning death, to his thirtieth year, the point at which the film begins.[12]

Truman takes this world for granted. He does not suspect the truth about his idyllic environment and his own role within it until a series of inexplicable occurrences prods him to examine the details of his life more closely than he has ever done before. A studio lamp suddenly falls out of the clear, blue sky. An elevator door opens to reveal a television crew on their coffee break. A severe rainstorm follows Truman around the beach much as a spotlight follows an actor on stage. From a flashback, we learn that Truman had missed a previous opportunity to learn the truth. Several years earlier, while he was still in college, a young woman, "Lauren" (whose real name is Sylvia) had attempted to reveal to Truman the fundamental facts of his own existence. But before she could tell all, a man posing as her father appeared out of nowhere and whisked her off the scene, never to return. Truman still pines for her but, until this recent spate of strange events, he did not ponder, let alone comprehend, what she had tried to tell him.

"Lauren's" attempt may have failed to register with Truman because he was not yet able to look beyond the surface of his own situation. A more recent breach of protocol on the part of a (former) cast member, by contrast, has an immediate effect on Truman: the unscripted resurrection of Truman's dead "father." Truman is thrilled to know that his father is alive after all, but "Kirk's" reappearance raises an even more frightening specter, that the tragedy that had shaped Truman's life was a fiction.

Truman's increasing determination to learn the truth prompts his evermore daring attempts to leave the island. These attempts are met by correspondingly frantic efforts on the part of Christof and his crew to keep Truman in ignorance and on Seahaven. Initially, Truman merely fantasizes about leaving; he then tries conventional modes of departure—plane, ferry, bus, and car. Stymied at every turn in bizarre and spectacular ways (a sudden shortage of airline tickets, the eruption of a brush fire, a nuclear plant disaster), he realizes that he cannot simply leave. He must escape! One night, Truman succeeds in eluding the cameras; he takes to the high seas in a small boat and prevails in a major storm. But, to his surprise, he does not reach a distant shore. Instead, he bumps into the artificial dome that is Seahaven's sky. Far from escaping into the wild, blue yonder, he has merely reached the far wall of the set. But all is not lost, for the wall is equipped with a staircase. Now fully aware of the truth, Truman climbs the stairs, opens the door, and walks through the wall into the real world.

USE OF THE BIBLE

Plot and Character

The basic plot structure of *The Truman Show* movie closely parallels that of the second creation account in Genesis 2:4b–3:24. Both stories feature a creator who is inherently larger than life (God) or believes that he is (Christof), and a man who is created, either literally (Adam) or socially (Truman) for the purposes of living in the perfect world that the creator has fashioned (Eden, Seahaven). In both cases, the man rebels against his creator; Adam eats the fruit that God has forbidden to him, and Truman escapes Christof's control.

In a more fundamental way, however, *The Truman Show* reverses certain key elements of the Genesis account. Adam's presumed reluctance to leave Eden contrasts with Truman's eagerness to leave Seahaven.[13] Whereas God drives Adam out of the garden, Truman propels himself out of Seahaven. In leaving Eden, Adam does not leave God's purview, for God is universal. By contrast, in leaving Seahaven, Truman effectively escapes all further control by and contact with Christof, who, after all, is not God but merely a television producer. If Genesis revolves around human disobedience and God's response, the film focuses on Truman's struggle for autonomy. Although Truman's departure from Seahaven is fraught with difficulty and uncertainty, it nevertheless fulfills his childhood desires and adult aspirations.

Even where it diverges and contrasts with Genesis 2–3, however, *The Truman Show* weaves the biblical creation accounts into its narrative, visual, and auditory fields. Structural parallels are signaled and reinforced by the film's numerous allusions to the Genesis accounts. Seahaven, like the garden in Genesis, is flawless—always sunny, always clean, and conspicuously free from the social ills of poverty and homelessness. A true paradise! Truman's "friends," as well as the local media, do not miss an opportunity to remark on Seahaven's perfection. As Truman drives to work, the morning radio host jovially proclaims that it's "another beautiful day in Paradise, folks." One of his "coworkers" at the insurance company points out a local newspaper headline that reads, "The Best Place on Earth." As in the Hollywood epics, Seahaven boasts a magnificent sunrise and sunset: wide-open skies with a beam of clear light poking through the fluffy clouds.[14] Only the divine hand could have created this paradise on Earth. So says Truman's "friend" Marlon, who, admiring the sunset, exclaims, "That's the 'Big Guy!' Quite a paintbrush he's got." True enough, but this "big guy" in the sky is not God but Christof, who is responsible for every single element of the elaborate set that is Seahaven.

The parallels between the garden of Eden and Seahaven Island go beyond such details, however. The biblical stories do not provide insight into God's motivations for creating the world or the garden within it. But they do imply two crucial points: that the world was created for the benefit of humankind, and that God gave considerable forethought to the essential ingredients of this world. In a similar fashion, Seahaven is a constructed world whose creator has paid meticulous attention to its every detail. Seahaven differs from the garden of Eden in that its principal inhabitant, Truman ("True man"), was not created by Christof but adopted by the corporation that sponsors the television world in which he is placed. But just as God in Genesis 2:8 places the first human being within the garden that God has created, Christof places Truman within a world that Christof himself has fashioned. Just as God remarks that this creation is "good," (Gen. 1:4, 10, 12, 18, 21, 25) and even "very good" (1:31), so does Christof repeatedly declare that Seahaven is the best place on Earth for Truman. Both the Genesis story and the film contrast the ideal world that the creator created and the real world as it has developed and changed throughout human history. From the point of view of both creators, their world is far superior to the real world in which the readers of Genesis and the viewers of *The Truman Show* (the soap and the film) must live. In paradise, human needs are met fully and with little human effort. Immortality, or, at least, freedom from mortal danger, is guaranteed.

The similarities between God's world and Christof's island imply an analogy between the two creators themselves, in relation both to the created world and to the human being who stands at its center. Christof's role both parallels and contrasts with that of God in the biblical creation narratives. Like God, he is known publicly as the creator of an all-encompassing world. Christof is identified as creator both implicitly and explicitly. According to the television show's opening credits, Christof is not the director or producer of *The Truman Show* so much as its creator. A television talk show host announces "a rare and exclusive interview with the [Truman] show's conceiver and creator." In his first and only direct conversation with Truman, Christof describes himself as the "creator . . . of a television series that brings hope and joy to millions." The pregnant pause that Christof inserts after the word "creator" invites a comparison between himself and God, the "Big Guy." Like God, Christof creates through the word. Just as God dispels the darkness by creating light, so does Christof, lamenting the darkness that hampers the nocturnal search for the escaped Truman. "Cue the sun," commands Christof, much as God had once proclaimed "Let there be light" (Gen. 1:10). And, like God, Christof unleashes a major rainstorm when his creation does not conform to the behavior that he requires (Genesis 7).

Adam, the one for whom the garden was created, provides the prototype for Truman, for whom Seahaven was created. The relationship between Christof and Truman is therefore analogous to that drawn in the book of Genesis between God and Adam. Brief visual references to Michelangelo's painting on the domed ceiling of the Sistine Chapel accentuate this parallel. In the scene commonly known as "The Creation of Man," God and Adam reach out to touch each other's hands but their fingers do not quite meet. Similarly, the camera occasionally lingers on the hand of Christof, as he lovingly and gently caresses the television monitor, a medium through which he can reach out but not quite touch *his* "Adam."[15] Yet another allusion to this image occurs after Truman's escape; the camera focuses on Truman's hand as he reaches out to touch the "sky" and realizes that it is the hard, painted surface of the set's wall, as illusory as Michelangelo's sky, painted on the hard, domed ceiling of the Sistine Chapel.

In both the Bible and the movie, ignorance and obedience are conditions of remaining in paradise. As long as he obeys God and refrains from eating the forbidden fruit, Adam will remain ignorant of the knowledge of good and evil, and he can remain in the garden. As long as he remains ignorant of the existence of *The Truman Show* and his starring role within it, Truman can, indeed must, stay on Seahaven and, unwittingly, dance to Christof's tune. In Genesis, God's command not to eat of the fruit of the tree of knowledge of good and evil signals to the reader the likelihood that sooner or later humankind will disobey. Truman's narrative also moves relentlessly towards its final moment, the departure of the True Man from the perfect world. In the film, as in Genesis 3, this departure is a consequence of newly gained knowledge that the creator had intended to withhold. For Truman, this is not knowledge of good and evil per se so much as knowledge about, or, more precisely, understanding of the truth of the artificial world in which he lives. Whereas God deplores and punishes humankind's disobedience but does not step in to prevent it, Christof determines every detail of Truman's life. God allows humankind fundamental autonomy, even when expressed as disobedience, whereas Christof's entire project rests on Truman's lack of autonomy.

Themes

Knowledge and Escape

The main plot line of the film focuses on Truman's attempts to leave Seahaven and to experience the world beyond this "paradise." His success, however, would spell the end of Christof's world, that is, of the television show, for in leaving Seahaven Truman would also learn the truth about his life. Thus *The Truman Show* television series, the reason for Seahaven's existence, would cease should Truman learn the truth. Its continuation, therefore, depends on Truman's ongoing ignorance.

When asked why Truman "has never come close to discovering the true nature of his world," Christof replies with a reflection about human nature itself: "We accept the reality of the world with which we are presented." But Truman's unawareness of his starring role in a television soap opera is not due simply to the human propensity to accept our known reality as a given; it also depends on Christof's deliberate efforts to keep him from straying from Seahaven. Christof achieves control over Truman in many ways, but principal among them is to inculcate in Truman a profound fear of large bodies of water. Until his thirtieth year, this fear made it impossible for Truman to leave Seahaven Island for even a short jaunt. Although he frequently sits on the beach alone or with his friend Marlon, he is afraid of entering the water, of traversing the water in a boat or ferry, or even of crossing a bridge by foot or by car. Christof created this fear by orchestrating his "father's" death by drowning during a fierce storm. Truman, a mere child, was with his father at the time.

Flashbacks reveal just how profoundly this tragedy and his inability to prevent it have troubled Truman throughout his life. Truman accepts the finality of his father's death, just as he accepts every other aspect of his life in Seahaven. But one day a strange thing happens. Truman sees an old, shabbily dressed man in the streets of Seahaven and immediately recognizes his father. As Truman approaches him, the man is hustled away by two people who appear out of nowhere; a crowd quickly interposes itself to prevent Truman from catching up. Later that day, Truman tells his mother all about it. She dismisses the possibility that the man might really have been Truman's father and opines, "You're just feeling bad because of what happened, you sailing off into that storm. But I've never blamed you, Truman, and I don't blame you now." This speech is meant ostensibly to reassure Truman, but the oily tone and the words themselves simply reinforce the guilt and fear that are intended to keep Truman on the island.

The sudden and unexpected appearance of Truman's "father" prompts a change in the script, one of the few that have been occasioned by actions beyond Christof's direct control. Rather than force the old man to disappear again, Christof brings him back for a tearful reunion with his son, to the accompaniment of a sentimental soundtrack. Not only the viewing audience, in bars and homes around the world, but also Christof and his crew, in their satellite station in the heavens above Seahaven, are visibly moved. The reunion, however, marks the beginning of the end of Truman's life on Seahaven. The return of his father requires Truman to rewrite his own biography;

if his father did not really die, then Truman no longer needs to feel morally responsible for his death. He also need not fear the water that perpetually reminds him of that traumatic event. And if he no longer fears water, he is no longer trapped on the island of Seahaven.

The first step towards freedom requires Truman to elude, at least temporarily, the many cameras that record his every move. Truman's dramatic escape from his house on Seahaven playfully reenacts another cinematic prison break: Andy Dufresnes's escape from Shawshank Prison in the 1994 movie *The Shawshank Redemption*. Andy escapes from Shawshank by slowly, patiently, and laboriously picking a hole in the cell wall. He keeps the growing hole covered with a poster of one voluptuous movie actress after another (Rita Hayworth, Marilyn Monroe, and Raquel Welch), until it is finally large enough for him to fit through. When Andy's absence is discovered at roll call on the morning after his escape, the prison warden furiously rips the poster off the wall, stares in utter disbelief at the gaping hole, and then pokes his head through it to view Andy's escape route. This scene is replayed, with slight variations, in *The Truman Show*. Truman also has a poster that represents freedom and desire: a map of Fiji and the South Pacific. This map hangs from the ceiling but covers a substantial portion of one wall of Truman's basement recreation room. Truman's "buddy" Marlon, who, like everyone else in Truman's life, is not only an actor but also, perforce, a jailor, discovers that Truman is gone. He frantically pulls on the string that rolls the map back up, sees the closet door, a ladder, and the debris. He then looks up and sees the hole marking Truman's escape route. The allusion to *The Shawshank Redemption* identifies Seahaven, Christof's paradise, as Truman's prison, whose walls, invisible as they are to Truman, both protect and confine him, as do the bars on the infant Truman's playpen, "captured" in a photograph in his "mother's" album.

Truman's escape is not only a prison break. It is also, more positively, the fulfillment of a lifelong desire to travel and to explore the world. The film traces this desire back to Truman's childhood. As a young schoolboy, he announces his intentions to be an explorer when he grows up, an intention strongly discouraged by his teachers. His desires remain alive, however, and focus on Fiji, where he (mistakenly) believes his college love, "Lauren," to be living.

Truman repeatedly discusses his travels plans with his "wife," Meryl, who is most unsympathetic, and with his "friend" Marlon, who, more subtly, responds by extolling the virtues of Seahaven. Truman's efforts to leave come to naught until the fateful night of his escape from the camera's ubiquitous eye. Truman reappears in the one place that Christof never thought to look, on the high seas. Having overcome his fear of the water, he has now become the adventurous explorer of his dreams. Again, this theme is reinforced by a number of clues. Truman's sailboat is called the Santa Maria, recalling the fleet of that most famous explorer, Christopher Columbus. Unlike Columbus, who challenged the commonly held view that the world was flat and hence had no edge, Truman reaches the end of his known world abruptly when he bumps into the blue wall at the back of the set.[16] This experience provides the final piece in the puzzle, confirming what Truman had begun to suspect: the artificiality, or "flatness," of Seahaven and the centrality of his own role within it. Armed with this knowledge, he is now able simply to climb up the stairs and leave the set forever, thereby defying the will of his creator. Like Adam, Truman can never return to the paradise that the creator had wrought for him. Whether the biblical Adam longed to return to Eden we do not know; Truman views the finality of his departure not as punishment but as triumph and liberation. As film critic Kenneth Turan notes, this film satisfies in vintage Hollywood fashion by providing us with a hero who must "live free or die" and by portraying, yet again, the "indomitability" of the human spirit.[17]

Television

The Bible has invited countless readers to look in on the lives of its characters, beginning with the primordial human being. Similarly, *The Truman Show* soap opera, like any movie or television show, invites its audience to view the lives of its characters. Television, according to some of its critics, encourages escapism; TV is simply a mindless distraction from the real world and the human situation. This criticism is implied by the plot of *The Truman Show* (the movie) as it celebrates Truman's escape from the television soap. As the film's audience, however, we are in an ambiguous position. As viewers of the film, we understand the truth long before Truman does. We recognize the film's basic premise early on, although we only gradually realize the magnitude of Truman's situation. Thus we are privy to the backstage discussions and crisis management that surround Truman's escapades and feel both joy and relief when Truman finally attains the knowledge that we have already achieved. We celebrate his escape from an artificially perfect paradise into the rough and tumble of our own realities.

At the same time, we viewers have another, less conventional role to play as the audience of Christof's television show *The Truman Show*. The first frames of the film place us immediately in this position by having Christof address the viewers directly. Christof's prologue is followed by footage of Truman's morning encounter with his mirror image in the bathroom, interspersed with opening credits as well as brief interviews with the actors who play Truman's wife, Meryl, and his best friend, Marlon. It takes us a moment to realize that this introduction, including the opening credits, pertain not to the producer, director, and actors in the film, but to the creator and the actors in the television show. This opening scene places the movie audience in the same position as the television viewers within the movie, whose reactions to the plot and characters are periodically shown on screen. The television audience within the movie parodies the popularity of the daily soaps but also mirrors, perhaps even prescribes, our own reactions to the ins and outs of Truman's daily life. Movie viewers therefore juggle two roles. At the same time as they view the television show alongside the television audience depicted in the film, they also watch themselves (via their counterparts in the film) watching the television show. This dual perspective criticizes our own role as consumers of entertainment at the same time as it reinforces that role by providing good entertainment itself.

In portraying the TV viewers' absorption with *The Truman Show*, this movie gently mocks our tendency to ascribe reality to the crafted, manipulated, and manipulative world of television.[18] In his prologue, Christof himself reflects on the play between craft and reality. "While the world that Truman inhabits is in some respects counterfeit," says Christof, "there is nothing fake about Truman himself—no scripts, no cue cards. It isn't always Shakespeare, but it's genuine. It's a life." According to Marlon, "It's all true. It's all real. Nothing here is fake. Nothing you see on this show is fake. It's merely controlled." Marlon's protestations themselves may be intended to reinforce Christof's own evaluation of the show, but they also raise the viewer's suspicions that in fact *everything* may be fake. Christof's first and only direct conversation with Truman, near the end of the film, addresses even more explicitly the conflict between the fake and the real. Christof, slow to admit defeat, tries to persuade the newly empowered Truman that "there is no more truth out there than there is in the world I created for you." To take Christof seriously on this score would imply that, for the television viewer as well, there is no more truth in the real world than there is in the television world circumscribed by the small screen.[19]

Numerous details contribute to *The Truman Show*'s affectionate critique of television. The main street of Seahaven itself looks uncannily like Main Street in Disneyland, with its immaculately clean, bricked roads, relentless sunshine, and ritualized joviality. The characters within the television show, with the exception of Truman himself, are named after famous movie stars: his friend is Marlon (Brando); his wife, Meryl (Streep); his father, Kirk (Douglas); his mother, Angela (Lansbury); and his would-be girlfriend, Lauren (Bacall). Lauren's last name in the show is Garland, an obvious allusion to *The Wizard of Oz*, another fabulously imagined alternate world in which escape—in this case, Dorothy's return home to Kansas—is a key theme. The family name Burbank—named after the location in California that has the highest concentration of movie studios—says it all. According to the backstory, the president and CEO of the OmniCam Corporation, the media conglomerate that produces *The Truman Show*, is called Moses, evoking that DeMille epic *The Ten*

Commandments.[20] Even the streets of Seahaven, such as Lancaster Plaza and DeMille Street, are named after actors and directors.

Also present are some of the economic elements of commercial television. Clearly, *The Truman Show* is a big-budget television program with a huge, global audience. Presumably it is also highly lucrative, not through commercials, of which there are none, but through product placement. As Christof boasts, everything on the show is for sale, from the actors' clothes to the houses they live in. The show does not content itself with the relatively subtle version in which brand names of products and appliances are shown briefly on the screen. Rather, Meryl periodically turns directly to the cameras and rhapsodizes about the qualities of specific brands and products, often at the least appropriate times. In the mist of the final, very tense, and potentially violent confrontation between Truman and Meryl, she flashes the housewifely smile of the 1950s television commercial and, speaking directly to the camera, offers, "Why don't you let me fix you some of this Mococo drink? All natural cocoa beans from the upper slopes of Mount Nicaragua, no artifical sweeteners." Even Truman, who has lived his whole life among these short scenes, is puzzled. "What the hell are you talking about?" he shouts. The disjunction between the emotional tenor of the scene and her brightly articulated advertising message is humorous to the movie audience, if not necessarily to the television audience portrayed in the film.[21]

Like *The Truman Show* film, the creation accounts in the Bible focus attention on the "constructedness" of the world as we know it. Of course, the emphasis in Genesis is not on the artificiality of our world but on the universal power of its creator. Yet while the garden that God creates is natural, it is also inaccessible to all ordinary mortals except through the medium of narrative, just as Seahaven is inaccessible to all but Truman and Christof's hired actors except through the medium of television.

Escape as Liberation

The notion that Truman's departure from Seahaven is not punishment but liberation is conveyed subtly by yet another set of biblical allusions and images, namely, those associated with Jesus as portrayed in the Gospels and in Christian tradition. Like Jesus, Truman is approximately thirty years old. Like Jesus, Truman quite literally walks on water when he steps off his sailboat after surviving Christof's major storm, and he is crucified, figuratively, if not literally, to serve his "father's" purposes.

Truman's "crucifixion" is foreshadowed in an early scene in which he steps in front of a bus and then stands in the middle of the intersection, arms outstretched, stopping all traffic around him. His shadow on the road's surface uncannily takes the classic shape of Christ on the cross.[22] His "real" crucifixion and resurrection occur at the climax of the film, which is a passion narrative of sorts. Just as the Gospels ascribe a role to God in the death of his Son, so does the film place responsibility for Truman's final trial upon Christof. When Christof sees that Truman has overcome his fear of the water and is determined to sail away from Seahaven, he unleashes a tempest of epic proportions. This storm recalls a variety of biblical storms: the one that Noah and his ark full of people and animals survive (Genesis 6–9; cf. 1 Peter), the one that Jesus stills (Matt. 8:24; Mark 4:37), as well as the storm that accompanies Jesus' crucifixion as portrayed in the epic *Ben Hur*. As wind and rain lash Truman's tiny boat, the fragile vessel capsizes and plunges Truman into the water in an eerie replay of his father's ostensible death by drowning. Truman, who has lashed himself to the boat, emerges from the water after what seems like an eternity and hangs over its railing in cruciform position. Is Truman dead? No! Truman's crucifixion, like that of Jesus, merely heralds his triumphant departure from the world as he has known it to a fuller, more complete life. Truman comes to, sputters, and continues on his way.

Just as Jesus' crucifixion and resurrection overshadow the last section of each Gospel, so also do Truman's life-threatening trials and tribulations hang over this film from the moment Marlon uncovers Truman's escape from the basement of his house. The possibility that Truman may have died is voiced by viewers the world over; we eavesdrop on one telephone conversation in which a French spokesperson reassures a caller, "Il n'est pas mort" ("He is not dead"). The television crew, from Christof's producers down to the technicians, is afraid and horrified that Christof may kill Truman in the violent storm that he unleashed. Truman's resuscitation and his final victory over Christof are cheered by the millions of viewers who have been following his life from day one. These allusions to Jesus and the passion narrative identify Truman's departure as liberation rather than punishment, in contrast to Adam's departure in the Genesis account, whose structure is paralleled within the plot of the film as a whole.

One element that binds this "Jesus" thread to the "Genesis" thread we have already traced is the filial relationship implied in each of the biblical accounts. In his letter to the Romans, the apostle Paul describes Adam as a "type" of "the one who is to come" (Rom. 5:14; cf. 5:12–21). The Gospel of Luke also draws a direct line from Adam to Jesus; his genealogy places Jesus as the final link in the human chain that began with Adam, who, like Jesus, was the son of God (Luke 3:23–38).

Truman is the son of Christof much as Adam and Jesus are sons of God. In none of these cases is the son a product of the father's biological procreative or generative powers. God creates Adam from earth and breath (Gen. 2:7). The infancy narratives of Matthew and Luke imply a nearly biological relationship between God and Jesus that is parallel but not identical to that of a human father and son. In the Gospel of John, on the other hand, the origins of the father-son relationship are not recounted; Jesus is portrayed as preexisting in the father's realm before he is sent into the world, but once there, incarnate, he is described preeminently as God's Son (John 1:14).[23] The Gospel of Mark implies that God adopted Jesus as his son at the baptism, and all four Gospels connect this act with God's declaration that Jesus is his beloved son.

But the origin of the father-son relationship is not the crucial element in the bond between God and Adam, on the one hand, and God and Jesus, on the other. Rather, the main point concerns the ways in which this relationship comes to expression throughout the lifetime of the "son." In both cases, God expects obedience from his son. Adam is to mind the garden and to refrain from eating the fruit of the tree of knowledge of good and evil; Jesus is to do God's will, to mediate between God and humankind, and to offer the world salvation through knowledge of God.

These elements are present in the relationship between Christof and Truman. Though Truman was clearly born in the normal way, he was chosen by Christof at birth and was adopted by the corporation that sponsored the show. Although Christof is not Truman's father in any biological or even adoptive sense, he loves him and takes the same pride in Truman as if he were his "real" father: Christof beams as he recalls Truman's first tooth, his first steps, his first day at school. He caresses the screen as if he were caressing Truman; he gives considered thought to every event that Truman will experience and engineers his every human encounter.

Like God (and the preexistent Christ whom his name recalls), Christof lives in the heavens above Truman's world and does not have direct, face-to-face contact with him. Nor does Christof communicate directly with Truman. Thus, in contrast to both Adam and Christ, who knew and spoke with their divine father, Truman is completely unaware of Christof's existence until the very end of the film. Only after Truman sails away from the island does he fully realize that there is a conscious, external power acting on him. When Christof unleashes the storm, Truman cries out, "Is that the best you can do? You're gonna have to kill me!" Truman may think he is raging at the heavens, but we know that a mere mortal (the technician) is up in the satellite working the weather controls on Christof's direct orders. Truman becomes aware of Christof only after the storm is over, when he hears Christof as the deep, masculine "voice of God" of the old-style documentaries, identifying himself as the creator of Truman's world. But by this point, Christof has lost all his power over Truman. Christof's invisibility to Truman adds irony to Truman's last words to Christof: "In case I don't *see* you, good afternoon, good evening, and good night" (emphasis added), the words with which Truman used to greet his

Seahaven neighbors every morning as he set off for work. Whereas Adam exemplifies the son who succumbs to temptation, and Christ epitomizes the son who is obedient even unto death, Truman actively rebels against his father by seeking to escape the world his father has created for him.

Finally, the use of Jesus imagery suggests that there may be yet another biblical verse lurking in the background of this film: John 8:32, in which Jesus declares, "You will know the truth, and the truth will make you free." Without the truth, Truman would not have been able to rid himself of the fear of water that had trapped him for so long on Seahaven nor would he have been able to resist the temptation to remain in the safe world that Christof had created for him. Although John 8:32 is not quoted in the film, it succinctly summarizes Truman's quest and the inextricable link that he makes between knowledge of the truth and his ability to escape his limited and artificial life.

Move from Dependence to Autonomy

This comedy encourages us to consider our society's and our individual relationship to television, Hollywood, and the entire media industry as it traces Truman's efforts to leave the island. But the film also goes beyond these specific themes to make a statement about human psychological and emotional development. Truman's departure from Seahaven is not only his escape from the fishbowl of television and his liberation from the oppressive authority of Christof. It also constitutes a progressive move from dependency to autonomy, from accepting the reality of his world to questioning it, from living a scripted existence to constructing a life for himself. The film illustrates the popular notion that our progress from childhood through adolescence to adult maturity entails the movement from the safety and control of our parents to the risk and adventure of autonomy.

Truman's desire to leave Seahaven and to explore the world is identified as immature by his "wife," Meryl. When he suggests that they take their savings and travel, she responds, in a voice dripping with condescension, "You're talking like a teenager. . . . Honey, you want to be an explorer. This will pass. We all think like this now and then." We too might see Truman's impulse as pure escapism were it not for the fact that it runs parallel to the more serious psychological theme of the struggle between dependency and autonomy.

The movement from childhood to adulthood is signaled by Truman's wardrobe. While he is a resident of Seaheaven, Truman dresses like an overgrown child, in short pants and plaid shirts that are ill-fitting and ill-matching. It is only on the high seas that he dresses as a mature and sober adult, in grey pants and sweater. This change of clothing symbolizes the notion that he is finally experiencing maturity and harmony. He has made an autonomous decision, figured out what is happening in his life, escaped the endless scrutiny under which he has lived all his life, and, most important, overcome his fear of the water. This is indicated in a beautiful shot that Christof himself admires: "That's our hero shot." Truman is standing in his boat, attractive and manly, smiling into the camera, face lifted up to the elements, hair windblown under his sailor's hat. This shot is modeled directly after one of the most famous photographs of the twentieth century: the young John F. Kennedy on PT 109, during World War II.[24] This photo shows a handsome, windswept (though bare-chested) Kennedy in a sailor's cap, smiling confidently into the camera. By mirroring this photo, the scene proclaims Truman's transformation from an immature and helpless loser into the all-American hero—courageous, carefree, and self-assured.

The process of maturation is desirable not only for the individual but also for society as a whole. The clothing worn by Truman, as well as the wardrobe of Meryl and of Truman's mother, are in the style of the 1950s, an era that has become synonymous with stability, static gender roles, and traditional family values as portrayed in such television shows as *Leave it to Beaver, Father Knows Best,* and *The Donna Reed Show.* Meryl's product placement pitches as well as the conventional platitudes uttered by the cast also evoke this era. Truman's dress on his escape not only implies his personal maturity but also reflects the conventional and casual male outfit of the 1990s, suggesting that the desire to remain in the world of Seahaven, hence in the well-ordered world of the 1950s, is in fact an immature impulse. We, like Truman, should embrace the "maturity" of our own era, with all of the chaos, adventure, and risk that it entails.

The theme of maturation also implies a psychological context for the progression from innocence to knowledge that we have already noted. Innocence is the condition of childhood and necessitates a level of protection that even the immature find chafing at times. On the other hand, knowledge, that is, an understanding of the workings of the social and physical world in which we live, accompanies maturation, freedom, and risk. Whereas the television show is about Truman's life on Seahaven, the movie is about his growing awareness of and dissatisfaction with the world created and controlled by Christof.

Viewed through the lens of the creation stories in Genesis, then, the film might be seen as a reenactment or, more accurately, a subversion of the expulsion from the garden. Truman, far from being expelled from paradise, can hardly wait to leave it. This desire flies in the face of Christof's insistence on the superiority, indeed, the perfection, of the world he created in comparison to the "real" world outside. If Truman had to leave Seahaven in order to develop and mature, so perhaps the primordial human beings also had to leave the protection and the perfection of the garden in order to lead a fully human existence. In both cases, departure from the ideal world is an expression, or perhaps a consequence, of the quintessentially human characteristic of free will. Truman can only be truly human, a "true man," by getting out from under Christof's (and Meryl's) thumb, and thereby exercising his natural human curiosity, making his own decisions, and opening himself up to the risk of making mistakes. In a similar manner, Adam and Eve can only get on with the essential business of living—family and work—by living out the consequences that God imposes on them after their act of disobedience.

This use of the second Genesis narrative may seem at odds with the widespread Christian reading that views the story as an account of the sin and "fall" of humankind. According to this reading, the story is intended to show that the propensity to sin and disobedience entered humankind when Adam and Eve ate the forbidden fruit.[25] Hence the expulsion from the garden is to be viewed as tragedy, the consequences of which affect humanity to this very day. The interpretation offered by *The Truman Show* is a much more positive, life-affirming account that perhaps deliberately reverses this negative assessment. Interestingly enough, however, the developmental theory implied in the film, in which departure from "paradise" accompanies the maturation of Truman from immaturity to adulthood, has also been proposed as an interpretation of Genesis 2:4–3:24.[26]

Perhaps the most detailed attempt to interpret the story from this point of view is that of Lyn Bechtel. Bechtel provides a "diachronic maturation interpretation" of Genesis 2:4–3:24. She views this story as a creation myth, the literary structure of which "portrays the general stages of maturation into adulthood." All of these stages are present in the text itself as we move sequentially through the narrative and are connected by sections marking the transitions between the stages. The stages are as follows: Nature Foreshadowing the Human Maturation Process (2:4b–6); Creation and Infancy (2:7–9); Transitional Foreshadowing of Maturation (2:10–15); Early and Middle Childhood (2:16–23); Transitional Foreshadowing of Maturation (2:24–25); Adolescent Maturation (3:1–19); Transition into Adulthood (3:20–24).[27] In this interpretation, "knowing" good and evil, that is, tasting the forbidden fruit, "involves the capacity to discern oppositional forces. It is forbidden only to children, and might otherwise be called 'the tree of mature knowledge of life.'"[28] Hence the story is not so much about disobedience and punishment or about the entry of sin into human experience as it is about "learning to accept the inherent oppositional forces of life created by God in the beginning and accepting death as a natural and essential part of life."[29]

Whether or not the filmmakers of *The Truman Show* were actually familiar with this approach to the second creation account, their portrayal of Truman's progression from immaturity to adulthood works well with the Genesis foundation on which this film is laid. The principal differences between the film and the Genesis account, on any interpretation, are the roles of the Creator and his relationship with humankind both within the garden and outside it. Christof's interest is not so much in humanity as a whole but in Truman specifically. On the other hand, his attachment to Truman does not benefit the man but rather satisfies Christof's own needs. God may have his ups and downs with the human species, as expressed, for example, in his attempts to wipe most of them out in the flood episode (Genesis 6–9); God's creation may defy him, betray him, and otherwise displease him on occasions too numerous to recount. But he remains engaged with humankind in general, and, later, with the people Israel in particular.[30]

The contrasts between the God of Genesis and the Christof of *The Truman Show* have led some reviewers to see an anti-Christian, perhaps even a gnostic, message in this film. Peter Chattaway suggests that "like the demiurge, who trapped divine spirit within the material universe according to Gnostic myth, Christof and his co-conspirators have sealed Truman within an artificial world because, through him, they hope to experience the perfect life, albeit vicariously."[31] Perhaps, but a more transparent motivation seems to be entertainment and profit. Elsewhere, Chattaway suggests that Christof, a "rip-off" of Christ, may be a metaphor for false God. Christof is evil, as is the world that he has created.[32] But there is little evidence within the film to support this conclusion. The film is neither pro- nor anti-Christian. Rather, the Genesis imagery encourages viewers to reflect on themes that are fundamental to the human experience in the late twentieth century, including the role of the media and the shaping of individual identity.

CONCLUSION

The creation stories provide a rich source for reflecting on the notion of an ideal world created by a consciousness that is external to that world (God in the case of Genesis and Christof in the case of *The Truman Show*), on the contrast between such an ideal world and the world that we know, and on the question of which world is ultimately the better environment for living a fully human life.

The movie's allusions to the fundamental biblical narratives in Genesis and the Gospels implicitly declare that *The Truman Show* is not just about one man, his television show, and those who create it and live by it. It is a movie about our own lives in the more or less artificial worlds within which we live and about the human condition as such. It offers a critique of our longing for some mythical time and place in our distant past (be it the garden of Eden or the 1950s sitcom), our desire for certainty, and our escape from responsibility for ourselves and our actions. Above all, it reminds us that with autonomy comes risk, but also adventure, love, and growth.

The struggle for autonomy is a religious struggle. This is intimated in a scene in which Sylvia is watching Truman's escape on TV. The scenes cut back and forth between her and Christof. She says, "Please God . . . you can do it." Off scene, Christof says, "You belong here (pause) with me." Like Sylvia, and the millions of viewers, we cheer when Truman finally escapes; his victory is not his alone but also our own. Truman knows that "life is fragile," as he says, presciently, to one of his insurance customers on the phone. But it has its joys and rewards as well. That very fragility—possible for Truman only by escaping the dome in which his life has been enclosed thus far—is a necessary condition of living a fully human life.

2

Magnolia and the Plague
of Frogs (Exodus)

If you refuse to let them go, I will plague your whole country
with frogs.

Exodus 8:2

INTRODUCTION

The book of Exodus, like the creation stories, is about departure. In contrast
to Genesis, however, Exodus is not about leaving home and going out into the
world, but about leaving exile and returning home. Indeed, Exodus is the classic biblical story of liberation. It tells of the Israelites' departure from Egypt,
the land of their enslavement, under the leadership of Moses. This departure
did not come easily. Rather, it was the dramatic climax of an extended and bitter power struggle between the God of Israel and the Pharaoh of Egypt. The
Pharaoh was considered by his subjects to be not only a human ruler but also
a divine being.[1] The conflict between God and Pharaoh therefore was part of
the larger struggle between monotheism and polytheism that is at stake at
numerous other points in the Hebrew Bible. The conflict is played out not
only with regard to the fate of the people Israel but also in the arena of the natural world. God's sovereignty is marked by his absolute control over nature as
demonstrated in his ability to turn the river, the sky, and the power of life and
death against the Pharaoh throughout the ten plagues. God turned the water
of the Nile into blood, and then plagued the Egyptians with frogs, gnats, flies,
disease, boils, hail, locusts, dense darkness, and, finally, the death of the firstborn male offspring of all Egyptian parents and livestock (Exodus 7–12).

According to the biblical account, it was the final plague—death of the firstborn—that hit Pharaoh's household and the entire Egyptian population with

greatest force. Pharaoh momentarily weakened his grip on the Israelites and allowed them to leave. He soon repented of this decision and ordered his army to chase the Israelites and forcibly to retrieve them, but by then it was too late. The Red Sea, which God had obligingly split to allow the Israelites to pass through, washed over the Egyptian army and killed them all.

If the death of the firstborn was ultimately the most effective plague in achieving the divine purpose, it is the plague of frogs that may be the most familiar to the general public. On the surface, this affliction appears to be the least dangerous and frightening of the entire lot. Frogs are inherently humorous creatures; they are sought and carried about by children; they often appear, clothed and talkative, in children's literature.[2] The plague of frogs is prominent in popular films based on Exodus, such as *The Ten Commandments* and *The Prince of Egypt*. It even appears in *The Simpsons*. In an episode entitled "Simpsons Bible Stories"[3] Homer dozes off in church and has a series of vivid dreams based on a selection of biblical stories. In the Exodus segment, two children that closely resemble Lisa and Millhouse unleash a plague of frogs on the Pharaoh. But Pharaoh, far from being frightened, welcomes these frogs like manna from heaven. He orders them to be cooked up and served to him as a gourmet dinner.[4]

A striking frog experience also features in the 1999 film *Magnolia*, written and directed by Paul Thomas Anderson. Approximately two hours into this long and complicated film, a single, giant frog falls from the sky onto the windshield of the car driven by an off-duty police officer. After smacking into the windshield, the frog oozes down the glass until it comes to rest on the hood of the car. Soon many others follow, until a slimy, bloody carpet of dead and dying frogs covers the roads. The frog rain is met with surprise and fear, such as the biblical plagues might well have aroused within the Egyptian population. The frog rain also causes surprising and frightening accidents: a man slips and smashes his face; an ambulance overturns, threatening the lives of its passengers; a gun goes off and kills its owner. No longer can the plague be seen as a humorous, harmless occurrence.

The inexplicable frog rain would seem to be a blatant allusion to the biblical plague of frogs, despite one major difference: whereas the biblical frogs come up out of the Nile (Exod. 8:3, 9–10), *Magnolia*'s frogs rain down from the sky. Nevertheless, the biblical allusion seems obvious. But an interview with the screenwriter and director, Paul Thomas Anderson, reveals that this scene was originally not at all intended to recall Exodus 8. Indeed, Anderson claims that he was completely unaware of the biblical passage until a friend drew it to his attention after reading a draft of the screenplay. He explains:

> I'd read about rains of frogs in the works of Charles Fort, who was a turn-of-the-century writer who wrote mainly about odd phenomena.

> Michael Penn was the one who turned me onto Fort, and who, when
> I went to one of Michael's shows in New York once, made reference
> on stage to "rains of frogs." At that moment I just went, Wow! How
> cool and scary and fun to do that would be—and what does it mean?
>   So I just started writing it into the script. It wasn't until after I got
> through with the writing that I began to discover what it might mean,
> which was this: You get to a point in your life, and shit is happening,
> and everything's out of your control, and suddenly, a rain of frogs just
> makes sense. . . . So then I began to decipher things about frogs and
> history, things like this famous notion that, as far back as the Romans,
> people have been able to judge the health of a society by the health of
> its frogs. . . . The frogs are a barometer for who we are as a people. . . .
> And I didn't even know it was in the Bible until Henry Gibson gave
> me a copy of the Bible, bookmarked to the appropriate frog passage.[5]

Once he learned of the biblical connection, however, Anderson exploited it to
the fullest. If Anderson's initial intention was unrelated to the Bible, the film
in its final form alludes frequently and playfully to Exodus 8:2. Someone in the
studio audience of a television game show briefly holds up a sign that says
"Exodus 8:2." The hanging victim in one of the short "documentaries" with
which the film opens is wearing a shirt with the number 82; a second "documentary" features a pilot in a red plane marked 82; a meeting announced in
the third "documentary" is scheduled for 8:20. A woman arrested by the police
officer on whose car the first falling frog perishes wears a prison number comprised of 8s and 2s; the officer's voice box number is 82; and at one point an
onscreen title forecasts 82% chance of rain. There are more than one hundred
such references and allusions.[6] In an interview in the *Austin American Statesman*, Anderson explains that after he found out about the biblical plague in
Exodus 8:2, he "just thought it was a fun directorial, bored-on-the-set thing
to do, to plant 8s and 2s all over the place."[7] If the inclusion of the frog rain in
the original screenplay was not initially intended as an allusion to scripture, its
presence and playful amplification in the film itself makes it an integral part
that sheds light on the film's plot and main themes.

FILM SUMMARY

Magnolia employs a narrative structure that has been a staple of the film industry since D. W. Griffith's silent film *Intolerance* (1916). This classic presents
several independent stories that are intercut in segments of different length.
The four stories that are woven together in *Intolerance* are of epic proportions.
Each traces the fate of its protagonists over a period of several years and connects thematically with the other stories. The transitions from one narrative

line to another are signaled clearly by means of intertitles (text projected on the screen) and the recurring image of a woman gently rocking a cradle. Similarly, *Magnolia* intercuts a number of independent stories that are related thematically, and, as eventually emerges, in many other ways as well. In contrast to *Intolerance*, however, *Magnolia*'s stories take place over a twenty-four hour period. Although they do exhibit thematic coherence, the transitions from one to another are quick and abrupt. Indeed, the film moves so quickly and so seamlessly from one story to another that a viewer must pay close attention in order to keep track, particularly at the beginning while the main characters and plot lines are being introduced. The effort is worth it.

The movie opens with a number of seemingly unrelated incidents, presented in documentary style, including voiceover by an unidentified and invisible male narrator. The stories include the murder of a man on Greenberry Hill by three men named Green, Berry, and Hill; the accidental death of a blackjack dealer caused by an amateur pilot to whom he had dealt unfavorable cards the day before; and the demise of a teenager who tries to commit suicide by jumping off the roof of his apartment building but who is shot accidentally by his mother when he sails past his parents' window. According to the anonymous and invisible narrator, these events, bizarre as they might be, are not merely a matter of coincidence. He states, "It is in the humble opinion of this narrator that this is not just 'Something That Happened.' This cannot be 'One of those things. . . .' This, please, cannot be that. And for what I would like to say, I can't. This Was Not Just A Matter of Chance. . . ."[8]

These incidents function as a preamble to the several stories that comprise the main part of the film, though the link between the "documentaries" and the body of the film is not initially apparent. After the narrator's summary, the camera moves us briskly through a sequence that presents the main characters of these stories as they begin their day. It then takes us back and forth from one story to another. Each character stars in a mini-drama of her or his own that comes to some measure of resolution over the course of a twenty-four-hour period.

In keeping with this structure, a summary of the film's plot is in essence a summary of these several plots. Here, then, are the main characters, in the order in which we first meet them, and a brief description of what happens to them from one morning to the next.

> Frank T. J. Mackey (Tom Cruise) is a young macho guy, the creator and guru of a self-help movement for men called "Seduce and Destroy." His workshops are highly popular and appear on television. He achieves reconciliation with his father and begins to accept the presence of his step-mother in his life.
>
> Claudia Wilson (Melora Walters) is a young cocaine addict who listens to music and watches television, simultaneously and at full volume. She

occasionally invites men that she meets in the Smiling Peanut Bar to come home with her for a night of sex. On this particular day, she makes a final break with her father, Jimmy Gator (Philip Baker Hall), and finds the possibility of love with the police officer, Jim Kurring (John C. Reilly).

Jimmy Gator is the sixty-ish host of a television game show, now in its thirtieth year. He is married to Rose (Melinda Dillon) but not faithfully so. He has been diagnosed with terminal cancer. As he faces his mortality, he confesses his adulteries to his wife, Rose, and tries to reconcile with his daughter, Claudia. Both reject him; he prepares to commit suicide, but as a direct result of the frog rain, he dies of a gun-shot wound without pulling the trigger himself.

Stanley Spector (Jeremy Blackman) is a clean-cut, ten-year-old genius, the star contestant on Jimmy Gator's television game show. He rebels against his genius role and finally is able to confront his father, who has been pushing Stanley's participation in the show for his own material gain.

Donnie Smith (William H. Macy) is a middle-aged and dissipated version of Stanley, a former child genius and star contestant on Jimmy's game show (from 1968, the first year of the show). He is now a failed appliance salesman infatuated with the male bartender at the Smiling Peanut Bar. Donnie believes that the young man, who wears braces on his teeth, will return his love if he, Donnie, gets braces too. In order to pay for this expensive and unnecessary orthodontic work, Donnie steals money from his former employers' safe. But before he can embarrass himself further, he is brought to his senses by Jim Kurring.

Earl Partridge (Jason Robards), the elderly producer of Jimmy's game show, is now in the terminal stages of lung cancer. He is tended by a devoted and caring nurse, Phil Parma (Philip Seymour Hoffman), and he is married to the highly distressed, and much younger, Linda Partridge (Julianne Moore). His final request is to see his son, Frank Mackey. Phil manages to arrange a meeting in the face of considerable obstacles, but whether Earl is aware of his son's presence is not clear. As Earl sinks further into his final coma, Phil assists him to a peaceful death.

Jim Kurring is a straight-laced police officer, a single, lonely, born-again Christian who has a habit of talking to himself as he drives his car as if he were being interviewed on the TV show *Cops*. He brings resolution to Donnie's situation and, with Claudia, creates the possibility of new love.

These disparate story lines are linked in a number of ways. The most obvious is suggested by the name of the film. "Magnolia" evokes the beautiful, spring-flowering tree that blooms briefly and spectacularly, after which its petals fall to the ground and decay. If there is any thematic connection between the tree and this film, it is to be found in the final stage of decayed beauty, which calls to mind the wronged wife of Jimmy Gator (Rose) and the long-dead first wife of Earl Partridge and beloved mother of Frank Mackey (Lily). For P. T. Anderson, however, the title signifies not a flower but a street in the San Fernando Valley (California) in and around which the action takes place. This location is never made explicit in the film. Nevertheless, it eventually becomes evident that the several narrative strands that comprise this film all converge on the same cityscape, namely, an intersection with a set of lights through which most of the characters in the various stories pass one or more times throughout the twenty-four-hour period covered by the film.

Other links among the various stories can best be described using the street metaphor that the name of the film implies. There are obvious intersections among the characters. Frank Mackey is Earl Partridge's estranged son; Claudia Wilson is Jimmy Gator's estranged daughter. Some characters are bound through the television game show: Donnie is a former contestant from the first year of the show; Stanley is a current contestant from what will prove to be the final year of the show; Jimmy is the host, and Earl is the producer of this same show. Other characters meet each other face-to-face for the first time on this particular day, when their paths cross for reasons that seem random but that perhaps, as the narrator has already warned us, were "Not Just A Matter of Chance." Jim Kurring, the police officer, meets Claudia in the line of duty, and, later that day, encounters Donnie when he is already off duty. These intersections draw attention to the role of roads, cars, and, yes, intersections, in this film. As the unidentified narrator muses in one of his philosophical interventions, "There are stories of coincidence and chance and intersections and strange things told and which is which and who only knows. . . ."[9]

Some of the characters do not intersect directly but travel parallel roads. The stories of Donnie and Stanley are the most obvious example. Both were child geniuses who were exploited by their parents and forced into long participation in this show, with detrimental consequences. During Donnie's long evening at the Smiling Peanut Bar, where he goes to get drunk and to moon over the young male bartender, we learn that his parents exploited him, took the money that he earned on the quiz show, and left him to fend for himself in his adulthood. He resorts to theft in order to finance the orthodontic work that he is convinced will bring him love and happiness. Donnie's pathetic state portends a similarly dismal future for Stanley, whose father urges, perhaps even coerces him into competing on the show. Stanley has excelled throughout; if he does well on this particular day, he is almost certain to win the championship in two days' time and to walk away with a sizeable sum. Although Stanley's father, somewhat hollowly, declares his love for Stanley on several occasions, he does not behave in a particularly loving way. He castigates Stanley for being late when their tardiness is in fact his own fault (he is a failed actor, scurrying from one unsuccessful audition to another). He swears at Stanley and squeezes his arm just a bit too hard when he falls short of perfect on the game show. Stanley is a lovable if eccentric child, and one cannot help but wish that he not turn out like Donnie, who is the film's loser par excellence.

A second set of parallels occurs in the stories of Jimmy Gator and Earl Partridge. Both are ill with cancer, and both will be dead by the film's end. Both have been guilty of adultery and worse; both seek death-bed reconciliations with their estranged adult children. Not surprisingly, both children are reluctant to reconnect with their fathers, but here the parallel ends. Jimmy's daughter, Claudia, ultimately denies reconciliation, while Earl's son, Frank, eventually, and with difficulty, comes around.

Finally, there are opposing roads that nevertheless meet, or, more precisely, collide. Such is the encounter between Jim and Claudia. Jim comes to Claudia's apartment in response to a neighbor's complaint about her loud music. He is immediately attracted to her despite himself; inexplicably, he either misses or overlooks the obvious signs of her habitual drug use. Claudia is the complete antithesis of the kind of woman Jim thinks he wants. We viewers know this, for playing in the background of Jim's first appearance in the film is the text of the personal ad that he has placed with a dating service. Jim claims to be seeking "someone special who likes quiet things." He says, "My life is very stressful and I hope to have a relationship that is very calm, and undemanding and loving." These attributes are indeed appropriate for a straitlaced Christian police officer. But Claudia hates the quiet. In fact, she surrounds herself with noise. She also swears profusely, has frequent emotional crises, and, as we learn late in the film, has probably been abused by her father, Jimmy. An intimate relationship with her is unlikely to be calm, quiet, and undemanding. Yet Jim seems to notice none of these things as he reaches out to her. If Claudia is the complete contrast to the kind of woman that Jim says he wants, Jim contrasts with the other man we associate with Claudia, namely, her father, Jimmy Gator, despite the similarity in name. Jim Kurring is a man of integrity rather than exploitative, straight rather than sneaky. Indeed, Jim and Claudia promise to be straight with each other, to tell each other everything. In the few hours that they have known each other, Jim and Claudia are awkward but nevertheless honest, even if they do not as yet tell all.

The interconnections among the characters and their story lines occur not just on the level of plot but on the level of theme as well. The characters are troubled by and preoccupied with the same kinds of issues. The soundtrack provides the most obvious clues to these thematic intersections. The lyrics of songs from a number of genres weave together the narrative threads and also articulate their main themes. Playing in the background of the scenes in which the main characters are introduced is the song "One," written by Harry Nillson and performed by Aimee Mann. The chorus, "One is the loneliest number . . ." describes the experience of the film's main characters, who go through their day with varying degrees of isolation, anger, and loneliness. Jim, Claudia, and Donnie long for love. Linda, Earl's wife, is out of control emotionally; she swears incessantly, rampages through the offices of her psychiatrist and lawyer, and finally takes an overdose of prescription drugs. She is distressed not only by Earl's impending death but also by the sense that she has squandered this opportunity for a loving relationship through her mercenary attitude and her many adulteries. Only now that he is at death's door does she come to love him. Jimmy Gator, although married to Rose, is also adulterous, as we see in an early scene. His recently diagnosed illness compels him to confess his adulteries to Rose. Because she suspects that he has in the past abused Claudia, their daughter, Rose abandons Jimmy, and he dies alone. Stanley has his father, but only superficially, since their relationship is fraught with tension over Stanley's participation in the game show.

Another sequence is played out against the background of the lyrics to an aria from Carmen. The aria is introduced at the game show; Stanley has to identify and sing the lyrics in French. In English, the text reads, "Love is a rebellious bird that nobody can tame, and it's all in vain to call it, if it chooses to refuse." They form the backdrop and musical commentary to Jim's strained first conversation with Claudia over very bitter coffee, which he tosses in the sink as soon as she leaves the room for a moment (to snort more coke). Will this be love or not?

A whimsical link is provided by Aimee Mann's song "Wise Up." Each of the characters sings along with Aimee Mann, even those who are unconscious at the time (Linda, who has overdosed in her car) or are near death (Earl, in a coma in his bed). Claudia, who is listening to a recording by Aimee in her apartment (at full volume, as usual), begins. Some characters just sing the chorus, others a verse, but clearly they all need to "wise up."

USE OF THE BIBLE

In light of Anderson's self-confessed ignorance of the biblical plague of frogs, it is not at all surprising that the film's plot and major themes can be summarized without recourse to the Bible at all. Nevertheless, the frog plague does play a crucial role in the film's narrative structure and also helps to illuminate its principal themes.

Plot and Character

The frog rain draws together and brings to a climax the familial, emotional, and thematic intersections that are explored in the film. To maintain the automotive motif, we might liken the frogs to the hub of a wheel through which all the spokes are connected. Despite the fact that the frogs' initial appearance in the screenplay was not intentionally related to their biblical role, their presence in the film draws attention to the ways in which the themes echo or mirror some of the important motifs in the Exodus story itself.

Within the plot, the plague of frogs, like the other visual and aural elements previously discussed, helps to connect the characters because it is an unusual phenomenon that they all experience simultaneously. It also has another function: to mark the turning point in each story line. In some cases it is the catalyst that leads directly to the resolution of the character's conflict or dilemma. A falling frog is ultimately responsible for Jimmy's death. As the frog rain subsides, Donnie meets up with Jim Kurring, who gently encourages Donnie to return the money Donnie has just stolen from the safe of his former employer and to reconcile himself to his own situation. In other story lines, the frogs do not directly contribute to the resolution but rather mark the point after which resolution occurs. Rose is on her way to see Claudia when the frog rain hits; she has an accident but nevertheless makes it to her daughter's apartment, where they wait out the rain and renew their relationship. Frank spends the night of the frog rain at his dying father's side; in the morning, after Earl's death, Frank visits Linda in the hospital and for the first time acknowledges her role in his father's life and her presence in his own. Stanley enjoys the frog rain, which seems to give him the courage later that night to wake his father up and to inform him calmly but firmly that he must be nicer from now on. After helping Donnie, Jim returns to Claudia's apartment, where she has huddled with her mother against the amphibian terrors of the night. He talks to her slowly and seriously, and so quietly that we viewers can barely catch a word. But we see the result: a slow, tentative, but radiant smile from Claudia, her first smile of the film and the final, cautiously optimistic image in the movie as a whole.

This seemingly random and extraordinary occurrence helps to turn things around for each character in the film. Those who needed to die in order to achieve peace do so (Earl, Jimmy). Those who had wanted to die but did not need to, survive (Linda). Those who are lonely achieve an authentic, if tentative, connection with someone else (Jim, Claudia). Those who are suppressed, like Stanley, emerge from the boxes into which others had put them. Those who are estranged reconcile (Frank and Earl, Rose and Claudia, Frank and Linda), and those who have railed against the past (Donnie) or tried to rewrite it (Frank) come to terms with their situations and move on.

Themes

The dual narrative function of the frog rain—to mark the intersections among the characters and to signal the point at which their stories move towards resolution—also connects to two of the main themes of the film. First and most prominent is the issue raised by the narrator periodically throughout the film: the nature and meaning of seemingly chance coincidences.

> There are stories of coincidence and chance and intersections and strange things told and which is which and who only knows . . . and we would generally say, "Well if that was in a movie I wouldn't believe it. . . . Someone's so and so meets someone else's so and so and so on. And it is in the humble opinion of this narrator that these strange things happen all the time. . . ."[10]

Indeed, the film seems intent on persuading its viewers that strange things can and do happen. During the frog rain, the camera moves slowly over a sign on the landscape that declares, "But it did happen." Stanley, the child genius who may be familiar with the same book of wonders that P. T. Anderson relied on, comments in wonderment and with satisfaction, "This is something that happens." The frog rain—a strange but true thing that really happens—exemplifies, or perhaps epitomizes, the possibility of strange events and inexplicable coincidences. Though it is more spectacular and surprising, it is not essentially different from the kinds of coincidences and chance encounters that we have all experienced and that sometimes have a lasting impact on our lives.

The frog rain alludes not only to the book of Exodus but also to cinematic renditions of this and other wondrous occurrences. The film draws attention to the camera's ability to conjure up the strange parallels between an artificial video world and the nitty gritty of our own real-life dramas. But there are strange coincidences not only within the lives and experiences of human beings but also between the lives we see on the screen (large or small) and the life that we experience directly.[11] This connection between the video world and our own is implied by the role of television in the film itself. Several of the characters regularly appear on television, where they are viewed by some of the other characters. Earl produces the TV game show that Jimmy hosts and on which Donnie and Stanley have appeared and that Jim, Claudia, and Phil watch; Frank, significantly, is estranged from Earl and has his own, competing TV presence. Both shows are exploitative, albeit in different ways. The game show exploits its child contestants, as when Stanley is denied permission to go to the bathroom and hence urinates in his pants. Frank's show advocates the sexual exploitation and manipulation of women and in doing so exploits men by promising them sexual success.[12]

More important, there are times when film or television imitate real life and vice versa, as Phil Parma, Earl's devoted nurse, knows well. After Earl asks to see his son, Frank, Phil does his utmost to arrange such a meeting. First he must track Frank down, however, and persuade Frank's handlers to convey his father's death-bed request. When he finally reaches a real person by telephone, Phil says,

> I know this all sounds silly. And I know that I might sound ridiculous, like this is the scene of the movie where the guy is trying to get ahold of the long-lost son, y'know, but this is that scene. This is that scene. And I think they have those scenes in movies because they're true, y'know, because they really happen. And you gotta believe me: This is really happening. . . . See, see, this is the scene of the movie where you help me out.

It would seem, then, that a major theme in the film is simply that strange things do happen, whether in the natural world (the frog rain) or in the world of human relations (the accidental death of a boy who has jumped off the roof; the chance encounter of Jim Kurring and Donnie Smith), or in the interactions between the natural and human worlds, on the one hand, and the video and human worlds, on the other hand. But the film goes one (tentative) step further than simply pointing this out. The movie cautions us that these parallels and intersections may not be coincidental. To repeat the narrator's final comment on the three stories of bizarre coincidence with which the film opens, "This Was Not Just A Matter of Chance."

If it is not chance, what is it? The film implies but stops short of claiming explicitly that a divine hand is at work. At the same time, there are a number of elements in the film that lead us precisely to that conclusion. One is the frog rain itself. As we have seen, the inclusion of this scene in the original screenplay was not intended as an allusion to Exodus 8, but the film itself makes that connection abundantly clear through the playful repetition of the numbers 8 and 2, and through several direct references to Exodus 8:2. These repetitions suggest that, Anderson's assertions to the contrary, we should view his frogs in light of their biblical counterparts in Exodus 8.

In this section of the Exodus story, as we have seen, God is in the process of afflicting the Egyptians with a series of ten plagues that are designed to demonstrate God's power. The intended objects of this demonstration are several: the Pharaoh himself, who, from the biblical perspective, has falsely set himself up as a rival to the one true God and hence must be taught a lesson; the Egyptian people, who suffer through the plagues and are guilty as a people of harboring the Israelites as slaves; and finally, the Israelites themselves, who must be persuaded of God's power to extricate them from Egypt and to return them to their own land (cf. Exodus 4).

The notion of liberation is alluded to in this film as well, in the text of a large billboard that we see from the window of Jim Kurring's car immediately before the frog rain hits: "Everything must go!" The biblical allusion—that the biblical Pharoah must let God's people go—does not render this sign less cryptic, however. Indeed, several different interpretations come to mind. Perhaps it is the frogs that must go, suggesting that God is unleashing his entire stock of frogs on this benighted block of the San Fernando Valley. Or it could mean that the frog plague is a sign that the characters in the film must learn to let go of the attitudes and to make peace with the memories that keep them in bondage. These meanings are not mutually exclusive, however, and perhaps both are in keeping with the message of the film as a whole.

Another thematic element is at work in this film: the power of the past to control us in the present. Virtually all of the characters are enslaved by their past to one degree or another. Some are haunted by past adulteries (Linda, Earl, Jimmy). Some have been guilty of abuse, physical or emotional (Earl, Jimmy); others have been abandoned (Frank), abused, or exploited in their childhood or youth (Donnie, Claudia, Stanley). Donnie makes this point explicitly. As he throws up in the bathroom of the Smiling Peanut Bar, he mutters, "the sins of the fathers . . . lay upon your children. . . . Exodus 20:5." The full text of this verse is as follows: "You shall not bow down to them or worship them; for I the Lord your God am a jealous God, punishing children for the iniquities of parents, to the third and the fourth generation of those who reject me."[13] This may provide the background for a statement that Jimmy Gator, Donnie, and the narrator himself make: "The Book says, we may be through with the past but the past ain't through with us."[14]

Hence the film alludes to at least two of the themes of the book of Exodus: liberation, here interpreted as personal reconciliation; and the relationship between the past and the present. The Israelites' enslavement comes as a consequence of their past, that is, the emigration of Jacob's sons to Egypt many generations earlier; so, too, are the predicaments of *Magnolia*'s main characters a consequence of their past actions, either brought upon themselves (Jimmy) or inflicted on them by their fathers and mothers (Frank, Claudia, Donnie, Stanley).[15] The various intersections allow the characters to come to terms with their situations and with their past, to "wise up," and to carry on. The connections with Exodus indirectly imply the presence of a divine hand. Just as God used the plague of frogs to aid in the liberation of the Israelites from Egyptian bondage, so God is using the frog rain to liberate these people who live on and around Magnolia Street.

In addition to these thematic links, a number of plot elements hint at the possibility of a divine hand. One striking clue comes in the form of Jim Kurring's gun. Upon leaving Claudia's apartment after their first meeting, Jim cruises around in his police car to complete his shift before returning to pick Claudia up for their dinner date. His suspicions are aroused when he glimpses a man running, and he gives chase on foot, in the pouring rain. At some point during this chase he loses his gun. He prays frantically that God return the gun to him: "God, please help me figure it out. . . . God, please help me find the gun." He is desperate; without his gun he faces penalties and loss of face in the eyes of his colleagues and peers. But his gun is nowhere to be found. Jim carries on to the end of his shift and then has dinner with Claudia. On his way home, the frog rain hits. Jim finds Donnie and sits down for a chat once the frog rain has subsided. Suddenly, his gun falls from the sky and lands in front him, in among the mess of dead frogs. Surely this is God responding to his prayer!

Some elements of characterization also allude, obliquely, to the possibility of a divine hand. It might be expected that a contemporary Hollywood film that explores the motifs of liberation and redemption would also have a Jesus figure or two among its cast of characters. This film is no exception. In fact, it presents us with three candidates for this role. One candidate is the black child rapper who pops up periodically and unexpectedly. He first appears to Jim Kurring, with a rap song in which he declares himself to be a prophet and in which he cryptically encodes information that would lead to the solving of a murder, if Jim could only understand it (he doesn't and the murder remains unsolved). He reappears alongside the car in which Linda is slumped, unconscious, after taking an overdose of prescription drugs. He gets into the car, searches her purse, and pockets her money, but then he dials 911 on her cell phone to call the ambulance, and in doing so, saves her life.[16]

A second, Frank Mackey, is a pseudo-Christ figure. The curtain opens on his "Seduce and Destroy" workshop and television show to the majestic strains of "Thus Spake Zarathustra," the theme music of *2001: A Space Odyssey*. Frank is silhouetted against a black background. He slowly raises his arms until they reach shoulder height; he holds this crucifixion pose for several long moments. Finally, he moves his elbows in to strike a strong fighter pose. Throughout his presentation he draws his students' attention to his own works, by book and page number, as if he were citing scripture. During his interview with the journalist, Gwenovier, he describes himself in the language of religious leadership: "I Am What I Believe. . . . I do as I say; I live by these rules as religiously as I preach them."[17] Yet the mission of Seduce and Destroy is decidedly unholy, to teach men how to dupe women into having sex with them, in the process also destroying their dignity. Finally, he has created an autobiography that provides himself with a live mother and dead father, an account that runs contrary to his real life story, which he cannot yet face: his father, Earl, abandoned him and his mother, Lily, during Lily's terminal bout with cancer, leaving the fourteen-year-old Frank to nurse his mother and watch her die. Frank too is redeemed, however. Phil tracks him down, and Frank, somewhat reluctantly, comes to his dying father's home. He sits at Earl's bedside and rages at his father, who may or may not be aware of him through his final coma. But in the end he breaks down, mourns his father's passing, and even summons the generosity of spirit to visit Linda in the hospital. He is no Christ figure, but he regains his humanity in the plague of frogs.

A third, and more conventional, Christ figure is found in Jim Kurring, whose initials almost, but not quite, match those of Jesus Christ himself. Jim is a lonely, humble man who is merely trying to do his job with integrity. He has a large crucifix on his bedroom wall; he says nightly prayers; he abhors swearing and strong language, particularly coming from a woman (he is perpetually shocked by Claudia, of course). He also sincerely experiences his relationship with God as a personal one. In the car after meeting Claudia, he says aloud—to God, to us viewers, and to himself—"That is what I wait for. . . . I pray, and sometimes Jesus says, Jim, I gotta surprise for you today. I want you to meet this young lady. Okay, now where it goes from there is up to you. God, I'm telling you right now, I will not screw it up. . . ."

Jim genuinely cares about people and wants to help them. Despite the loss of his gun, he somehow has the ability truly to set aside his own needs and concerns in order to think about the needs of others around him. This appears most clearly with Donnie. After Donnie confesses his theft to Jim Kurring, in the aftermath of the frog rain, we hear Jim's voiceover and watch him escort Donnie back to the employers' office, put the money back in the safe, and part with a handshake. Being off duty, Jim does not have to arrest Donnie. Instead, he senses what Donnie needs: forgiveness. As Jim says, "Sometimes people need a little help. Sometimes people need to be forgiven and sometimes they need to go to jail. And that's a very tricky thing on my part . . . making that call . . . the law is the law and heck if I'm gonna break it . . . but you can forgive someone . . . ? Well, that's the tough part . . . What Do We Forgive?"[18] This speech calls to mind John 20:23, in which the resurrected Jesus returns to his disciples and gives them the power to forgive sins or to sustain them, thus thrusting them into the same dilemma that Jim Kurring faces every day in his job as a police officer.

The film does not explicitly make a religious statement. While it asserts that strange things can happen in "real life" (and not just in the movies)—and that these strange things are not necessarily coincidence or chance—it does not openly attribute these happenings to a divine or overarching consciousness. It does leave this possibility open, and perhaps even leads us, if tentatively, in that direction. On a psychological level, however, the message is clear: we cannot be free from the power of the past until we have come to terms with it.

Finally, lurking beneath the surface of both Exodus and *Magnolia* is the theme of personal responsibility. In Exodus it would seem that Pharaoh bears final responsibility for the suffering of the enslaved Israelites, on the one hand, and of the plagued Egyptians, on the other, for he is the one who has the power to heed Moses' (and God's) word or to ignore it. But the biblical account complicates this notion by declaring periodically that God hardened Pharaoh's heart (e.g., Exod. 9:12), thus implying that God, not Pharaoh, may ultimately be responsible for everyone's suffering. In the film, personal responsibility is not addressed explicitly, but it is implied in each of the individual plot lines. Each person is caught in a situation that is not directly of his or her own choosing. In most cases, however, resolution comes when the character takes responsibility for the situation and for his or her ability to emerge from it. In this sense, each person's liberation, like Israel's exodus from Egypt, comes about when he or she finally stops wallowing in self-pity and risks the first step towards a new life.

CONCLUSION

The film displays what we might well call an inadvertent use of scripture, insofar as the central and most powerful biblical image—the plague of frogs—was not initially intended, or known to be, a biblical allusion at all. But there is no doubt that the film itself capitalizes on the biblical context of this image; magnifies it through many details, both obvious and playful; and thereby adds another dimension and another whole set of questions to the film as a whole, questions that I wish we could pose to that anonymous off-screen narrator who gives us his opinion so freely.

Perhaps Anderson's frogs are yet another example of a coincidence that could not possibly be chance. Given the degree to which these biblical images and motifs have enriched the film, we might speculate that his attraction to the "weird-but-true" is merely a prelude to his encounter with a book that has outsold even Frank Mackey's popular tomes. Or perhaps it remains only coincidence.

3

Dead Man Walking and the Riddle of Divine Justice (Leviticus)

You shall give life for life, eye for eye, tooth for tooth, hand for hand, foot for foot, burn for burn, wound for wound, stripe for stripe.

Exodus 21:23–25

Anyone who kills a human being shall be put to death. Anyone who kills an animal shall make restitution for it, life for life. Anyone who maims another shall suffer the same injury in return: fracture for fracture, eye for eye, tooth for tooth; the injury inflicted is the injury to be suffered. One who kills an animal shall make restitution for it; but one who kills a human being shall be put to death. You shall have one law for the alien and for the citizen: for I am the LORD your God.

Leviticus 24:17–22

INTRODUCTION

The Bible is a narrative work that describes the creation of the world and of human society and recounts the early history of Israel, from the patriarchs and matriarchs through the Israelite settlement in Egypt, the exodus, the return to "the promised land," and their adventures and misadventures through successive political regimes. But as anyone who has ever attempted to read the Bible cover to cover will know, this set of books contains not only stories—of family intrigue, successes and failures, conflicts and resolutions—but also many laws that pertain to the lives of individuals and society. Most famous, of course, is the Decalogue, the "Ten Commandments," that, according to the biblical story, were given by God to Moses at Mount Sinai some three months after the Israelites left Egypt (Exod. 20:1–17; Deut. 5:6–21). In addition to these ten basic injunctions, the books of Exodus, Leviticus, Numbers, and Deuteronomy contain hundreds of legal precepts concerning property, restitution, justice, slaves, dress, family status, and activities of the priesthood, among dozens of other topics. From our perspective some laws seem archaic and obsolete, such as the numerous laws governing the daily, weekly, and festival sacrifices of oil, grains, birds, and animals. Others, such as the liability of a person whose ox gores a man or woman to death, sound strange at first but have obvious application to issues of liability and responsibility that remain relevant today. Finally, some laws continue directly to inform many contemporary debates. The biblical laws against homosexuality, which prescribe the death penalty for a man who "lies with a male as with a woman" (Lev. 20:13; cf. Lev. 18:22–23), are a case in point.

Equally controversial are the biblical injunctions regarding the death penalty. *Lex talionis*, the law of retaliation (Exod. 21:23–25; Lev. 24:17–22), when read literally, indicates that those who hurt, maim, or kill others should suffer those same consequences themselves. The biblical context implies that *lex talionis* is an expression of the divine will; the solemn statement "for I am the LORD your God" that seals the discussion in Leviticus strengthens this idea.[1] Thus it would seem that a human system of justice that applies the *lex talionis* to crimes against other human beings would emulate divine justice as much as is humanly possible. Jewish law, Christian canon law, and Western criminal law have generally incorporated the fundamental principle of the law of retaliation but in a nonliteral way, namely, by assessing monetary damages and by sentencing the perpetrators to prison sentences of varying lengths. The area of capital crime itself arouses vigorous debate and passionate disagreement regarding the application of *lex talionis*. Thus "an eye for an eye" is a biblical statement that has highly charged meanings legally, politically, and morally.[2]

FILM SUMMARY

A powerful illustration of the political use of this biblical phrase is found in the 1995 film *Dead Man Walking*, directed by Tim Robbins and based on an autobiographical account by Sister Helen Prejean.[3] This film is about the relationship between Sister Helen (Susan Sarandon) and a death row inmate, Matthew Ponselet (Sean Penn).[4] Sister Helen works and lives in the St. Thomas Projects, a poor, black urban neighborhood in Louisiana. She teaches literacy to adults and is involved closely if informally in the lives of the children and families in her neighborhood. During class one day, a colleague approaches her with a request to respond to a letter from a death row inmate

at Angola State Prison. Somewhat distractedly, she agrees. So begins her relationship with Matthew Ponselet. After a brief correspondence, Helen visits
Matthew and eventually becomes his spiritual advisor. Matt has been sentenced to die by lethal injection for his role in the rape and murder of Hope
Percy and murder of Walter Delacroix, both teenagers. Sister Helen is
repulsed by Matt's crime, by his racist, sexist, and white-supremacist attitudes,
and by his unflinching denial of any responsibility in the acts for which he has
been convicted. Despite these feelings, she is willing to help him.

Matt has a clear idea of what such help should entail: free legal counsel in
order to achieve a pardon or, at the very least, to commute his death penalty
to life imprisonment, which was the same sentence handed down to Matt's
accomplice. Sister Helen tries her best, reluctantly at first, but with increasing
conviction as she herself becomes more sensitive to the issue of capital punishment and the political, social, and economic factors that influence whether
or not a death sentence will be handed down and carried out. But as she gets
to know Matt better, she sees that her more difficult and more important goal
is to help Matt acknowledge his role in the crimes and thereby to achieve a
measure of reconciliation with himself and, from her perspective, with God as
well. By the end of the film, she fails to achieve the goal that Matt had set for
her; all avenues of appeal are ultimately denied to him and he is executed by
lethal injection as scheduled. However, she succeeds in her spiritual goal: Matt
ultimately takes responsibility for the violent crimes against Walter and Hope.

ROLE OF THE BIBLE

Plot and Character

The theme of spiritual salvation is a counterpoint in the film to the theme of
physical salvation. At the same time as the main plot moves inexorably from
political and legal activity to failure, culminating in Matt's execution, the
thread that follows Matt's spiritual progress moves from despair to redemption, culminating in divine-human love. Not surprisingly, biblical passages and
images play an explicit as well as an implicit role in both of these plot lines.

Political and Legal Redemption

Although the film takes a clear stand against the death penalty, it does not
demonize the opposing viewpoint. On the contrary, through the representation of the parents of Matt's young victims, the film does not flinch from the
powerful emotions that help to fuel the political and religious arguments in
favor of the death penalty.

One such emotion is the desire for vengeance. Clyde, the father of victim Hope Percy, states in a television interview, "It's been six years, now, and as far as I'm concerned, it's about time the state got on with it. Call me sentimental, but I'd rather see him fry [than die by lethal injection]."[5] Politics also plays a role. A governor in a conservative state who decides to run for reelection cannot afford to pardon Matt lest he be seen as "soft" on violent crime. As Matt tells Hilton, the lawyer whom Helen has persuaded to handle Matt's final appeals, "Day before Governor Benedict says he's gonna run for reelection they set a date for my execution to show how tough he is on crime." Hilton concedes that there is a political dimension to the decision to keep Matt on death row, and notes that the pardon board is "full of political appointees, the governor's appointees."

In these ways, the film points out the political and personal factors that complicate the capital punishment debate as well as the fate of individuals on death row. The film's main focus, however, is on the biblically based argument. Shortly after Helen has begun to visit Matt on death row, a man named Wayne Purcell is executed at Angola. During the execution, pro- and anti-death-penalty groups demonstrate outside the prison. Members of the large crowd in support of the death penalty carry posters with the slogan "Eye for an eye"; they count down the seconds to the execution, and they cheer when it is over. The atmosphere is festive and celebratory. Underlying their actions is the notion that human justice must mirror divine justice. If divine justice is expressed in the literal interpretation of *lex talionis*, then the state is justified in taking the life of someone who is guilty of murder.

A short distance away, a small and subdued group that includes Sister Helen and several other nuns hold a candle-light vigil in silent protest. Their protest may at first glance seem misplaced. If the justification for the death penalty is to be found in the Bible itself, surely those people who have dedicated themselves to a religious life should be among the staunch supporters of capital punishment. The very fact that this movie's critique of the death penalty is articulated by a nun challenges the notion that capital punishment expresses the ideal of divine justice.

This point comes to the fore in a conversation that takes place between Captain Beliveau and Sister Helen on the day of Matt's execution. Sister Helen and the Captain are waiting for Matt to complete the lie detector test that he had insisted would prove his innocence. "Tell me something, Sister," says Beliveau. "What is a nun doing in a place like this? Shouldn't you be teaching children? Do you know what this man has done; how he killed them kids?" Helen answers, "What he was involved with was evil; I don't condone it. I just don't see the sense of killing people just to say that killing people is wrong." To this Beliveau declares, emphatically, "You know how the Bible says, 'An eye for an eye,'" as if this clinches the argument. Helen, however, has an answer for him: "You know what else the Bible asks for? Death as punishment for adultery, prostitution, homosexuality, trespass upon sacred ground, profaning the Sabbath, and contempt of parents." Beliveau concedes defeat: "I ain't gettin' into no bible-quotin' with no nun, cuz I'm gonna lose." Helen smiles triumphantly.

Sister Helen, who has dedicated her life to the service of God, has a more complex view of Scripture than does the captain, who may or may not give the Bible much thought under other circumstances. Helen is deeply engaged with the biblical text, as we learn from the ways in which she tries to introduce the Bible into Matt's way of thinking about himself and his situation. But she does not have a simplistic or literal view of scripture. Rather, she recognizes the distance between the original social context of the Bible, in which the prescription of the death penalty for mortal transgressions may have made some sense, and the situation in the late twentieth century, in which acts like profaning the Sabbath and trespassing on sacred ground are scarcely noteworthy, let alone punishable by law.

The view that the death penalty is a just punishment for murder is expressed by others in addition to Beliveau. At a last minute hearing of the state pardon board, the lawyer for the state pulls the emotional strings very effectively: "These families will never see their children graduate from college; they will never attend their wedding; they will never have a Christmas with them again. There will be no grandchildren. All they ask of you is simple justice for their unbearable loss. . . . I ask you to take a breath, steel your spine, and proceed with the execution of Matthew Ponselet." Not surprisingly, the victims' parents concur. Hope's father, Clyde Percy, tells Sister Helen, "If you really are sorry and you really do care about us, you'll want to see justice done for our murdered child." Even Matt, eventually, can sympathize with the Percys' sorrow and anger at the murder of their child and their desire to see him dead in just retribution.

Far more offensive than the lawyer or the parents is the "Shock radio jock," as the shooting script refers to the radio personality who mocks the anti-death-penalty lobby.[6] He may be targeting Helen herself, whose activities on Matt's behalf have been reported widely in the media: "Oh please, don't kill him. He is a child of God, he deserves more, he is reformed, he's a poet. Blah blah blah. Attention. All ye folks, ye advocates of killers and child molesters, ye opponents of execution: Ye cannot walk upon the high ground, ye do not have the moral authority to walk there. Ye traverse with scum, and scum is where ye lay."

As this radio clip suggests, the media play a central role in this film, as they do in the others that we have discussed thus far. The film uses newspapers, radio, and television newscasts to convey the backstory to the film audience; at the same time, it criticizes the role of the media in shaping public response to capital punishment. The information given out by the media influences the public against Matt, his family, and his spiritual advisor, Helen; clips and photos of Matt's behavior during the trial emphasize his obnoxious behavior in the courtroom and dwell on the premeditated and truly offensive nature of the crime itself.

Television also serves as a platform for political statements and political posturing. One of the candidates for governor declares that it is time to "get tough on sentencing, get tough on lenient parole boards, get tough on judges who pass light sentences." Hilton requests a private meeting with the incumbent, who is "a reluctant supporter of capital punishment," thinking that the governor may be sympathetic to Matt's case. But the governor, unbeknownst to Hilton, has invited the media, thereby turning their private meeting into a media circus. The governor admits, at least indirectly, to opposing the death penalty, but makes it clear to Hilton and Helen that he will not intervene on Matt's behalf: "You must understand that in representing the state I must carry out the laws and must submerge my own personal views to carry out the expressed will of the people."

The media coverage has a profound and negative impact on others who are associated with Matt but not implicated in his crimes. His mother Lucille tells Helen that she is now famous: "Yesterday I was in this store and I seen these two ladies eyeing me and when I get closer I hear one of them say, 'I just can't wait to hear that they have executed that monster, Matthew Ponselet.'" Helen is also affected. Her sister tells her at the Easter dinner table that "Mom's friends, the Pierres, they read an article which mentioned your name as being associated with Ponselet." The neighborhood kids start to avoid her and other friends criticize her for neglecting her duties in order to spend time with a death row inmate.

Television is also a medium through which the Bible or, more specifically, the literalist readings of the Bible are disseminated, especially in religious programming and by televangelists. But we must not overlook the fact that the movie itself is a powerful medium that has the potential for influencing public opinion. Tim Robbins, the film's director, denies that there is a strong political dimension to the film. He claims that ethics and politics clash only in the scene in which Sister Helen and Hilton pay a visit to the governor, who then rebuffs their request on the grounds that he must represent the viewpoint of his constituency. Otherwise, the film is not political because it is not directed at either Democrats or Republicans but rather at morality as such.[7] While it is true that one should not reduce this film to its political dimensions, Robbins is being disingenuous here, for the film makes a powerful statement against capital punishment and also, in the process, against the use of the Bible to support the death penalty.

In Sister Helen the film has created a compelling spokesperson against the death penalty. As we have seen, she answers the biblical argument by noting that a literalist reading of the Bible is not workable. As viewers, we take her viewpoint seriously, precisely because her representation throughout the film as someone joyously and thoughtfully religious in the most profound sense. This point is alluded to in an encounter that occurs one day as she drives home from the prison. Sister Helen is stopped by a state trooper for speeding. When he realizes that she is a nun, he decides not give her a ticket, apparently out of respect for her status. He tells her that he once gave a ticket to a man who was an employee of the Internal Revenue Service, and the next year he was audited. Presumably he fears that giving a ticket to a nun may involve him in an even more powerful reckoning.[8]

The film directs its audience to view Matt's situation through Sister Helen's eyes in a number of other ways. The opening of the film contains scenes from the home movie taken at the time of Helen's entry into her religious community as a novice. She is dressed in a white gown and veil, and has the radiant glow of a bride on her wedding day. Her piety and happiness are palpable. Second, the film allows us to witness in detail her own dilemmas in relation to Matt and the ways in which she strives to overcome them. Third, the film shows Helen's attempts to reach out to the victims' parents, on the one hand, and to Matt's mother, on the other. Finally, we view Matt's execution through her eyes. The focus on Sister Helen's viewpoint does not by any means minimize Matt's crimes, which Helen imagines frequently and with horror, but it does show Matt's execution as a violation rather than a fulfillment of God's justice and will.

The film's construction of character therefore encourages viewers to identify with Sister Helen or at least to perceive Matt, Sister Helen's role as his advisor, and the experience of Matt's last days and moments from her perspective. This experience, vicarious as it might be, nevertheless requires us to respond to the issue of the death penalty not in an abstract or theoretical way, but very personally.[9]

Spiritual Redemption

In the end, all avenues of appeal fail, and Matt is executed. Despite her best efforts, Sister Helen does not succeed in helping Matt avoid the death penalty, as he had hoped she would. But by this point in the film, we know that this does not spell Helen's failure. Despite Matt's hopes and wishes, Helen had signed on not as his legal counsel but as his spiritual advisor. What exactly this role entails, as the film shows, is open to interpretation. The prison chaplain, who can barely contain his disdain for Helen, views this role in a narrow way: the advisor's sole function is to get Matthew to utter the formal confession and to accept the sacraments before his death. But Helen takes a much broader view. As Matthew's spiritual advisor, she intends to bring him to the point of acknowledging his own role in and responsibility for the deaths of Walter and Hope. Only then will he stop deceiving himself, and only then can he be reconciled with God.

In the plot line that traces Sister Helen's impact on Matt's spiritual development, the Bible plays an even larger and more varied role than it does in the legal and political narrative. The tension between Helen and Chaplain Farley is palpable from their first meeting and further helps to align the viewer with Helen's perspective. Chaplain Farley is the foil to Sister Helen. He is male where she is female, jaded where she is idealistic, domineering where she is charismatic, legalistic where she is spiritual. He disapproves of the fact that she does not wear a nun's habit, and he does not seem to know that habits have not been required for many years. He is most aggravated, however, by her quiet resistance to his authority, and, by extension, or so he implies, to the authority of the Bible. The chaplain challenges her, "Are you familiar with the Old Testament, 'Thou shalt not kill but if you shed the blood of man by man shall your blood be shed?'" (Gen 9:6).[10] Helen has a swift and faintly disrespectful rejoinder, "Yes. Are you familiar with the New Testament where Jesus speaks of grace and reconciliation?"[11] The contrast between them, and the Bible-quoting contest that Helen wins yet again, helps to define Sister Helen as a figure who can be trusted by Matt, even before he is able truly to understand and appreciate her aims, and by the viewer, who is further encouraged to be sympathetic to her role in Matt's life and to side with her on the issue of capital punishment.

Sister Helen takes the spiritual element of her formal role as Matt's advisor seriously indeed. The theme of spiritual salvation is signaled by the fact that Matt's execution, and hence Helen's most impassioned efforts on his behalf, take place during the Easter season, evoking the theme of salvation and redemption through Christ's own death and resurrection. Her task is to bring Matthew from his defensive, argumentative, angry, and hateful self to an acknowledgment of his human responsibility and the pain that he has caused others. The Bible, whose effectiveness as a tool in the hands of the pro-death-penalty lobby has been neutralized in this film, becomes a crucial instrument in her success.

The Bible plays a variety of roles in Helen's campaign for Matt's soul. The frequent references to the Bible and to the importance of reading the Bible are most conspicuous. In one of their early meetings, Helen asks Matt whether he reads the Bible. Matt confesses that he is not much of a Bible reader, but, he hastens to add, he does pick it up from time to time. Helen comments, "Like W. C. Fields read his Bible? . . . W. C. Fields, he used to play this drunken character in the movies. So he's on his deathbed and a friend comes to visit, and he sees him reading the Bible. And the friend says, 'W. C. you don't believe in God. What are you doin' reading the Bible?' And Fields says [here Helen drawls broadly], 'I'm lookin' for a loophole.'"

This joke is disarming. For one thing, it reveals that Helen has a sense of humor, even about matters as serious as death and religion. Second, the joke implies that she has some sympathy for and understanding of people who, unlike herself, do not attempt to live the sorts of lives in which the Bible is central. Third, the joke introduces, indirectly, the belief that in the final analysis, each person—W. C. Fields, Sister Helen, Matt—will face God's judgment; it is not yet too late for Matt to "look for a loophole" that will set matters right with God, if not with the state judicial system.

After Matt has been moved to the death house, he reminds Helen of this joke. "So this is the end, huh? My death house vacation. Three days of quiet. Plenty of time to read my Bible. Look for a loophole." But Helen is not in the mood to joke. She urgently wants to know, "Did you read anything about Jesus in that Bible?" Matt mechanically recites a brief catechism: "Holy man, did good, in heaven, praise Jesus." Helen ignores this flippant response and continues, "There are passages in there about when Jesus was facing death alone that you might wanna check out." Matt dismisses the idea: "Uh, I think me 'n Jesus had a different way of dealing with things. He was one of them turn the other cheek guys." Helen responds: "It takes a lot of strength to turn the other cheek, Matt. You say you like rebels. What do you think Jesus was? . . . He was a dangerous man." Matt sneers, "What's so dangerous about 'love your brother'?" Helen: "Because his love changed things, his . . . his love changes things. People that nobody cared about, the prostitutes, the beggars, the poor, finally had someone who respected them, loved them, made 'em realize their own worth. They had dignity and were becoming so powerful, that made the guys on top get real nervous so they had to kill Jesus." Matt says, "Kinda like me, huh." Helen retorts, "No, Matt, not at all like you. Jesus changed the world with his love. You watched while two kids were murdered."

Helen tries to describe Jesus in a way that will make sense to Matt and at the same time to introduce what she sees as Jesus' central contribution: the love of others, which means respecting them as human beings regardless of their social status or wealth. But she rejects Matt's misguided response. Later, on the day before his execution, Helen asks again, "You been readin' your Bible?" Matt says, "I tried to last night . . . makes me want to sleep. I'm trying to stay conscious. I appreciate you trying to save me, but me and God, we got our things squared away. I know Jesus died on the cross for us and I know he's gonna be there to take care of me when I appear before God on judgment day." These last words, like his earlier rote recitation, sound more like a Sunday School formulation than a mature expression of Christian faith. Helen comments, "Matt, redemption isn't some kind of free ticket admission that you get because Jesus paid the price. You gotta participate in your own redemption. You got some work to do."

The film's talk about the Bible keeps faith and salvation front and center as an issue between Helen and Matt. Another prominent feature is direct quotation of the Bible. One passage that appeals to Matt is John 8:32: "You shall know the truth and the truth shall set you free." "The truth shall make you free," he repeats. "I like that. So I pass that lie detector test and I'm home free." This is obviously not how Helen understands this verse, but she ignores the discrepancy in their notions of freedom and continues: "Matt, if you do die, as your friend, I wanna help you to die with dignity. And I don't see how you can do that unless you start to own up to the part you played in Walter and Hope's death." Her words subtly redefine the meaning of freedom. John 8:32 refers not to physical freedom but to spiritual redemption. For Matt, real freedom does not entail release from death row but rather dying with dignity, that is, in full recognition of his own culpability. Just as Helen had to revise and broaden Captain Beliveau's literal understanding of biblical law, so she must challenge and revise Matt's reading of John 8:32.

The camera then turns to Matt's unsuccessful appeal to the governor, his inconclusive polygraph test, and, poignantly, his family's last visit. At parting, his mother and brothers are allowed to say good bye and to take his things, but they are not permitted any physical contact: no hugs, no kisses. A final phone call is allowed, however. The process of final separation has begun.

As it turns out, this last phone conversation with his mother marks the moment of breakthrough. As Matt tells Helen later, his mother persisted in blaming Vitello, Matt's accomplice, even in this final phone call. Matt says, "I didn't want her thinking that. Something you said. I coulda walked away [from Vitello on the night of the murders]. But I didn't. I was a victim. I told my mother I was yellow. She kept saying, 'It wasn't you, Matt, it wasn't you.'" Helen tells him, "Your mama loves you, Matt."

Matt breaks down. He confesses to killing Walter and to raping Hope. This moment of truth is sealed by a rite of confession, more meaningful if less conventional than the prescribed formulation that the chaplain expected. Helen asks, "Do you take responsibility for both of their deaths?" Matt replies, "Yes, ma'am." He continues: "When the lights dimmed on the tier [last] night I kneeled down by my bunk and prayed for them kids. I never done that before." Helen replies, with great emotion, "Oh, Matt, there are spaces of sorrow only God can touch. You did a terrible thing, Matt, a terrible thing. But you have dignity now and no one can take that from you. You are a son of God, Matthew Poncelet."

Matt's recognition of his crime and his sincere prayer for his victims bestow dignity upon him, the type of dignity that Sister Helen had earlier connected with the spiritual freedom to which John 8:32 refers. Matt has been transformed from a subhuman monster (in the eyes of the media) or an irresponsible, immature, arrogant, and weak-willed convict (as he appears to Sister

Helen and hence to us) into a "child of God." The term "son of God" is used in the New Testament primarily to refer to Jesus, but John 1:12 applies this label to believers in God: "To all who received him, who believed in his name, he gave power to become children of God." Matt finds some amusement in Helen's words. "Nobody ever called me no son of God before." But he immediately becomes serious again: "I just hope my death can give them parents some relief. I really do. . . ."

As Helen and Matt walk slowly towards the execution chamber, she reads to him from Isaiah 43:1–2: "I have called thee by thy name, thou art mine. Should you pass through the sea, I shall be with thee; should thou walk through fire thou shalt not be scorched, and the flame shall not burn you." In Isaiah, this section is preceded by the words: "But now thus says the LORD, he who created you, O Jacob, he who formed you, O Israel: Do not fear, for I have redeemed you." By reading these words of salvation, Helen comforts Matt with the promise of divine protection and assures him that he has been redeemed, not only in her eyes but in the eyes of God.

The physical book itself also plays a role in the development of this spiritual plot line. In this movie, the Bible is a "prop" whose significance shifts as the movie progresses. Initially, the Bible is a book that represents the institutional variety of religion that affects Matt only in a superficial way. Sister Helen, through her story about W. C. Fields, introduces the notion of a "loophole," touching lightly but meaningfully on the possibility that the Bible may offer relief and release even for a transgressor like Matt. By the end of the film, the Bible has come to symbolize the divine word and Matt's connection with Sister Helen. Before he sets off for the execution chamber, Matt gives Sister Helen his own Bible, freshly inscribed with his date of death. The Bible now constitutes a token of his knowledge and understanding of the gift that she has given him. Through the Bible, the best part of him will live on, at least in Sister Helen's memory.

Themes

The Image of God

Yet another theme developed in this film is the notion that human beings are made in the image of God: "Then God said, 'Let us make humankind in our image, according to our likeness'" (Gen. 1:26). Although this passage is not quoted, the idea that every human being is worthy of respect is a thread that weaves throughout the film. Helen unfailingly treats Matt with dignity, even as she becomes increasingly haunted by her imaginings—portrayed in stark black and white—of what went on in the forest when Matt and Carl raped and murdered Hope and Walter. Matt, in turn, struggles with the concept of human dignity. To some extent, he accords Helen respect for coming to see him and for *not* preaching fire and brimstone, as other clerics may have done. But he repeatedly reverts to treating her as a potential sex object, as he has been accustomed to viewing all women with the exception of his mother, and, one hopes, his estranged daughter. At one point he leers at Helen, "I like being alone with you. You're looking real good to me." She immediately snaps back, "Look at you. Death is breathing down your neck and here you are, playing your lil' Matt-on-the-make games. I'm not here for your amusement, Matt; show some respect." Matt says, rudely, "Why should I respect you? Because you're a nun and you wear that little cross around your neck?" Helen responds, "Because I'm a person; every person deserves respect."

Just as his crime, and more generally, his attitude to other people imply that Matt does not see others as fully human, so do these attitudes diminish his own humanity and influence the ways that others see him. As they prepare for the pardon-board hearing, Hilton tells him, "They're thinking of the crime and you as a monster. It's easy to kill a monster but it's hard to kill a human being." Matt does not help matters when, during a television interview, he expresses his admiration for Hitler and proclaims his own ambition to join a terrorist group. Helen loses her temper and rages at him: "You're a fool. You are making it so easy for them to kill you, coming across as some sort of a crazed animal, Nazi racist terrorist mad dog who deserves to die." Thus not only Matt but also those who seek his death are guilty of not viewing other human beings—all other human beings—as fully human, in the image of God, and hence as deserving or even requiring our respect.

Spiritual Love

Another major theme is love, not as a sexual or romantic emotion, but as a reflection of the spiritual love that characterizes the ideal relationship between God and humankind. In the film, this theme is expressed through the deepening friendship between Matt and Helen. The two do have a few things in common. As Helen points out playfully, they both live with the poor: he, in prison; she, in her neighborhood. And like Helen, Matt enjoys his mother's love and also cares about her, at least to some extent. But the movie generally emphasizes the differences between these two people: she comes from an upper-middle class family, has always been supported by her family, and has dedicated her life to helping others, from a foundation of profound faith. Unlike Helen, he comes from a poor family, with little education; he is both racist and sexist, preoccupied with alcohol, drugs, and sex. At home, Helen says to her mother, "He's so full of hate he doesn't trust anybody; he just keeps pushing me away." Worst of all, he is a man convicted of the most heinous crimes imaginable but unable to admit his culpability even to himself. Matt consistently shifts the blame onto his erstwhile friend, Carl Vitello, who, luckier, or perhaps wealthier, than Matthew, is not on death row but serving a life sentence. Helen, on the other hand, has dedicated her life to God. She personifies the divine and represents Christ in the world.

The simple silver cross that Helen wears symbolizes her Christian faith, which is the instrument that she will wield in her battle for Matt's soul. The potency of the cross as a weapon is intimated in the scene depicting her first visit to Angola Prison. As she goes through the security check, her cross sets off the alarm, and the camera focuses on it intently as the guard passes her scanner over it repeatedly. The cross is not a lethal weapon in the usual sense but in the terms set out by this film, it poses a vital threat to the institution's official religiosity as represented by the chaplain and a challenge to the belief, held by most if not all officials at the prison, that capital punishment is an expression of divine and human justice.

The gap between Helen and Matt is symbolized throughout much of the film by the steel mesh and prison bars that separate them physically. These have a realistic basis insofar as they are familiar to viewers—if not for most of us from firsthand experience, then from many other depictions of prisons in film and on television.[12] We expect to find a physical barrier between a death row convict and his visitors. But the encounters between Matt and Helen are set up and framed by the camera in such a way as to draw the eye relentlessly to the symbolic meaning of this physical barrier.

The change in Matthew's consciousness is accompanied by a change in their physical positioning on the screen. On the day of his death, after his confession, he knows that he has found love—not sexual love but spiritual love—for the first time in his life: "I've never had no real love myself, never loved a woman or anybody else much good. . . . Well it figures I'd have to die to find love. . . . Thank you for loving me." The change in Matt's understanding is genuine. For the first time in his life he is able to see beyond his own needs and desires and recognize the needs of another. He realizes how hard his impending death will be for Helen and as they wait out the last few moments together before he must walk his last steps, he asks her if she is alright. She replies, "Yeah, Matt. I'm OK. Christ is here. . . . Look, I want the last thing you see in this world to be a face of love. So look at me. When they do this thing you look at me. I'll be the face of love for you."[13] As he moves down towards the execution chamber, she holds on to his shoulder—the first and only affectionate touch that he has experienced while on death row, and perhaps long before that. She reads a section of Isaiah aloud from the Bible he has given her, and then kisses his shoulder when they must finally separate. For Matt's last moments, then, the physical barriers between him and Helen have fallen away, just as the spiritual barriers have done.

The moment is brief; soon Matt takes his place on the execution table, and Helen takes hers in the observation area, along with the victims' parents and other witnesses. But they continue to touch through their gazes until the moment that he loses consciousness. He tells her that he loves her; she responds in kind and holds out her arm to "touch him" in an action that, as in *The Truman Show*, evokes God reaching out to his creation Adam in Michelangelo's "Creation of Man" on the ceiling of the Sistine Chapel. It is in this way that she fulfills her promise to be the face of love or, one might say, the face of Christ for him, holding him close as he meets his death. Again, these changes in physical proximity are realistic in that they accompany the steps in the inexorable process towards execution, but they also serve a symbolic function. As Matt moves closer to death, an event that signifies the failure of his and Helen's legal and political efforts, he is also moving towards spiritual redemption and, from a Christian point of view, the possibility of eternal life.

Abiding

Closely related to the theme of divine love is a third biblical motif, that of abiding. Abiding is a divine attribute associated with both Jesus and God throughout the Gospel of John (e.g., 15:4). Helen promises that she will stay with Matt, and she violates that promise only once, inadvertently, when she faints in the death house and must be taken to the infirmary. Others, including Captain Beliveau and Chaplain Farley, disapprove of her faithful attendance, as do the victims' parents, whose concerns are presented in detail and with gravity. Earl Delacroix, Walter's father, confronts Helen during the recess in the pardon-board hearing and accuses her of neglecting him and the Percys in her zeal to support Matt. She takes this criticism to heart and visits Mr. Delacroix and the Percys. They all express their anger and resentment of Matthew, but the Percys go further and argue that she cannot provide support both to them and to him at the same time. Only by supporting the death penalty for Matt can she truly help them. Mr. Delacroix, however, is more open and indeed reaches out to Helen. She accompanies him to a meeting of a support group for parents of murdered children, and after Matt's execution they meet for prayer at a small church. Helen, too, is changed, not only by her meeting with Matt, which requires her to draw on all of her intellectual, emotional, and spiritual resources, but by her encounter with Mr. Delacroix, which allows her to view the situation in its full moral complexity.

Redemption

Finally, the theme of redemption is signaled by the presence of Jesus imagery. The chaplain, the prison's formal and official representative of Christ, is shown as a decidedly un-Christlike figure, empty of the spirit of forgiveness and understanding. Sister Helen, on the other hand, embodies these qualities, despite the fact that she is female and does not wear a habit. But the most explicit Christ imagery is associated not with either of these characters but with Matt. Like all those who are executed by lethal injection, Matt is strapped to a narrow table, in cruciform position, with his arms outstretched and his legs slightly apart. For his final words to his victims, the table is tipped upright so that Matt can face them through the glass. The tableau, while realistic, is also a striking parallel to Christ at Golgotha, nailed to the cross and flanked on both sides, in Jesus' case, by two criminals (Matt. 27:38) and, in Matt's case, by two prison guards, who, though not criminal in any formal sense, are from the film's perspective guilty of murder by virtue of their collusion in this act of state-sponsored execution. This image conveys that Matt, like Christ, has indeed been killed unjustly by the state for political reasons at the same time as it symbolizes his spiritual redemption and his rebirth as a son of God. While the words of the priest who presides over his funeral ("With the love of God and the peace of our dear Lord Jesus Christ bless and console us and gently wipe every tear from our eyes, Amen") may reflect a standard liturgy, it takes on new meaning in the context of Matt's own spiritual journey.

CONCLUSION

The themes of capital punishment and spiritual redemption are linked by the question of divine and human justice. The use of the biblical *lex talionis* in the arguments in favor of capital punishment imply that by executing a man who is guilty of murder, the government, and by extension, human society are acting in accordance with divine justice. But Sister Helen's personal campaign for Matt's redemption implies the opposite, that divine justice is served not by punishing the physical body but by saving the soul. Divine justice has been done the moment that Matthew accepts responsibility for his own actions, expresses sincere regret for those actions, and asks forgiveness from those whom he has hurt so deeply. The title of the movie captures both of these senses. A "Dead Man Walking" is a man on his way to his execution, but this phrase may also designate a man who is dead to that which makes us human: to respect, to love, to genuine empathy and concern for the other. At the moment that he becomes a "Dead Man Walking" in the judicial sense, Matt has ceased to be one in a spiritual sense.

4

Fried Green Tomatoes and the Power of Female Friendships (Ruth)

Naomi said, "Turn back, my daughters, why will you go with me? Do I still have sons in my womb that they may become your husbands?" . . . But Ruth said, "Do not press me to leave you or to turn back from following you! Where you go, I will go; Where you lodge, I will lodge; your people shall be my people, and your God my God."

Ruth 1:11, 16

INTRODUCTION

Female friendship, while not as ubiquitous as male-female romance, is nevertheless present in many Hollywood films. The theme is most obvious in female buddy films such as *Thelma and Louise* (1991), where the protagonists are women, but it is also explored in many other films where women's relationships are only incidental to the main theme or plot line; the comedy *About a Boy* (2002) is only one example among many. In the Bible, on the other hand, female friendship is a significant theme in only one book: Ruth. The book of Ruth tells the story of an Israelite woman named Naomi, who leaves her native Bethlehem for the wilds of Moab in times of famine. While in Moab, her two sons marry Moabite women but have no children. Her husband and her sons die, leaving Naomi alone except for her two daughters-in-law. She decides to return to Bethelehem and instructs her daughters-in-law to return to their Moabite families so that they may remarry and have children, for Naomi will have no more sons to offer them. One daughter-in-law, Orpah, tearfully agrees; the other, Ruth, refuses to leave, uttering the famous words quoted in the epigraph. The rest of the book narrates their return to Bethlehem, Ruth's efforts to support them by gleaning in the field of Boaz, the discovery that Boaz is a blood relative, and finally, the marriage of Ruth and Boaz and the birth of their child. The story revolves around the movement from emptiness to plenty on two planes: that of agriculture, in which the story moves from famine to a plentiful harvest, and that of Naomi's emotional life, in which she moves from emptiness—the death of her husband and two sons—to fullness, realized with the birth of Ruth's son.[1]

It would be far-fetched to claim that the biblical book of Ruth underlies, either directly or indirectly, Hollywood's treatment of female friendship. Given the fact that friendship is a fundamental source of satisfaction and strength in the lives of many women of all ages, its presence in the cinema requires no specific antecedent source. However, at least one film self-consciously models elements of the relationship between female characters on the story of Ruth and Naomi: *Fried Green Tomatoes* (1991), directed by Jon Avnet and based on the book *Fried Green Tomatoes at the Whistle Stop Cafe*, by Fannie Flagg.[2]

FILM SUMMARY

The film has two distinct plot lines that parallel one another and also intersect at significant points. The first is played out in a frame narrative, set in the present, that focuses on the friendship between a middle-aged woman, Evelyn Couch (Cathy Bates), and an elderly woman, Ninny Threadgoode (Jessica Tandy), whom she visits regularly at the Rose Hill Nursing Home. Evelyn and Ninny first meet in the sitting room of the nursing home. Evelyn and her husband, Ed, had come to Rose Hill to visit Ed's aunt. For reasons unknown, this aunt takes extreme exception to Evelyn and orders her out of the room. As Evelyn waits for Ed in the common sitting room, Ninny comes over and strikes up a conversation about nothing in particular. Evelyn is wary at first, unsure of Ninny's state of mind or her sanity. But as Ninny reminisces about her long-ago childhood in the tiny hamlet of Whistle Stop, not far from this very nursing home, Evelyn is captivated. She begins to visit Ninny regularly to hear further installments, so absorbed is she with the characters and events that Ninny describes so vividly.

The story that Ninny tells constitutes a second narrative that occupies the majority of the film's attention. This story also features the friendship between two women, Ruth Jameson and Idgie Threadgoode (Mary Stuart Masterson), the latter of whom is ostensibly a childhood friend of Ninny's who later becomes her sister-in-law. The story begins in Idgie's childhood, just after World War I, at the wedding of her oldest sister. Ruth (Mary-Louise Parker) has come for the wedding and, not incidentally, to visit with Bud, Idgie's adored older brother. The idyll is shattered by a tragic accident. As Bud, Ruth, and Idgie are out strolling, a gust of wind lifts Ruth's wide-brimmed hat off her head. Bud chases after it along the railroad tracks until his foot becomes wedged in the track. Unable to free himself, he is killed by an oncoming train.

Bud's death overshadows the rest of Idgie's childhood and much of the rest of the story. Ruth returns home; Idgie retreats from her family and moves in with their black hired hand, Big George. He looks after her tenderly but she nevertheless becomes involved with the town's lowlife. Some years later, Ruth Jameson returns to spend the summer with Idgie's family. She has a job teaching Bible stories to young children at the church's summer school, but her real purpose, assigned to her by Idgie's mother, is to draw Idgie out of her depression and back to her family. Idgie initially resists Ruth's overtures at friendship. But she is also intrigued and goads Ruth into taking some daring chances. Idgie dares Ruth to jump with her onto a freight train, rob it of its goods (packaged food that Idgie distributes to the poor), and then jump off again. To Idgie's surprise, Ruth does not hesitate, at least, not much. Ironically, it is Idgie, and not Ruth, who get hurts in this adventure. Ruth helps her to hobble the two miles home. This incident transforms Idgie's attitude toward Ruth. Ruth, in turn, is won over when Idgie, a self-described "bee charmer," retrieves honeycomb directly from the hive, without any protection, and emerges completely unscathed. For the rest of the summer, the two are inseparable. Only it seems that it is Idgie who has influenced Ruth, not the other way around. Although Ruth continues to be a regular churchgoer, she also joins Idgie in her drinking and poker games at the River Club.

At the very end of her summer stay, Ruth tells Idgie that, as soon as she returns home, she will be married to a man named Frank Bennett. Upset, Idgie cuts all ties with Ruth, though she does drive to the wedding to watch from afar. Ruth and Idgie continue their separate lives; we see little of Ruth's life but follow along with Idgie as she continues to drink, gamble, and live with the black servants on her mother's estate.

After some time, Idgie's mother again steps in to reconnect the two friends. She bakes a pie for Ruth and asks Idgie to deliver it to Ruth's door. Idgie is shocked to see Ruth. From Ruth's evasive manner and from the huge "shiner" on her right eye, Idgie realizes immediately that Frank has been beating her. Idgie loses her temper and threatens to kill Frank if he should ever touch Ruth again. Some time later, Ruth, now pregnant, leaves Frank and returns to live with Idgie and her family. When her baby boy is born, she calls him Bud Jr., or Buddy. Idgie's father lends them money to start the Whistle Stop Cafe, whose specialty is fried green tomatoes. There is some trouble from the local Klansmen, who are not pleased with the fact that the cafe serves blacks and hobos, but otherwise they are managing very well.[3] One day, Frank returns;

first, together with his fellow Klansmen from Georgia, he ties up Big George and beats him until the town sheriff, who has had a crush on Idgie for years, puts a stop to their sport. Then Frank returns alone and smuggles Ruth's baby out of the house. Just as he is about to put little Buddy in the truck and drive off, he is stopped by some of Ruth and Idgie's loyal friends. He goes missing, mysteriously, and the sheriff from his Georgia town starts hanging about. He makes it clear to Idgie that he will have her tried for murder should there be even a shred of evidence linking her to Frank's disappearance. Five years pass; then one day torrential rains stir up the river bed and bring Frank's truck to light. Idgie is arrested, tried, and acquitted. Life returns to normal, more or less, until Ruth's death from cancer. Ninny speculates that Ruth likely died not knowing whether or not Idgie had really killed Frank.[4]

The film cuts back and forth from the "present," in which Evelyn visits Ninny regularly at the nursing home, to the "past," the story of Idgie and Ruth that Ninny tells to Evelyn, serial fashion. Ninny's tale not only holds Evelyn spellbound but gives her the courage to make changes in her own life. As Ninny tells Evelyn the story of an extraordinary friendship between two young women, the friendship between Ninny and Evelyn also develops.

The plot lines intersect at the very end of the film. One day, Evelyn arrives at the nursing home only to find Ninny's room empty. She panics until she learns that it is Mrs. Otis who has died. Ninny has gone home as she has said she would do all along. But Evelyn knows something that Ninny does not: Ninny has no home to which to return. During her lengthy stay at Rose Hill, her house in Whistle Stop was condemned and torn down. Evelyn finds Ninny sitting on her suitcase in front of the lot where her house used to stand. Together, they visit the cemetery and stop in front of Ruth's gravestone. Magically, there sits a fresh jar of honey and a loving note to Ruth from the "bee charmer." Is Ninny in fact Idgie? Perhaps. We know that Idgie was eight or nine years old when Bud was killed in 1920, which would make her eighty-three years old, exactly Ninny's age in the frame narrative. The movie does not, however, make the identification any more explicit than that and leaves each viewer to decide.

USE OF THE BIBLE

The Bible appears in this film primarily through the quotation of or reference to specific biblical passages or books. These references fit naturally into the film's settings and plot. Films set in the southern United States often portray characters that attend church, cite the occasional biblical passage, and inter-act with clergy.[5] So, for example, it is not surprising to hear Psalm 23 ("The

Lord is my shepherd") recited at Bud's funeral, as this psalm is often said as part of the funerary liturgy or by characters facing mortal danger or death.[6] The recitation of Psalm 23 here contributes to the verisimilitude of the film and does not become the object of specific reflection. Other biblical quotations and references not only enhance the film's realism but also illuminate its major plot, characters, and themes.

Plot and Character

During the summer that Ruth spends with Idgie and her family, Ruth and Idgie's mother faithfully attend church, but Idgie refuses to step inside the building, let alone attend a service. One Sunday, the billboard outside the church displays the following message: "Why did Noah let two snakes on the boat, when he had a chance to get rid of them once & for all?"[7] This question provides the theme for Reverend Sproggett's sermon, in which he expounds on snakes and serpents within the community that tempt upright and honest citizens to gamble, drink, and worse. As he is delivering this message, Idgie rides by on a wagon, off to the very den of iniquity against which Reverend Sproggett is railing so passionately. She laughs mockingly as she passes the church. The Reverend comments, "Snakes and serpents take many disguises."

This scene identifies Idgie as a rebel, someone who thumbs her nose at social and religious norms and institutions. Just as she is physically outside the church while her family and neighbors are inside, so she lives outside the norms of the conventional, middle-class, white southern society to which all the others adhere. The scene also sets her apart from two of the people who love her most, her mother and Ruth, who sit inside the church as Idgie rides by.

The Reverend expresses and reinforces the social concerns of the church-going members of the community about other segments of their society. But at the same time the film also insists that, contrary to Sproggett's sermon, these social distinctions do not correlate neatly with the moral categories of good and evil. Though Idgie's mother and Ruth listen attentively to Sproggett's rantings, they obviously, openly, and lavishly love Idgie and support her in every way possible. However willing Idgie may be to transgress social and religious norms, she also maintains a high standard of morality that was frowned on in her own time but is publicly acceptable in the 1990s, the "now" of the frame narrative. Idgie drinks and carouses with the lowlife, but she also goes out of her way to help hobos and black laborers in ways both licit and illicit. Even the Reverend is not entirely the one-dimensional character that his sermon would suggest. He appears in a more complex and hypocritical light at Idgie's murder trial, in which he lies on the witness stand (swearing on a book that looks to all the world like a Bible but is in fact a copy of *Moby Dick*). It might seem odd that he should perjure himself in order to testify on behalf of this "snake and serpent," but we later learn that it is Ruth who put him up to it, dangling before him the enticement of Idgie's possible repentance and salvation.

The billboard query about Noah's hospitality to the serpents therefore contributes to the complex social networks that are essential to this film, and also, thereby, to its verisimilitude. Even viewers whose own social contexts are far removed from the south of the 1920s and 1930s will recognize the message that social demarcations are not to be equated with moral categories.

Much later in the film, the Noah motif reappears, this time in the African American church to which Evelyn accompanies Ninny one Sunday morning. A gospel singer provides a rousing rendition of a song about Noah that, in contrast to Reverend Sproggett's sermon, emphasizes the positive elements of the story. As she sings, the woman moves down the aisle toward Ninny. The scene hints at the possibility that emerges fully only in the film's final scenes, namely, that Ninny is not Idgie's sister-in-law but Idgie herself. Far from being the wily and lowly "serpent," Ninny (Idgie) is the righteous one, who, despite her lack of faith and absence from church, saves others from extinction, just as Noah did.

Reverend Sproggett's Whistle Stop church is the setting for yet another biblical reference. Shortly after Idgie rides by and thumbs her nose at minister and church alike, the camera focuses on Ruth as she reads a children's version of the book of Job aloud to her young students in the summer Bible school. Ruth spies Idgie through the window just at the moment in her story that God finally agrees to let Satan put Job to the test. As Ruth tells her young charges, Job, who had been on top of the world, is plunged down into the deepest of pits, losing his wife, his children, and his wealth. At this point in Ruth's story, the camera cuts to Idgie looking at Ruth through the window.[8] Idgie has come to take Ruth to her surprise birthday party, held at that very den of iniquity against which the preacher had railed so passionately.

Are we to see the life to which Idgie has tempted Ruth as the moral equivalent of Job's trial and despair? Hardly. The film conveys a playful contrast between official southern religiosity and the ideas of morality that accompany it. The movie not only shows Ruth having the time of her life at this birthday party among Idgie's friends; it also provides ample evidence later on that her fundamental faith and piety have remained intact. One might say that Idgie, already identified by the pastor as a snake, and hence associated with Satan, has come to "test" Ruth; the outcome, however, is not sinister but joyous. The film resists any temptation to make Idgie a fallen figure or to show Ruth herself as succumbing to temptation. Instead, it consistently portrays their relationship as positive and life-sustaining for them both.

Job's trial is even more subtly related to the lives of Idgie and Ruth, however. At the point when Ninny begins to narrate their story, both Idgie and

Ruth have everything that young girls could want: youth, love, family, and material comfort. Buddy's death is an accident, hence undeserved, as are Job's sorrows, and his death destroys the charmed life that the girls have led to this point. Whereas Job retains his faith in God, Idgie has no use for God, religion, or any of the mainstays of middle-class, white life in the South. But when Ruth returns to live with her, and especially when Ruth's baby is born, Idgie's life, including love and family, is restored, and she settles down to a more or less stable and satisfying life. Bud Jr.'s name implies that he fills the emptiness left in both Ruth and Idgie's life by the death of his namesake.

Themes

Even more than Job, however, the book of Ruth illuminates the central themes of this film. The biblical book of Ruth is also the source of the most striking biblical quotation in the film. After her mother dies, Ruth gathers the courage to leave her husband. Because of Frank's possessive and abusive nature, and his suspicion of Idgie, Ruth communicates her plans in code. She sends a letter to Idgie and Idgie's mother containing only two documents: a news clipping announcing her own mother's death and a page torn from her Bible. The page contains the first chapter of the book of Ruth. Ruth has underscored chapter 1, verse 16: "Where you go I will go, where you lodge, I will lodge; your people shall be my people, and your God my God." Idgie's mother reads this section aloud to Idgie, and they prepare to welcome Ruth into their home. Like Psalm 23 and the references to Noah and Job, this quotation seems entirely natural in the context of the film's characters and plot. The film has already established that Ruth is a churchgoing woman who knows her Bible; due to her name, the page from the biblical book can be viewed simply as a plot device, a coded petition to Idgie and her mother that she be allowed to move in with the Thread-goodes. But those who are familiar with the content of the book of Ruth will easily see the strong parallels between Ruth and Naomi of Moab and Bethlehem, on the one hand, and Idgie and Ruth of the southern United States several millenia later.

The main thematic connection concerns deep friendship and love between women. In the biblical book, Naomi is the older and Ruth the younger; they are separated by a generation. Their love for each other is expressed in their efforts to look after each other's interests in ways that are possible within their social contexts. Naomi seeks to orchestrate a good marriage for Ruth, and Ruth produces a child that becomes Naomi's, thereby filling the void left by the death of her own sons.[9] In the story of Idgie and Ruth, Ruth is the older one chronologically, but Idgie plays the role of Naomi in the sense that she is the one who offers protection and refuge to Ruth after she leaves Frank Bennett. Just as Naomi is initially reluctant to accept Ruth's loyalty, so is Idgie initially wary of Ruth. But the more important element is the lifelong devotion between them. They set up the Whistle Stop Cafe, develop their specialties (including fried green tomatoes), and thereby provide for one another's sustenance as well as the needs of their employees and the homeless who wander their way. Most significantly, Ruth's child also becomes Idgie's, thus filling the void left by her brother's death; Bud Jr. is raised by both women. Thus Ruth Jameson restores family to Idgie, just as the biblical Ruth did for Naomi.

The strength of their relationship emerges most clearly when Frank begins to show up at the Whistle Stop Cafe, thereby threatening the happiness and stability of their small family. Ruth feels unsettled and regrets Idgie's involvement in her own troubles. She tells Idgie, "I just don't want you to feel like you have to look out for us. I just don't want to be selfish, that's all. Maybe if I wasn't here you'd settle down." Idgie is distraught at the possibility that Ruth may leave. She insists, "I'm as settled as I ever hope to be . . . Believe me when I tell you I don't want you to move out." Ruth describes how she used to thank God for the strength to endure Frank's beatings and for every day that her mother was alive. Now she realizes that prayer is not always the answer. "If that bastard Frank Bennett ever tries to take my child, I won't pray . . . I'll break his neck." Idgie tells Ruth, "Frank Bennett won't be bothering you no more, you understand?" Ruth confronts Idgie: "You killed him, didn't you?" Idgie denies it, but Ruth doesn't believe her.

Frank indeed disappears, thereby removing the threat to Ruth and Bud, though his disappearance too causes trouble for Idgie, who is charged with murder along with her hired man, Big George. Ruth and Idgie continue to live together for the rest of Ruth's life. Ruth provides a focus for Idgie's life, an object for Idgie's affections, and a child to help care for; Ruth's ingenuity contributes to the dropping of the murder charge against Idgie and Big George. Idgie helps Ruth to escape her abusive husband and gives her a home and her love. After Ruth's death, so the film implies, Idgie continues to raise Bud Jr. on her own.

Somewhat less intense, but equally meaningful, is the friendship between Ninny and Evelyn in the frame narrative. Ninny's capacity for friendship is illustrated by her devotion to Mrs. Otis, to the point where she is willing to enter a nursing home herself in order to look out for her.[10] As in the book of Ruth, there is a generational difference between Ninny and Evelyn, and an initial wariness on the part of one woman towards the other. In this plot line, however, it is the younger woman who is needy.

Evelyn's "emptiness" is not related to the death of a person but to a failing marriage. Evelyn feels that she must change in order to salvage her relationship with Ed. Her efforts to repair their marriage lead her to behave in ways both hilarious and pathetic. Evelyn signs up for various personal development courses without telling Ed what she is up to. The first course is intended to teach her how to be a better wife. In doing so, it simply reinforces the message that she must change in order to refocus Ed's attention on her. Initially Evelyn follows through on the prescribed exercises faithfully. On one occasion she prepares Ed's favorite dinner and sets the table beautifully, in hope and anticipation of a romantic dinner together. Ed, unaware of her distress and oblivious to her efforts, breezes in from work directly to the dinner table. He does indeed compliment her on dinner but, far from lavishing attention on Evelyn, takes the plate into the den and settles down to eat dinner in front of the television. Evelyn's friend supplies a trenchant analysis of the situation: "What we really need is an assertiveness training class for southern women. . . . Especially you, sweetheart, you're living in the dark ages." Evelyn consoles herself with chocolate bars and donuts, in bulk.

Having failed to increase her marital satisfaction by conventional means, Evelyn tries another class. This one focuses on "reclaim[ing] our own power as women." At the first session the group leader announces, "Tonight we're going to begin to explore our own femaleness by examining the source of our strength and our separateness, our vaginas." She then instructs her students to slip off their panties and straddle a mirror on the floor. This is too much for Evelyn, but of course she is too polite to say so. As she excuses herself, the teacher asks, "Do you have a problem with your sexuality?" Evelyn replies, "No, ma'am, but I do have a problem with my girdle."

Evelyn is so fascinated with the story of Frank Bennett's death that Ninny begins to worry that one day she will hit Ed over the head with a frying pan in exasperation. The danger exists, perhaps. One day, as she passes through the supermarket checkout counter, she stands transfixed by a tabloid headline that screams luridly, "Wife kills husband and sells his body parts to aliens." Evelyn comes face to face with her own passivity and her overdone southern niceness towards men when she is jostled roughly and rudely by a young man in the supermarket, and then again outside by the same man in the parking lot. If she is the quintessential southern wife, this man, like the other men in her life, is hardly a perfect southern gentleman. Evelyn finally confides her distress to Ninny, who diagnoses her basic problem: menopause. Ninny prescribes hormones and a paying job. Evelyn follows this advice to the letter. She also takes up vigorous exercise and switches from candy bars to raw vegetables in order to lose weight and improve her self-image.

She also begins to stand up to Ed. She single-handedly tears down the wall of their grown son's room and finally tells Ed what she feels when he takes his dinner into the television room instead of sharing a quiet meal with her. It is Evelyn's friendship with Ninny and Ninny's narrative of Ruth and Idgie that encourage Evelyn to assert herself and finally to shed the persona of the southern wife. Just as the biblical Ruth made Naomi's empty life full, so Ninny causes Evelyn to regain her self-esteem and derive enjoyment from life again.

Evelyn reciprocates Ninny's affection and concern. Because Ninny has no home after she leaves Rose Hill Nursing Home, Evelyn announces to Ed that Ninny will come to live with them. The following conversation ensues:

> **Ed:** She's an old woman; what if she got sick or something? . . . She isn't even family.
>
> **Evelyn:** She's family to me.

When Evelyn admits that she has not yet broached the subject with Ninny, Ed responds:

> **Ed:** Well, good. Then we'll just pretend it never happened.
>
> **Evelyn:** I'm making my own money now. I'll pay for everything. You don't have to do a thing.
>
> **Ed:** Evelyn, it's never gonna happen, so just forget about it.

Evelyn suddenly becomes formidable:

> **Evelyn:** Don't you ever say never to me! . . . Someone helped put a mirror up in front of my face. And I didn't like what I saw one bit. And you know what I did? I changed. And that someone was Mrs. Threadgoode. She needs my love and care now. And I'm gonna give it to her.

Thus Ninny and Evelyn will become family, just as Ruth and Idgie did, and Ruth and Naomi long before them.

These three narrative lines—Ruth and Naomi, Ruth and Idgie, Ninny and Evelyn—are not entirely parallel, but each of them illustrates the power of women's friendship to transform and to sustain. All three fulfill one of Ninny's proverbs: "God never shuts one door without opening another."

The possibility that Ninny may indeed be Idgie adds another element to this analysis of friendship. If Ninny is in fact Idgie, the film does not show us two parallel relationships (Idgie and Ruth, Ninny and Evelyn) but rather portrays Ninny/Idgie as someone with a deep capacity for friendship, reaching out to Ruth in her youth, to Evelyn in her old age, and no doubt to others, including Mrs. Otis, in between. The ambiguity around Ninny's identity meshes with yet another ambiguity in the film itself: the possibility that Idgie and Ruth are not merely friends but also lovers. This ambiguity also constitutes a point of connection to the biblical book of Ruth, about which similar questions have been raised.

In the book of Ruth, Ruth is Naomi's daughter-in-law. Much of the plot focuses on their efforts to find a suitable husband for Ruth and thereby to secure their future in one of the few ways open to women in the biblical period. In the context of biblical literature, the bond between them is striking. In no other biblical book is the friendship between women, whether related by blood or not, such a major theme. Most other female relationships are between sisters and/or co-wives. In Genesis 19, the two daughters of Lot collude with one another to make their father drunk and to commit incest with him in order to get pregnant and have children. In most other cases the narrative emphasizes the rivalry between women. Hagar, pregnant with Abraham's son Ishmael, flaunts her fertility in the face of her mistress Sarah (Genesis 16); Rachel and Leah, the daughters of Laban and wives of Jacob, are rivals for Jacob's love and his seed (Genesis 30); Peninah, married to Elhanan, teases her co-wife Hannah about her barrenness (1 Samuel 1). Ruth, by contrast, insists on accompanying Naomi on her return journey from Moab to Bethlehem, despite the fact that Naomi has no son to give her in marriage. Naomi is initially unwilling to accept Ruth's decision to stay with her. Naomi's ongoing laments for her "empty" condition, as she continues to mourn for her dead husband and sons, suggest her failure to recognize the depth of Ruth's devotion and the life-giving importance of Ruth's presence in her life. But Ruth persists. She gleans in the field to provide food for them both, marries Boaz, and gives Naomi a son. Naomi provides ideas and advice that help Ruth to move Boaz towards a marriage proposal, and in other ways looks out for Ruth's future.

There is no direct or explicit indication of a sexual or romantic element in the relationship between Ruth and Naomi. But the text leaves an opening for a lesbian interpretation of the book, particularly in Ruth's famous declaration (Ruth 1:16–17a): "Where you go, I will go; where you lodge, I will lodge; your people shall be my people, and your God my God. Where you die, I will die— there will I be buried." This declaration is sealed with a solemn and binding vow: "May the LORD do thus and so to me, and more as well, if even death parts me from you!" (1:17b). This declaration implies that Ruth does not see this relationship as being superseded at some further point by remarriage. It also shows that Ruth's devotion to the God of Israel is integrally linked to her devotion to Naomi. Most strikingly, the verb translated in the New Revised Standard Version as "lodge" literally means "to sleep" or "spend the night." Hence a literal translation of this part of Ruth's declaration would read, "Where you sleep, I will sleep."

It is not surprising, therefore, that the book of Ruth, and 1:16–17 in particular, have had a special appeal to lesbians, both Jewish and Christian, who often use Ruth and Naomi as role models and incorporate these verses into lesbian ceremonies of commitment.[11] While it may not be possible to retrieve the historical reality of the relationship between Ruth and Naomi,[12] the story is ambiguous enough to allow for this interpretation.

Like the book of Ruth, the film is open to a lesbian interpretation. Idgie and Ruth, perhaps even more explicitly than the biblical Naomi and Ruth, live together, raise a child together, and apparently have no sexual relationships with men once Ruth has left Frank. Although each has connections to other people, it is obvious that theirs is the primary, most fundamental relationship in each of their lives.

Some viewers have criticized the film for failing to be even more explicit with regard to lesbianism. In their eyes, the film shies away from this theme and reduces a beautiful love affair to mere friendship.[13] Others comment that the lesbian relationship is obvious to those who choose to see it, and particularly to lesbians themselves. These viewers criticize the need on the part of some critics to see sexual intimacy on screen before they will acknowledge the presence of lesbian or gay relationships, a criterion that is not applied to cinematic heterosexual relationships.[14] If the lesbian element has been played down, it is likely due to box office concerns, though it must be noted that in more recent films, the presence of lesbian relationships has been much more explicit and has likely contributed to rather than detracted from box office success.[15] Nevertheless, the possibility that the film represents a lesbian relationship does not negate the interpretation that the fundamental theme is female friendship and not sexuality as such.

Both the biblical book and this film are clearly open to lesbian interpretations, just as they are open to other interpretations as well. In both cases, however, the possibility of a lesbian reading does not rule out or override the fundamental emphasis on profound friendship as an element both in sexual and in nonsexual relationships between women.

CONCLUSION

In *Fried Green Tomatoes*, the Bible, through biblical allusions and quotations, is woven so naturally into the plot and characterization that an average viewer might overlook its thematic importance. Certainly the film's celebration of female friendship is such an obvious theme that specific attention to and knowledge about the Bible are not required in order to discern or to appreciate this motif. But including the book of Ruth and, to a lesser extent, the stories of Job and Noah, among the resources that one brings to a viewing of this film does add an extra dimension. The film demonstrates the plasticity of biblical texts, and the different, even contradictory, ways that they can be interpreted and applied in our own lives. The Reverend, for example, can use Noah as a vehicle for his disapproval of Idgie's way of life, which violates the conventional norms of middle-class society in the South in the 1920s, while the gospel singer, many years later, can imply that Idgie is akin to Noah in her right-eousness and in her courage in saving others from the situations that can destroy them. The narrative structure of the books of Job and Ruth, which depicts the pattern of suffering and restoration, is mirrored not only in the experiences of the characters in this film—Ruth, Idgie, Evelyn—but also in many of our own lives as well. Finally, adding the biblical Naomi and Ruth to the examples of female friendship shown in this film not only testifies to the antiquity of the need and power of such relationships but also illustrates the different ways that such bonds can be expressed and the different ways in which women can help one another to live fruitful and satisfying lives.

5

Cape Fear and the Devil
as Savior (Job)

One day the heavenly beings came to present themselves before the LORD, and Satan also came among them. The LORD said to Satan, "Where have you come from?" Satan answered the LORD, "From going to and fro on the earth, and from walking up and down on it." The LORD said to Satan, "Have you considered my servant Job? There is no one like him on the earth, a blameless and upright man who fears God and turns away from evil." Then Satan answered the LORD, "Does Job fear God for nothing? Have you not put a fence around him and his house and all that he has, on every side? You have blessed the work of his hands, and his possessions have increased in the land. But stretch out your hand now, and touch all that he has, and he will curse you to your face." The LORD said to Satan, "Very well, all that he has is in your power; only do not stretch out your hand against him!" So Satan went out from the presence of the LORD.

Job 1:6–12

INTRODUCTION

The opening verses of the biblical book of Job portray Job, a non-Israelite but God-fearing man, as the pawn in an argument between God and Satan. In raising doubts that Job's faith runs deeper than gratitude for his good fortune, Satan has clearly touched a nerve with God. The matter can be settled only by putting Job to the test. God agrees, but on one condition: that Job himself not be harmed. Everything else is fair game. Satan is obviously known to God. He is not yet the devil, the epitome and prince of evil that he becomes in post-biblical Jewish and Christian literature.[1] Rather, he is a member of the divine entourage, charged with the task of seeking and reporting the faithless. He will be the one to carry out the trial of Job.

By the end of the first chapter, Job has lost his entire wealth: all of his oxen, donkeys, and camels; all the servants; and, most tragically, his children. Job mourns and laments, but "in all this Job did not sin or charge God with wrong-doing" (1:22). God feels vindicated, telling Satan at the next meeting of the heavenly beings, "He still persists in his integrity, although you incited me against him, to destroy him for no reason" (2:3). Satan, however, does not back down. "But stretch out your hand now and touch his bone and his flesh, and he will curse you to your face" (2:6). God agrees to take the test one step fur-ther. Satan can hurt Job physically but not kill him. Immediately Job is afflicted with terrible sores from head to toe. His wife mocks his integrity and urges him to "curse God, and die" (2:9), but he silences her, saying, "Shall we receive the good at the hand of God, and not receive the bad?" (2:10). The next thirty-nine chapters of the book of Job debate the relationship between divine jus-tice and human suffering from all angles, in the form of lengthy speeches and by a variety of parties: Job and his friends (chapters 3–31); another friend Elihu, who rebukes both Job and his friends (32–37); and, finally, God and Job directly (38–42:6). The frame narrative concludes in 42:7–17, when Job's for-tunes are restored: he regains a wife and his wealth, and he enjoys a long life graced by numerous descendants.

The book of Job is an example of biblical Wisdom literature. Works in this genre, which also includes some of the Psalms, Proverbs, Ecclesiastes and the Song of Songs, do not focus specifically on Israel, as do most of the other bib-lical books. Rather, they reflect on universal and perennial issues such as jus-tice, knowledge, morality, and the role of the individual in society and in relationship with the divine.[2]

The book of Job provides the central motifs and plot structure for Martin Scorsese's terrifying 1991 film *Cape Fear*. This film is a remake of the earlier film noir classic directed by J. Lee Thompson (1962) and starring Gregory Peck, Robert Mitchum, and Polly Bergen. Scorsese's version retains the basic story line of the earlier film, which itself is based on a crime novel by John R. Macdonald, *The Executioners* (1957). However, the 1991 film develops the moral ambiguities of the situation in far greater detail than do either the book or the 1962 movie. In the process, Scorsese also adds a significant number of references to and quotations from the Bible, and, most significantly, uses the book of Job as a structuring device and a key to the major themes and characters.

FILM SUMMARY

Sam Bowden (Nick Nolte) is a lawyer living a comfortable life in New Essex, North Carolina, with his wife Leigh (Jessica Lange), a graphic artist, and his fifteen-year-old daughter Danielle (Juliette Lewis). They have a beautiful house, a dog, and a houseboat on the Atlantic coast at Cape Fear, North Carolina. Life is perfect until the day that Max Cady (Robert De Niro) blows into town. Max Cady is a psychopath just released from prison where he has served a fourteen-year sentence for battery. What he had done, in fact, was brutally rape and assault a sixteen-year-old girl; Bowden, Cady's defense lawyer, had managed to get the charge reduced to battery.

Should not Cady be grateful to Bowden for getting his sentence reduced? In fact, there is an important unresolved issue between them. Although he was the lawyer for the defense, Bowden intentionally suppressed evidence concerning the prior sexual experience of the victim that might have acquitted Cady or significantly lessened his sentence. Bowden's aim, as he admits to one of his colleagues, was to ensure Cady's conviction. In doing so, Bowden had set himself up as judge and jury, thereby compromising his obligation to his client, to the judicial system, and to the truth. Now Cady has come back to haunt Bowden. Cady intends to make Bowden suffer as he himself has done, and, as we soon find out, he has the ability and the power to do so.

From their first meeting, Cady applies increasing pressure on Bowden by threatening those in his immediate circle. He poisons Mrs. Bowden's beloved dog; a few days later he casually drops by to return the dog collar in a manner that is all the more sinister for its feigned innocence and congeniality. He rapes and then viciously assaults Lori, Bowden's racquetball partner and would-be lover, a young law clerk who is infatuated with Bowden though the relationship is not consummated sexually. By posing as her drama teacher, Cady lures Sam's daughter Danielle (Danny) to the deserted auditorium at her high school and gains her trust and sympathy by appealing to her adolescent sexuality and dissatisfaction with her parents.[3] Cady goads Sam into threatening him, and then uses those threats to obtain a restraining order against Bowden. He later initiates proceedings that result in Sam's disbarment. He repeatedly enters the Bowdens' house undetected, and finally confronts the family as the plot reaches its climax on their houseboat on Cape Fear.

Max Cady threatens Sam's sense of personal and professional integrity and security as well as the health, well-being, and lives of his family. He senses and exploits every weakness in Sam, his wife, his daughter, and his environment in order to take vengeance for Sam's breach of legal process and lawyer-client ethics. In prison, Cady has learned how to read and has studied enough law to run his own appeals. Indeed, he now considers himself to be Sam's colleague in the law, as he often taunts Sam. For this reason he feels entitled to have what Sam has. He is more than a (self-trained and self-appointed) lawyer, however. In fact, he has set himself up as a one-man, full-service judicial system. Not only has he investigated the case, in the process uncovering the evidence about Sam's professional breach of conduct, but he has also charged, judged, and sentenced Sam. At Cape Fear he proposes to carry out the execution. If Sam had set himself up as judge and jury when he buried information that could have helped Cady, Cady has now followed in his path and even outdone him.

Sam, for his part, pays lip service to the rule of law and takes refuge in the apparent solidity of his middle-class values and lifestyle. But the fabric of his life is flawed by the considerable tension in his family: between Sam and his wife, Leigh, over marital infidelity; and between Danielle and her parents for the usual adolescent reasons. Professionally, Sam is also not as upright as he would like to be seen.[4] His decision to bury evidence can perhaps be explained in light of Sam's belief that his vicious client did not deserve to benefit from the evidence about the sexual behavior of his victim, but it also points to a lapse in his professional conduct.

The faultlines in Sam's character and his home and professional lives widen as Sam reacts to Max's progressively more violent threats and behavior. The film tracks the progressive degeneration of Sam's civilized conscience and actions. Cady watches this descent with great interest and exploits each successive step. Initially Sam tries to neutralize Cady by legally acceptable means. He seeks and obtains a restraining order, and he informs his legal associates as well as his friends on the police force. Next, he tries to bribe Cady into leaving him and his family alone. Then he hires a private investigator. As Cady's actions escalate relentlessly, Sam finally accedes to the investigator's suggestion that he hire several men to "teach Cady a lesson" with a persuasive beating. This lesson proves unsuccessful; Cady takes them all on in a superhuman show of strength that causes Sam's fear and panic to escalate.[5] Soon Bowden acquires his own gun, a move he had initially resisted vigorously, and, with the detective's help, attempts to entrap and kill Cady. This plan fails spectacularly. Not only does Cady elude them, but he manages to enter the house undetected and to murder the housekeeper and the private investigator. The Bowdens flee to their houseboat on Cape Fear. But this is no escape, for, unbeknownst to them, Cady is hitching a ride by clinging to the chassis of their car.[6] During their final confrontation in the houseboat, the Bowdens are completely stripped of their civilized selves and simply fight for their lives. Mrs. Bowden prepares to sacrifice herself in order to protect Danielle, while Sam's sole goal is to kill Cady. Finally, the boat sinks, as does Cady, and the three Bowdens survive, but just barely. In the final scene, they all emerge from the mud, an eloquent comment on the fact that the encounter has reduced them to an animal-like state. But this image is also a hint of their rebirth from the primeval earth of the cape's shore, with new knowledge of just what they can endure in order to survive and to ensure the survival of one another. As Danielle tells us in the final voice-over, they rarely spoke of this episode again, but it is hard to imagine that it did not leave its mark on them all.

These two intertwining movements—Cady's ever-tightening noose and Sam's ever-loosening humanity—create the aura of suspense and terror that pervades the movie. The pressure does not let up; Cady is relentless and positively diabolical in his ability to get at each of his victims by exploiting the approaches that are most likely to succeed. Bowden's growing despair is palpable; his dilemma—to stick to his ethical and professional principles or to succumb to his fear and desire for vengeance—draws us in as we react with either horror or understanding to his progressively more desperate measures.

In many respects, Scorsese's *Cape Fear* turns our expectations upside down. It keeps us off kilter and wary from the very first moment of the film to the very end. One device that contributes strongly to this destabilizing effect is the use of off-center camera angles, many images are tilted and unbalanced. This unconventional camera work symbolizes the film's topsy-turvy world, in which the victim, Bowden, is under a restraining order while his oppressor, Cady, is allowed to move freely. This comes through most clearly in the scene in which Cady initially contacts Danielle by posing as her drama teacher. At the same time as he is talking with her on the phone, he is also exercising in his apartment, hanging upside down from the door frame of the room. After establishing this position, the camera then moves upside down, so that we viewers see Cady as if he is right side up. This mirrors the moral situation in which Cady, a perverted psychopath, presents himself to Danielle as "righteous," right side up so to speak, as an adult in whom she can confide, whom she can trust, and who can say just the right thing to soothe her troubled adolescent soul. This moral inversion is reflected in Danny's own judgment that Cady may not be so bad, perhaps he did not kill the dog, perhaps her parents have (typically!) misjudged him. She soon learns, however, that her parents have in fact underestimated the violence of which he is capable.

The disconcerting effect of the camera work is intensified by the use of color. At significant points in the film, including its opening and closing frames, the camera lingers at length on a scene, then superimposes on it a close-up of a face, focusing on the eyes. The filter then changes to red, and finally to a silver-gray "negative" shot, which looks like x-ray vision. This movement from positive to negative, like the reversals of camera angle, also symbolizes the inversion of moral values that drives the film's plot.

The color shifts often occur in shots that focus closely on Danielle's eyes. This focus reminds us of her role as narrator at the beginning and end of the film. Yet this narrative role, like the tilt and tint of the camera work, does not remain stable. Although Danny is the one who introduces the story and brings it to its conclusion, her point of view is not maintained throughout the film.[7] These elements also tie directly and not very subtly into the movie's main themes, signifying both the blood and horror that drives the plot and emotional tenor of the film, and the effect of the horror in stripping the mundane of its color and its civilized veneer.

The soundtrack amplifies these effects. The music is ominous and overbearing from the outset; it is neither subtle nor inobtrusive. On the contrary, it intrudes continuously on our consciousness, relentlessly keeping us focused on the fear, suffering, and terror that lurk everywhere for the main characters and hence for ourselves to the extent that we identify with their plight. The music and this ominous mood are maintained even in scenes that are brightly lit and that do not seem to contain any perceptible danger. Hence even when Sam and his family go to the movies, enjoy a meal at home, or watch a parade, danger is never far away.[8]

USE OF THE BIBLE

Plot and Character

The inversions of everyday reality and conventional morality, as well as the mood of fear and horror, are enhanced by the film's direct and nearly exclusive association of the Bible with Max Cady. True, other characters occasionally allude to the Bible or use biblical phraseology. For example, when Sam Bowden initially rejects a violent solution to the Cady problem he tells his friend that "maybe 2000 years ago we might have taken this guy out and stoned him to death. I can't operate outside the law. The law's my business."[9] Cady's lawyer is also fond of vague biblical phraseology. Referring to Mr. Bowden's threats that Cady had recorded, the lawyer says, "Mr. Bowden made good on his threat. . . . [j]ust as God arose to judgment to save all the meek of the earth I hope and pray that you will do the same" (cf. Matt 5:5). He calls on the court to validate the restraining order in the interests of Christian charity and declares, bombastically and fawningly, to the judge, that "King Solomon could not have adjudicated more wisely your honor" (cf. 1 Kings 3). His petition for the disbarment of Mr. Bowden on grounds of moral turpitude implies that Sam has violated not only the law but also biblical morality.[10]

But it is Cady who most often quotes, refers to, or alludes to the Bible, and he does so with an authority that in itself is shocking. Insofar as the Bible represents the divine word, someone who quotes the Bible can be seen as invoking divine support for his own person and actions, even if, as a human being, he or she naturally falls short of the ideal.[11] Here, however, there is not the slightest doubt from the outset that Cady, biblically knowledgable and Bible-quoting as he is, is a truly evil person. Cady's use of the Bible is confusing to Sam and to others, and it also debases the Bible in that it is being coopted as moral legitimation for extortion and murder. The dissonance between the cultural expectations we associate with the Bible and our immediate perceptions of this character contributes to the sustained horror of the film, which forces us to live for two long hours in a state of moral inversion that is as complete and absolute as the upside-down Cady's sweet-talking manner towards Danielle would suggest.

Cady, more precisely than either Sam or Cady's own lawyer, quotes scripture and sprinkles his conversation with biblical allusions. In his conversations with Sam, Cady often compares the suffering he endured in prison to that of Paul the apostle as he traveled around the Roman empire preaching to the Gentiles and running up against the authorities (cf. Paul's letter to Philemon). "You don't know what suffering is, Councillor. Like it says in Galatians 3, have you suffered so many things in vain. . . ." In other words, Cady claims that he, like Paul, suffered for the truth as he understands it. As Cady sees it, a failure to act against Sam would render his own suffering meaningless. When Cady lures Danielle to a meeting in the deserted theater of her high school, he appeals to her by using formulas that resonate with biblical language. He advises her not to damn her parents nor to judge them but "just forgive them for they know not what they do," words that some versions of the Gospel of Luke attribute to Jesus on the cross.[12] This quotation implies that Danielle's parents, unlike Cady and now, he hopes, Danielle herself, do not understand his real role in their lives. The entire scene is sinister and terrifying. Having heard Sam's description of Cady's brutal rape of a teenage girl, and having witnessed his vicious assault on Lori, we fear that Cady has the same evil intentions towards Danny. Perhaps so; certainly his antipathy towards Sam coupled with his own powerful inclinations towards sexual violence would make this outcome plausible. But he does not act on this possibility yet. Rather, he is patiently saving this "satisfaction" for the grand finale, his final majestic confrontation with Sam and his whole family on Cape Fear. In this final dramatic sequence, too, he uses biblical allusions in a manner that is threateningly sexual and violent. When he is about to assault Sam's wife, Leigh, he says, "Ready to be born again, Mizz Bowden? A few minutes alone with me, darlin', and you'll be speakin' in tongues." He rips off her blouse and kisses her violently.

The Bible appears not only in Cady's dialogue but also on his very person. His entire upper body is covered in tattoos, many of them composed of biblical quotations, complete with references to chapter and verse. In a physical sense, then, Max Cady "embodies" the scriptures. We catch a glimpse of these quotations in the opening sequence of the film, which briefly frames Cady's tattooed back as he is exercising in his prison cell shortly before his release. We see the tattoos more clearly when Cady is strip-searched by the New Essex police. Observing Cady through a one-way glass, Sam's lawyer exclaims, "I don't know whether to look at him or read him."

The following quotations appear on Cady's arms and chest: "Vengeance is Mine" (Rom. 12:19); "My Time is at Hand" (Matt. 26:18); "The Lord is the Avenger" (1 Thess. 4:6); "I have put my trust in the Lord God, in him will I trust" (Ps. 91:2); and "My time is not yet come" (John 7:6; 7:8). Beneath this final quotation, the image of a sad clown emerges from behind prison bars, holding a smoking gun and the Bible. Cady's back displays a large tattooed cross supporting the scales of justice and truth.

With the exception of Psalm 91, these quotations focus on two themes: patience and vengeance, which is Cady's explicit reason for pursuing Bowden and his family. Patience may allude to the fourteen years that Cady spent in prison, a period of time which recalls the fourteen generations from Abraham to David, from David to the Babylonian exile, and from the exile to the birth of Jesus (Matt. 1:17). More specifically, it also draws attention to the measured pace with which Cady plans and carries out his revenge. The two elements of patience and vengeance are also present in another, albeit nonbiblical, tattoo: "Time is the Avenger." Cady is avenging the fact that he had to do time, and he is doing so in his own time and on his own terms. The tattooed quotations suggest that the Bible, and hence God, support and justify Cady's campaign for vengeance. A similar message is conveyed by the depiction of the cross as the beam supporting the scales of justice and truth. From Cady's point of view, his goal is to see that the "truth" is finally told about his own case and that "justice" is done by making Bowden suffer as Cady has done due to Bowden's act so long ago.

More puzzling is the passage from Psalm 91:2. The notion of trusting in God does not sit well with the Cady that we encounter in the film; Cady leaves nothing to God but rather sees himself as the instrument of divine vengeance. Perhaps the purpose of this quotation is to establish an element of Cady's psychopathic character, namely, that Cady truly does see himself as God's agent, a "white-trash Wrath of God," as one critic has called him.[13] That is, he views his vengeance against Bowden as a fulfillment of God's will. If so, then the passage contributes to the sinister effect of the tattooed and embodied Bible: Cady's appropriation of the Bible has inverted the scriptures' true meaning and perverted their sustaining and positive power; it profoundly violates and demeans the Bible as sacred book. The scriptures that Cady has carved into his own flesh therefore express his own self-understanding as someone who is on a divine mission of vengeance, planned carefully and patiently. Even more than this, Cady's embodiment of scripture implies that he is identifying himself as God or as God-like. This is implied in Cady's quotation from a seventeenth-century theologian Angelus Silesius: "I am like God and God like me. I am as large as God, he is as small as I. He came not above me nor I beneath him."[14]

The fact that Cady alludes to scripture, cites scriptures, and carves scripture into his body implies that he is extremely familiar with it and sees himself, his life, and his ambitions therein. Moreover, he believes that he is orchestrating the fate of Sam in a manner that corresponds with and perhaps is even prophesied by scripture. The use of the Bible as a paradigm is evident in a pivotal scene in which Sam bursts into a café where Cady is sitting at a booth leafing through his Bible. Sam orders Cady to stop harassing him "or else." Cady notes that Sam is threatening him and then tells him, "Check out the Bible, councillor, the book between Esther and Psalms."

His statement is a puzzle to Sam, who obviously is not so familiar with the Bible as Max Cady has become. That night, too tense to sleep, Bowden thumbs through his Bible, remarking to Leigh, "Cady said to read the book between Esther and Psalms"—the book of Job. When he summarizes the biblical account: "God took away everything he had, even his children," Leigh immediately makes the connection between the biblical book and their own tortured situation: "You want some answers. Me too. I'd like to know just how strong we are, or how weak. But I guess the only way we're gonna find out is just by going through this." In contrast to Job's wife, who urged Job to take a spectacular stand against God and then die (Job 2:9), Leigh, like God and Satan in the book of Job, is curious to see whether and how they will survive.

The entire plot of the film, as the parallel with Job leads us to expect, proves the prescience of Leigh's words. Cady's reading recommendation provides Sam, as well as the viewer, with the key to an enigmatic comment that Cady had made in one of their early encounters. Sam does not quite catch it at the time, but, as he later tells his wife, it was something like "I'm going to make you learn about loss," or "I'm gonna make you think about loss." Cady's advice regarding "the book between Esther and Psalms" indicates that the events that Cady has planned for Sam as well as the plot of Scorsese's film take the story of Job as their paradigm. By systematically threatening everything that Sam has, Cady will teach Sam about loss; test the mettle of Sam, Leigh, and Danielle; and ensure that justice, or at least his own perverted version thereof, will be done.

The trials of Job therefore resonate through this film. God's interest in Satan's plan is precisely to see how Job bears up under pressure. Can he retain his faith in God, or will he renounce God in the face of his unjustified suffering? In the film, Cady's test does not address the Bowdens' ability to retain faith in God—religious faith is not an issue in this film—but whether they can maintain their principles and their civilized humanity in the face of the fear that Cady raises in them and the threat of suffering that he imposes.

The film's answer is equivocal. The Bowdens survive physically, but in doing so they shed all vestiges of civilized behavior. As they rise from the mud of Cape Fear, are they reborn to a new life free from the fear of Cady's menacing presence? Or have they shed all human vestiges and become animals who have returned to the jungle environment from which, according to popular Darwinism, humankind originally emerged? We suspect the latter, for in their last battle with Cady they no longer behaved like human beings, with forethought and reason, but like animals, lashing out instinctively for self-protection. This is symbolized by the fact that they have relinquished or lost all manufactured weapons; in the end, Sam kills Cady not with a gun but by pounding on Cady's head with a large rock. Terence Rafferty has suggested that the film is intended to illustrate the Christian idea that suffering is good for the soul. Thus, Sam's suffering leads to purification of his soul.[15] But this idea is not entirely clear in the film, in which Cady views Bowden's suffering as just retribution for the suffering that Bowden has caused Cady, whose soul did not seem to benefit at all from the suffering that he experienced in prison.

On the other hand, the Bowdens' final confrontation with Cady tested their mettle in the manner that Leigh Bowden had predicted. It is only through superhuman courage, strength, and single-minded purpose that they were able to prevail. At the same time that they lost the veneer of civilization, they also let go of the problems that they had with one another. This is clear particularly in the behavior of Leigh and Danielle. The film earlier had emphasized the tensions between them; each felt misunderstood and to some degree betrayed by the other. But on the houseboat, they act entirely to ensure each other's survival. Leigh is ready to do and to suffer anything for Danielle; Danielle, in turn, does what she can to combat a man whose evil nature she has now fully comprehended: she unleashes upon him one of the basic elements of existence. What has survived, therefore, is not faith in Western civilization, good manners, and inhibitions, but raw human courage and the instinct for self-preservation. To the end it remains uncertain whether Sam parallels Job in this regard or contrasts with him. It is also unclear whether Cady has had his revenge. Cady does succeed in bringing Sam down to his own level of violence and primal emotion, but he does not succeed in killing him or his family.

If Sam is to be compared with Job, then Cady plays the part of Satan. Cady accepts this identification when he directs Sam to the book of Job as a key to understanding Cady's plans for him. Just as Satan will make Job suffer, so will Cady do with respect to Sam. Various elements of Cady's characterization support his narrative role as Satan. He appears larger than life; far from being bound by social rules or conventions, he takes delight in flouting them, as he does by lighting up a cigar in a movie theater and laughing raucously throughout. He seems to have the ability to walk through walls; at least he shows up in the most unexpected places and eludes the most elaborate traps. He is also diabolical in the ways in which he succeeds in corrupting others, particularly Sam, and turns their acts against themselves.

The identification of Cady with Satan is made most explicit in the final sequence on the houseboat. Cady has confined Danielle in the hold, perhaps a figurative equivalent to the underworld and a foreshadowing of the grave to which we fear he will send her before our very eyes. Danielle is resourceful, strong, and frightened enough to risk everything. She manages to free herself, and, armed with a barbecue lighter, waits for an opportune moment to attack. As Cady lights up his trademark cigar, she sprays him with the lighter fluid and sets him on fire. This blaze seals Cady's identification as Satan, now no longer the chief prosecutor of the heavenly realm but the Satan of hellfire.

More subtle hints regarding Cady's diabolical identity are also present. The most striking is his association with Christian symbols. We have already noted the crucifix and the New Testament quotations tattooed on his back. Cady has appropriated Christian symbols to express his own sense of self and his mission in New Essex. In some scenes he appears in cruciform position, as he is when he calls Danielle and poses as her new drama teacher, or when Sam chains him to one of the houseboat's poles with his arms outstretched. In both of these scenes, however, his inverted posture implies that he is the opposite of Christ. Similarly, he takes biblical quotations and images out of their literary and theological contexts and perverts their meaning in order to legitimate a quest that is contrary to both the letter and the spirit of the Bible.

Yet Cady presents himself not in diabolical terms but as someone who is serving a divinely sanctioned mission. He has a very personal and direct relationship with the Bible; everything in it seems applicable to his own situation; indeed, it seems to be all about him. Like Christ, Cady claims that he came to save Sam Bowden, a salvation to be enacted through suffering. This claim is reinforced by Cady's allusions to Dante's *Inferno*. Cady addresses Sam, whom he has bound with rope on the houseboat, in the following way: "I'm Virgil, Councillor, and I'm guiding you through the gates of Hell. We are now in the ninth circle, the circle of traitors to country, traitors to their fellow man, traitors to God! You, sir, are charged with betraying the principles of our trade.... And I find you guilty of betraying your fellow man, guilty of betraying your country, guilty of abrogating your oath, guilty of judging me and guilty of selling me out! With the power invested in me by the Kingdom of God, I sentence you to the ninth circle of hell; there where you will learn about loss, the loss of freedom, and loss of humanity. You and I will be the same."

Diabolical as Cady seems to us, the film suggests that he may even have seen himself as God, or at least, as a superhuman divine spirit. As Deacy has noted, Cady resembles the stereotypical vengeful God of the Old Testament, trying to redeem his errant people from transgressions.[16] Certainly the theme of salvation—the Bowdens' or Cady's—is alluded to at various points in the film. On the way to Cape Fear, for example, the family, unwittingly towing Cady along with them, passes a road sign in the form of a cross, and inscribed on it are the words "How will you spend eternity?" As he is drowning in Cape Fear, Cady holds Sam's gaze and chants, mockingly, "I'm bound for the promised land; I am bound for the promised land." His voice continues to echo as he slowly sinks. But the film retains some ambiguity as to whether Cady is motivated by Sam's evident need for redemption or by his own need for vengeance. The former is certainly present, but the latter still dominates.

Themes

In providing a paradigm for the film's narrative, the book of Job also signals the main theme of this film: the effects of suffering, specifically, the effects of extreme fear, on human character. The film's use of the Bible also connects, if more subtly, to the themes of justice, human and divine, and the perversion of justice—legal, moral, and personal. The relationship between Sam and Cady is initially defined by the legal system: Cady is the defendant; Sam is his defense attorney. Cady's conviction ends that relationship and, in Sam Bowden's view, should have ended any further contact between them. But what Sam, the movie audience, and, as it turns out, Cady all know is that Sam himself breached one element of the law. In refusing to reveal evidence that could have worked in this client's favor, Sam has violated his role in the legal relationship, a violation that Sam acknowledges but justifies as being in accordance with a higher, moral good, namely, the imprisonment of a violent and depraved rapist. For Cady, Sam's action legitimates all Cady's own subsequent behavior towards Sam and his family. On his release from prison, Cady does what he perceives Sam to have done fourteen years earlier at his trial; Cady takes the law into his own hands. Sam responds in kind, so that by the end of the film both Sam and Cady have exceeded and violated state law in countless ways, but each has found ways to justify these violations. This notion is implied in a bumper sticker that adorns Cady's 1967 red Mustang convertible: "You're a VIP on Earth, I'm a VIP in Heaven."

The Job paradigm helps to ground the theme of justice in a biblical context and sharpens the central question of the film by relating it to the theme at the heart of the book of Job: how does unwarranted suffering affect people's relationship with God? In the biblical book, as well as in the 1962 version of the film, it is obvious that the main character does not deserve the loss and suffering that is inflicted on him. Not so in the Scorsese version. As we have seen, the 1992 film introduces moral ambiguity to all of the principal characters. The suffering that Cady brings on Sam—while cruel, diabolical, and illegal—is not entirely random. Though viewers are unlikely to agree with Cady's point of view, the connection between Sam's earlier breach and Cady's current campaign is clear. In this sense, the plot of the film departs from that of Job and that of the earlier film of *Cape Fear*.

The most problematic element of this film remains Cady's persistent use of the Bible, biblical quotations, and the biblical paradigm of Job in a quest that is profoundly evil. Some critics have suggested that the film is a critique of fundamentalist Christianity, especially as it is practiced in the South, and argue that it expresses Scorsese's lack of appreciation of Protestant Christianity and his disdain toward any location outside of New York City.[17] According to Les Keyser, the remake of *Cape Fear* was Scorsese's opportunity to pay back some of the religious fundamentalists from the South who had lambasted Scorsese's 1989 film *The Last Temptation of Christ*. In this reading, Cady is the evil twin of the Jesus of *Last Temptation* and serves up southern Pentecostalism for ridicule.[18] Support for this view comes from one of the bumper stickers on Cady's car: "American by birth. Southern by the Grace of God."

If one were, in fact, to see Cady as representative of the South more generally, this criticism would have some merit. But the film makes it clear that Cady is an affront to the South and to its middle-class aspirations and conventions. Thus, while the film's portrayal of the South is not altogether complimentary, Cady's diabolical reading of scripture is not portrayed as representative of southern religiosity but rather as an anomaly. Cady's use of the Bible may be attributed to the fact that Cady learned to read only as an adult in prison, after which he concentrated on law books, the Bible, and Medieval literature and theology. But Cady is a psychopath; he does not have meaningful relationships with any human beings, and he does not participate in any social groups, including religious ones. His reading of the Bible takes place entirely in isolation from a community of interpretation. A community in which the Bible is valued and revered as a source of life could potentially have tempered Cady's tendency to take sections out of context and his proclivity for seeing the Bible as speaking directly and specifically to his own life situation in such a violent way.[19] Unfettered by a religious or Bible-reading community, Cady used the Bible as a powerful weapon of destruction, and he used it to legitimate a violent and diabolical path. The film is not so much a critique of southern fundamentalism as it is a warning that even a book as revered and as supportive of morality as the Bible can be an instrument of destruction through which justice and morality can be perverted. Reading the Bible in the context of an interpretative community may not prevent its use to further discrimination and injustice, but it is unlikely to lead to as inverted a path as the one that Cady has chosen.

Scorsese's *Cape Fear* demonstrates what we might call the diabolical use of the Bible, that is, use of the Bible to support purposes that are contrary to the fundamental ethos of the Bible itself. In doing so, it shatters the commonplace illusion that the Bible is necessarily and always a positive force in an individual's life and that living by the Bible or reading the Bible will always have a salutary effect on oneself and others.

6

The Sixth Sense and the Quest for Eternal Rest (Psalms)

Out of the depths I cry to you, O LORD.
    Lord, hear my voice!
Let your ears be attentive to the voice of my supplications!

If you, O LORD, should mark iniquities,
    Lord, who could stand?
But there is forgiveness with you, so that you may be revered.

I wait for the LORD, my soul waits,
    and in his word I hope;
my soul waits for the Lord
    more than those who watch for the morning,
    more than those who watch for the morning.

O Israel, hope in the LORD!
    For with the LORD there is steadfast love,
    and with him is great power to redeem.
It is he who will redeem Israel from all its iniquities.

Psalm 130

INTRODUCTION

Like Job and the other works of Wisdom literature, the Psalms, while composed thousands of years ago, speak as directly to the universal human condition as to a particular social and historical situation. They have a timeless and timely quality that has contributed to their ongoing ability to move and console us. The

Psalms are a collection of poems or songs that were probably written for use in worship in the Jerusalem Temple. Although many of them are attributed to David, they were likely written and collected over a period of several centuries rather than by a single person. They may have been accompanied by ancient string, percussion, or wind instruments; some of them have headings that may be instructions for their performance. For example, Psalm 22 begins with the superscription "To the leader: according to the Deer of the Dawn. A Psalm of David." The words translated as "to the Deer of the Dawn" may be a musical instruction, much as we might find the note in a contemporary songbook that a set of verses is to be sung to the tune of "My Bonnie Lies over the Ocean."

The Psalms can be assigned to a variety of genres depending on content. Psalm 130 is generally seen as a lament though it does not share all the features of other psalms in this genre.[1] Laments are often written in the first person. The psalmist invokes the name of God, describes an experience of distress, and implicitly or explicitly asks for divine aid. Psalm 130 does not describe the distressful experience directly, but the supplicant's location in the "depths" and his or her cry for forgiveness suggest that such an experience, perhaps involving the psalmist's own actions and their consequences, has occurred.

What these depths are, and where they and the supplicant are to be found are matters of some controversy.[2] According to some commentators, the depths are the watery deeps and should be viewed as a metaphorical description of the supplicant's frame of mind. He or she is very "low" due to illness and despair, so low that the psalmist feels dead already. Another line of interpretation goes further to suggest that the supplicant is already in the world of the dead and is here begging for forgiveness and resurrection. While to modern ears the metaphorical interpretation may be more palatable, the latter would be consistent with the ancient Israelite understanding of death and the afterlife. According to the Bible, Israelites did not believe in life after death. As he prepares to expel Adam from the garden of Eden, God promises,

> "By the sweat of your face
>   you shall eat bread
> until you return to the ground,
>   for out of it you were taken;
> you are dust,
>   and to dust you shall return."
>   (Gen. 3:19)

Death and life are different stages in the same biological process.[3] The book of Psalms reflects the belief that the souls of the dead descended to Sheol (Job 8:9–10), a place that is much like the Greek Hades, a cavernous area beneath the earth or under the waters that run beneath the earth (Pss. 18:4–5; 69:1–2), where they continued in some weak form of existence (Pss. 6:5; 88:3–6, 10–12). The "depths" may then refer to Sheol, and the psalm as a whole may be interpreted in two ways: as the lament of the dead soul who seeks forgiveness and the ability either to rise up from the depths or to rest there peacefully; or, metaphorically, as the lament of an individual who seeks God's help and forgiveness in his or her time of despair.[4]

These meanings are not mutually exclusive; both come into play in the 2000 film *The Sixth Sense*, directed by M. Night Shyamalan, but only for those who are able to recognize the psalm's presence in the film.

FILM SUMMARY

The Sixth Sense crosses several genres. Its main focus is the complex relationship between a boy and a man, but at the same time it is a psychological thriller and a love story. Most intriguing, it is also a puzzle that teases and mystifies. But readers who have not yet seen *The Sixth Sense*, be warned. This is a very spooky film, complete with ghosts and spirits, haunted houses, and unexpected surprises of the most unpleasant sort. Now a second warning: view the film before reading this essay! It is impossible to discuss this film without revealing the ending, but knowing the ending before viewing the film will rob readers of the surprise and, yes, the delight, that attends a first viewing.

Each element of the film conveys its creepiness and provides pieces of the puzzle that challenges the viewer. The camera lingers on empty rooms, shoots scenes from strange angles, and often looks down at the action from far above. The colors are muted, but the periodic burst of brilliant red—on church doors, basement doorknobs, clothing, and fingernails—shock the eye. The soundtrack sometimes mirrors, sometimes anticipates, the action on the screen, augmenting the suspense and tension of the plot. Barely audible but nonetheless palpable are the whispers and breaths that animate each scene and convey the sense of invisible presence.

These elements support and enhance a plot that is simultaneously scary and intriguing. The film opens with a lone light bulb that lights up slowly and mysteriously. We then catch sight of Anna Crowe (Olivia Williams), a beautiful young woman, festively dressed. Soon it becomes apparent that she is in the basement of her home, looking for a bottle of wine. No doubt she is the one who turned on the light to guide her down the basement stairs. But the sense of mystery and foreboding does not dissipate completely. Anna is ill at ease, chilly, and anxious to go back upstairs where her husband, Malcolm (Bruce Willis), awaits. She returns with sweaters for them both. Soon we learn the occasion for the wine and her festive attire. Malcolm and Anna have just returned from a ceremony at which Malcolm was presented with the Mayor of Philadelphia's citation for professional excellence in the field of child psychology. They are slightly drunk and amorous. Malcolm is pleased with the citation, but he makes light of it. The lone hint of trouble comes in Anna's comment that his success has sometimes been at the expense of their relationship. But the brief chill of this moment is dispelled as Malcolm and Anna go upstairs to their bedroom and playfully prepare to make love.

There the mood alters abruptly. Anna sees shards of glass on the floor; someone has broken in through their bedroom window and is now in their bathroom. The intruder is one of Malcolm's former patients, Vincent Gray (Donnie Wahlberg). Vincent is either drugged, crazed, or both. He stands half naked in the bathroom doorway, facing Malcolm, who is standing near his bed. He weepingly accuses Malcolm of failing to help him—an accusation that brings Malcolm face to face with his greatest failure, on this night of his greatest honor. Switching into psychologist mode, Malcolm tries to talk him down. Vincent turns his back briefly, then suddenly turns around again; he shoots Malcolm in the stomach and then puts the gun to his own head. As the scene fades out, Anna is crouched by the bed where Malcolm is lying with eyes open. He is clutching his stomach but strangely calm. We viewers are left with the question, Does Malcolm survive?

The question appears to be answered by the next scene, which takes place "Next fall." Malcolm is sitting on a bench in a residential neighborhood, apparently hale and hearty. He is glancing over some notes that pertain to a new patient, a child named Cole (Haley Joel Osment). We follow his glance as he watches Cole leave the house, put on a pair of lensless, oversized glasses, and run down the street, quickly and furtively, to a dark stone church with a bright red door. Malcolm follows him into the church and spots Cole playing with a set of toy soldiers. Malcolm introduces himself; Cole is not particularly happy to see Malcolm but seems resigned to his presence as well as to the idea that he will see Malcolm again.

From this starting point, the plot develops primarily around the connection between Malcolm and Cole. This relationship, in turn, has a significant impact on two others: that between Cole and his mother (Toni Collette) and that between Malcolm and his wife Anna.

Malcolm's and Cole's roles are clear from the outset. Malcolm is the psychologist; Cole is the patient who needs help. Cole reminds Malcolm very much of Vincent Gray, who was also fearful and weighed down by unknown and unseen troubles. Cole's peers call him a freak and shun him. He finds respite only in the church, where he goes frequently to play with his lead soldiers. Malcolm must win Cole over, try to figure out what is troubling him, and help him to overcome his fears. He acknowledges an element of self-interest in his desire to help Cole. Succeeding with Cole, he believes, will assuage the guilt he still feels over his failure to help Vincent Gray.

Initially Cole is wary of Malcolm, as any eight-year-old would be in this situation. Their sessions take place everywhere—in Cole's apartment, at school, and in the neighborhood—except in Malcolm's office. Simply by spending time with Cole in these varied settings, Malcolm gradually gains his trust. Cole tells him some things—about his father, about getting in trouble at school for drawing violent pictures, and about his troubled relationships, or, more accurately, nonrelationships, with his peers at school. Malcolm knows that Cole has a secret, but he does not know what it is. Still, there are clues. He has observed that Cole has deep scratch marks on his body. Malcolm believes that these may be signs of parental abuse or perhaps of self-abuse. Having observed the loving relationship between this single mother and her son, Malcolm considers the latter to be more likely than the former.

One day, at a classmate's birthday party, Cole has an extremely unsettling experience. He hears voices upstairs behind a door on the landing and goes to investigate. Two of his classmates follow him, open the landing door, and shove him inside. His mother, who has just arrived to pick him up, hears his screams and with effort succeeds in opening the door and rescuing him. Cole is unconscious.

The camera cuts to the hospital, to which Cole has been admitted for observation. Malcolm comes to see him before bedtime and attempts to tell Cole a bedtime story.

> Once upon a time there was this young prince, and he decided that he wanted to go for a drive, and he got his driver and they started driving . . . driving and driving . . . they drove so much that he fell asleep . . . and then he woke up and he realized that they were still driving . . . this was a very long trip.

Cole interrupts, "Dr. Crowe . . . You haven't told bedtime stories before . . . you have to add some twists and stuff. . . . Maybe they run out of gas." Malcolm responds, "They run outta gas, that's good, 'cause they're driving, right." Cole interrupts Malcolm again:

Cole: Tell me a story about why you're sad.

Malcolm: Do you think I'm sad?

Cole: (nodding) Yes.

Malcolm: What makes you think that?

Cole: Your eyes told me.

Malcolm says, mechanically, "I'm not supposed to talk about stuff like that." Cole looks away, and sighs. Malcolm stares at him, then moves his chair closer to Cole's bed.[5]

Once upon a time there was this person named Malcolm. He worked with children. . . . He loved it more than anything else. (smiles) And then one night, he found out that he made a mistake with one of them. Couldn't help that one. And he can't stop thinking about it; he can't forget. Ever since then, things have been different. He's not the same person that he used to be. And his wife doesn't like the person he's become. They barely speak anymore; they're like strangers. And then one day Malcolm meets this wonderful little boy . . . who reminds him a lot of the other one. And Malcolm decides to try and help this new boy. 'Cause he feels that if he could help this new boy, it would be like helping that one too. . . .

Cole asks, "How does the story end?" Malcolm admits, "I don't know." Malcolm's confession prompts Cole's own revelation: "I want to tell you my secret now." The room is quiet and tense.

> **Cole:**   I see dead people.
>
> **Malcolm:** In your dreams? (Cole shakes his head.)
>
> **Malcolm:** When you're awake? (Cole nods.)
>
> **Malcolm:** Dead people, like, in graves and coffins?
>
> **Cole:**   Walking around, like regular people. . . . They don't see each other; they only see what they wanna see. They don't know they're dead.
>
> **Malcolm:** How often do you see them?
>
> **Cole:**   All the time. They're everywhere (pause). You won't tell anyone my secret, right?
>
> **Malcolm:** No, I promise.
>
> **Cole:**   Will you stay here till I fall asleep?
>
> **Malcolm:** (nodding) Of course.

Unlike Malcolm, the viewer already knows Cole's secret. The camera has already shown us a number of the real-looking "dead people" who appear to Cole at home and at school. These are the most frightening scenes in the movie, and they all take the same pattern. The temperature drops, and a tiny cloud of condensation emerges from Cole's mouth. Then there appears a person who looks alive and well until suddenly he or she turns around and reveals a violent wound, still oozing blood.

Malcolm, not privy to these scenes, initially does not believe Cole's secret. Instead, he sees Cole's confession as evidence that Cole is even more disturbed than Malcolm had originally thought, and he despairs of helping him. This despair, coupled with the concern that his preoccupation with Cole is seriously damaging his marriage, leads him to a decision: he must resign from Cole's case.

But something prompts Malcolm to return to the tapes that he had made years earlier of his sessions with Vincent. He hears Vincent's childhood voice:

> **Vincent:**   Do you know why you're afraid when you're alone? I do. . . .
>
> **Malcolm:**   Whoo, It's cold in here. Vincent, why are you crying?
>
> **Vincent:**   You won't believe.

Malcolm plays the tape repeatedly. At one point during this therapy session, Malcolm had excused himself to take a phone call, but the tape remained running. As Malcolm now replays this section, he hears faint sounds that could be whispers and turns up the volume to the maximum. What he hears shocks him: the sound of a chair screeching across the floor and then a voice saying in Spanish, "Yo no quiero morir [I don't want to die]."

Suddenly Malcolm understands everything. He runs to find Cole in the church. Cole feigns surprise. Malcolm asks, "What do you think these ghosts want when they talk to you? I want you to think about it, Cole. . . ." Cole says, "They just want help." Malcolm says, "That's right, that's what I think, too. They just want help, even the scary ones." Now that Malcolm believes Cole's secret, he can help Cole to move forward to a solution of his problems. He advises Cole to listen to the ghosts and to attempt to help them.

Cole is still fearful. What if some of the ghosts do not really want help but are just angry and out to hurt somebody? Nevertheless, he follows Malcolm's advice. That evening he receives a visit from a young, dead girl, who vomits copiously inside the makeshift red tent Cole has set up in his room. Cole gathers his courage to ask, "Do you want to tell me something?" We are not privy to the conversation; the camera cuts quickly to the next scene: the interior of a bus carrying Cole and Malcolm to an unnamed destination. Soon they disembark and merge with a large group of people who are dressed in black mourning attire and stream into a suburban house. It is the home of the dead young girl who had paid Cole a nocturnal visit; Malcolm and Cole have arrived for the postfuneral reception. Cole goes upstairs to the girl's room. The music builds ominously. Just when the tension reaches the breaking point, a hand suddenly reaches out from under the bed and grabs Cole's foot. Cole (along with the viewing audience) is frightened out of his wits. It is the young girl. She gives him a box, which he takes down to the girl's mourning father. It contains a video tape, the contents of which we see in full. The video shows, clearly and unequivocally, that the girl had not died of any natural illness, but she was systematically poisoned by her mother. This is the unfinished business that the girl needed Cole to complete. With this information, the father not only knows exactly what happened to his daughter but can also prevent it from happening again to her younger sister, who was already beginning to exhibit the same symptoms as those that had afflicted the older girl.

Thus Cole makes peace with his "sixth sense"; he no longer runs away from the ghosts but accepts them and his ability both to see them and to help them. This successful conclusion is a satisfying resolution to the relationship between Malcolm and Cole. Cole has been helped by Malcolm; in helping Cole, Malcolm has also resolved the sense of failure that had attended his inability to help that earlier boy, Vincent, who, Malcolm now realizes, was tormented by a similar sixth sense.

The resolution of this relationship also has positive repercussions for the two other relationships that are explored in this film: that between Cole and his mother and that between Malcolm and his wife. Cole's mother is a single parent who works several jobs in order to support herself and her son. She is utterly devoted to him, and at the same time she is both puzzled by and concerned about him. Strange things are happening in her house. She leaves the kitchen for a brief moment and returns to find all the cabinet doors open. Her beloved bumblebee pin goes missing, only to surface in Cole's room. She blames Cole for these mishaps, but with some uncertainty. Worst of all, she notices welts and wounds on his back and is convinced that someone or something is out to harm him. Other mysterious things occur. One day, while cleaning the apartment, she gazes with love at the photos of Cole that are hung in the hallway: Cole's birthday parties, a day at the amusement park, a barbecue. For the first time, she notices a thin streak of light in each photo, illuminating Cole subtly.

These events are extremely distressing for Cole's mother. She knows that Cole is hiding a secret. When he refuses to confess to taking the bumblebee pendant, she tells him, "God, I am so tired, Cole. . . . I need some help. . . . I've been praying, but I must not be praying right. Looks like we're just gonna have to answer each other's prayers. If we can't talk to each other we're not gonna make it." The turning point in this relationship occurs after Malcolm has helped Cole to accept and to work with his "sixth sense." On the way home from the school play, Cole and his mother are caught in a serious traffic jam. Cole chooses this moment to tell his mother: "I'm ready to communicate with you now." To explain his gift, he tells her that the traffic jam is caused by an accident in which a woman died. As he says this, the woman appears outside Cole's window, unseen by his mother but acknowledged quietly by Cole. "You're scaring me," she tells him, alarmed and upset. Cole persists: "They [the ghosts] scare me too sometimes. . . . They want me to do things for them. . . . They're the ones that used to hurt me. . . . You think I'm a freak?" She responds, "I would never think that about you, ever." Still, she is not convinced. But her skepticism changes to belief when Cole begins to talk to her about her own mother, his grandmother. "Grandma says hi. She says she's sorry for taking the bumblebee pendant. She just likes it a lot. Grandma comes to visit me sometimes. . . . She wanted me to tell you she saw you dance. She said, when you were little, you and her had a fight right before your dance recital. You thought she didn't come to see you dance. She did. She hid in the back so you wouldn't see. She said you were like an angel. She said you came to the place where they buried her. Asked her a question. She said, The answer is, every day. What did you ask?" The question, says his mother, now crying, is, "Do I make her proud?" Malcolm has not only healed Cole but provided a way for Cole to communicate with his mother and thereby to heal that all-important relationship as well.

Malcolm's relationship with his wife also needs healing. Since the night of the shooting, Malcolm and Anna have become more and more estranged. They do not speak to each other. In fact, they do not interact at all. He returns home from his meetings with Cole to find that she has eaten alone and has not even set the table for him. When he joins her, late, at their favorite restaurant for an anniversary dinner, she ignores him, pays the bill for her solo meal, and says, angrily, as she leaves, "Happy anniversary." Worst of all, he sees her young, attractive male employee (she runs a jewelry and gift store) leave their home, obviously smitten with love for Anna, and later he catches them in a kiss at the store after she has given the young man a birthday gift. At this point he decides that his work with Cole is harming his marriage; perhaps he is mindful of her reproach to him on the night of the awards presentation, that he has put his work before her. Yet he knows that she still loves him, for he has on occasion returned home to find her asleep in front of the television with their wedding video playing.

Neither Malcolm nor we, the viewing audience, can put our fingers on the specific problem or its solution. But Anna knows, and so does Cole. Indeed, Cole has known from the moment that he has laid eyes on Malcolm in the church. MALCOLM IS DEAD. Like the other ghosts who appear to Cole, Malcolm does not *know* that he is dead, and, like them, he needs Cole to help him resolve his unfinished business so that he can finally rest in peace. This unfinished business involved Vincent, to be sure, but it also involved Anna. He died unable to assure her that despite his dedication to his work and to the children whom he tried to help, she was always first for him. His confession to Cole during Cole's hospital stay not only encouraged Cole to share his secret with Malcolm, but it also revealed to Cole the problem that this particular ghost had to resolve. Cole offers advice: "I got an idea how you can talk to your wife. Wait till she's asleep, then she'll listen to you and she won't even know it."

Malcolm returns home and finds his wife asleep in front of the wedding video. She talks in her sleep:

Anna: I miss you.

Malcolm: I miss you too.

Anna: Why, Malcolm?

Malcom: Why? What is it?

Anna: Why did you leave me?

Malcolm: (startled) I didn't leave you.

A ring drops out of her hand and rolls along on the floor. It is his wedding ring. Malcolm, in a flash, realizes that he is dead. Suddenly everything makes sense: her meals alone, her sadness, even the scenes between her and her assistant. For the first time since he was shot, he staggers up the stairs, as if in pain, and reenters the setting of the opening scene. Sprawled on his bed, a bullet wound in his stomach, he quietly dies with Anna in shock and crying at his side. He (or his ghost) returns now to the room where Anna has dozed off and watches her; her breath condenses, as does Cole's when a ghost is visiting him. "I think I can go now," he tells her. "I just needed to do a couple of things. I needed to help someone. I think I did. And I needed to tell you something. You were never second. Ever. I love you." She smiles in her sleep. He continues: "You sleep now. Everything will be different in the morning." She responds, "Good night, Malcolm." "Good night, sweetheart," he answers. He closes his eyes, and the screen is flooded by a bright white light.

The recognition that Malcolm, too, is a dead person makes sense not only of Anna's behavior throughout the film but also of several other scenes in the film. The film plays an elaborate and skillful trick on the first-time viewer through careful editing and the use of color and sound. For example, Cole speaks frequently of "seeing" Malcolm. When they first meet in the church, Cole is wary of Malcolm and says matter of factly, "I'm going to see you again." Once all is resolved, he says, "I'm not going to see you anymore, am I?" Against the background of Cole's confession that he sees dead people, we realize that Malcolm is one of those dead people who appear to Cole seeking his help.

Careful editing also contributes to the mystery. When Malcolm first meets with Cole at his home, we see that Cole's mother is sitting in the living room across from Malcolm. They are not speaking to each other, but their poses suggest that Cole's arrival has simply interrupted their conversation. In the context of his mother's concerns, the audience naturally believes that his mother has engaged him in his capacity as a child psychologist. Later we realize that, in fact, Malcolm was invisible to his mother; she was simply sitting and waiting for Cole, completely unaware of Malcolm's presence, though he is fully aware of hers.

Perhaps most obvious, at least in retrospect, is the striking use of the color red. As the filmmakers explain in the DVD and video versions of the film, the color red is used for items that have been touched by the restless dead, such as the doorknob to the basement, where Malcolm spends an inordinate amount of time; the door of the church, where Cole goes to play with his soldiers; and the red dress and shawl that Anna wears during the period that Malcolm's ghostly presence prevents her from coming to terms with his death.

Finally, aspects of the setting are also telling. In particular, we note that Malcolm frequents the basement of his home. As the lowest part of the house, this location may symbolize his status as a person who is dead and buried but who refuses to rest, emerging periodically from this symbolic grave to wander around the house and in the world. Only after we learn that he is dead do we understand why his books, files, and tapes have all been packed away in boxes in the basement.

Surely one of the film's intentions is to play this trick on the viewing audience. In this regard, the film plays with the notion of verisimilitude and the expectations that viewers bring to the movie theatre. Because we are accustomed to narrative continuity, we interpret the sequence of events in a particular way. The first scene, in which Malcolm is shot but in which we do not see him die, is followed immediately by his first glimpse of Cole, which took place the following autumn. Because it does not occur to us that, in this genre of realistic film, a man walking around the streets of Philadelphia can be anything other than a living human being, we now believe that Malcolm could not have died at Vincent's hand, though perhaps we are puzzled by the absence of ambulance and hospital scenes that would have filled in that gap for us. It is only at the end that we understand the truth.[6]

USE OF THE BIBLE

As our summary indicates, the film's plot and main premise are easily described without any recourse to the Bible. Nevertheless, the Bible plays an important, if subtle, role. When Malcolm first enters the church and watches Cole playing with his lead soldiers, he hears Cole recite, speaking for one of his toys, "De profundis clamo ad te domine." Malcolm asks Cole what this phrase means. Cole is evasive: "It's called Latin," says Cole. "It's a language." Malcolm asks, "All your soldiers speak Latin?" "No," says Cole, "Just one." At home, Malcolm digs his Latin dictionary out of a box in the basement and

translates the phrase word by word: "Out of the depths, I cry to you, Lord."
"Mass for the dead," says Malcolm aloud, and in part he is correct, for this
Psalm is frequently recited at both Catholic and Protestant funerals.

But there are two other points related to this quotation that are not made
explicit in the film. The first is its role not only at funerals but in the Catholic
liturgy for Halloween and All Saints' Day.[7] In the film, these words are uttered
just as Malcolm enters the church. The significance of this "coincidence,"
however, will not emerge except to those who identify the phrase, understand
its traditional association with Halloween, and know that Malcolm himself is
a ghost. By having his toy soldier say these words, Cole is acting out his own
troubled relationship with "dead people" and foreshadowing its eventual resolution in which he will be able to help the ghosts who call out to him just as
he can "help" the toy soldier with whom he is playing.

Plot and Character

The Latin words, quoting the first few words from Psalm 130, imply a particular relationship between the one who cries out and the one who listens. In
the psalm, the one who cries is the supplicant, who, as we have already discussed, is either dead or in deep despair, and the one to whom he or she cries
out is God. It is not clear that Malcolm, or even Cole, knows the biblical source
of this quotation. Certainly its source is never made clear in the film. Nevertheless, its relevance to the film is immediately apparent. In the film, the sup-
plicants are dead people, and the one to whom they cry out is Cole. The
despair and longing of the speaker correspond in intensity to the longing of
the dead people in the film to reach out to someone in the world of the living
who will be attentive to their words and make it possible for them to resolve
the issues that prevent them from achieving eternal rest. These issues are not
necessarily terrible sins, as they seem for the supplicant in the psalm, but, at
least in Malcolm's case, they represent tasks left undone such that undue pain
was caused to others.

If the dead people in the film can be seen as analogous to the speaker in the
psalm, then perhaps we may push the connection between the psalm and the
film even further to suggest that Cole's potential role in the lives of "his" dead
people corresponds to the role of the Lord in the psalm in the life of the supplicant. Like the Lord, Cole is the object of the dead people's supplications.
They ask of him what the speaker asks of the Lord: to listen to them and to
aid in their redemption.

Certainly Cole himself is not directly represented as anything but fully
human, except for his sixth sense, an ability that is rare and unexpected, perhaps, but not unique to him, as the case of Vincent demonstrates. But there

are elements of the film that hint at a quasi-divine role, or, at least, at his potential for fulfilling a role that is denied to most people. This role is filtered through the images associated with Christ.

Like Truman in *The Truman Show*, Cole is portrayed briefly in a cruciform position, during one of the rare carefree moments that we glimpse in the film. He and his mother have just done grocery shopping. In the store's parking lot, Cole sits in the laden shopping cart as his mother pushes it towards the car. She playfully begins to run, pushing the cart ahead of her. Cole enjoys every moment, arms outstretched, outlined like a joyous Christ figure against the clear blue sky. Cole's comfort in the church also alludes to his Christ-like redemptive role. Although Malcolm "psychologizes" the importance of the church in Cole's tortured life, Cole himself simply treats the church as home. He is very comfortable there, where he plays freely; he also helps himself, in a proprietary manner, to the objects that are in the church. Thus on his way out of the sanctuary after meeting Malcolm for the first time, he slips a small Jesus figurine into his pocket. The fact that the figurine is dressed in red may reinforce the idea that Jesus, whose presence is associated with the church, also has unfinished business with the living, just like the dead people who terrify Cole.

That Cole feels the church is his natural domain is illustrated in a second scene. When Malcolm suddenly understands Cole's true situation, he rushes to the church. There he finds Cole walking back and forth on the church balcony. Cole looks down from this height onto Malcolm, and, disguising his anger, speaks imperiously to him in a way that belies the usual adult/child and doctor/patient hierarchies. Their relative positions in this scene mirror the postures implied in the psalm, in which the speaker is calling up to the Lord on high from the depths, just as Malcolm must call up to Cole on the church balcony from where he stands on the sanctuary floor. This scene also calls to mind the despairing words that Cole's mother addresses to him: "God, I am so tired . . . ," a profound sigh that may well be her own psalm of supplication and lament.

In taking on the Lord's role, at least in this limited way, Cole is responsible for the redemption of the dead people who call out to him. His own suffering has been caused by his unwillingness to accept this responsibility due to his fear of the supplicating dead themselves. Once he is able to listen to them, and thereby to help them resolve the issues that were keeping them from resting peacefully for eternity, he is also released from his own fears as well as from his "freakish" social status at school. Thus he is able to help Malcolm both to redeem his own failure with Vincent Gray and to resolve his relationship with his wife.

Malcolm facilitates Cole's redemption from fear. When he first meets Malcolm, Cole is like one of the dead people of whom he is afraid. His fear has made him unable to enjoy life as any child would, to achieve friendship and recognition by his peers. In trusting Malcolm with his secret, he is also crying out to Malcolm for help. Malcolm's initial inability to believe and his temporary withdrawal from Cole's treatment are painful to Cole and lead him to be angry and to try to hurt Malcolm, much as the dead people were angry and hurtful to Cole when he refused to or was unable to listen to them.

After Cole comes to accept his sixth sense, he becomes a lively child, confident and full of the vitality that characterizes healthy eight-year-old children. This change comes through beautifully in the contrast between the two school plays in which Cole participates. In the first play, he has only a minor role, and he is clearly envious of his erstwhile friend, Thomas Thomasino, who is a star. In the second play, a rendition of *The Sword in the Stone,* Cole plays the young King Arthur, a young man of special powers—like Cole—and the only one who can remove the magic sword from the stone in which it has been embedded. At the end of the play, the children carry Cole on their shoulders and collapse, laughing, on the floor. No longer is Cole an outsider, who is reviled by the others. He is honored in the play and honored also by participating in the happy and childish laughter of his peers.

Malcolm is as proud of Cole as any father would be. Cole's dramatic success also marks his cure. Both he and Cole know that they no longer need each other. But, unlike his feelings towards the other dead people whom he sees, and in contrast to his initial attitude towards Malcolm, Cole is now reluctant to let Malcolm leave. As Cole comes to terms with Malcolm's departure ("I'm not gonna see you again, right?"), Malcolm replies, "I think we said everything we needed to say. Maybe it's time to say things to someone closer to you," by which he means Cole's mother. Cole does not want to let go: "Maybe we can pretend like we're going to see each other tomorrow. Just for pretend." Malcolm agrees and says, deliberately, "I'm going to go now. . . . I'll see you tomorrow, Cole."

Themes

The film develops a number of themes related to human relationships. One is grief and the need to come to terms with the unfinished business that physical death and the death of a relationship inevitably leave behind. Another is the focus on communication, both between the living—Cole and his mother—and, in a different way, between the living and the dead—Anna and Malcolm. In fact, communication is seen as central to the appropriate resolution of all three of the interlocking relationships portrayed in this film. Malcolm cannot help Cole until Cole communicates his secret to him, but Cole does not do so until Malcolm tells Cole why he is so sad. Malcolm, in turn, encourages Cole to speak with the dead who haunt him and the living, his mother, who loves him. Cole's decision to tell his mother his secret in the car on the way home from the play resolves her concerns and fears about him. Malcolm and Anna can both come to terms with his death after he is able to tell of his undying love for her.

In this regard, this film is typical of many other relationship movies where communication is shown to be essential to the resolution of conflict and the expression of love.[8] The added twist here is the supernatural element. The premise of the film requires that we, along with Malcolm, gradually suspend our disbelief in the permeability of the boundaries between the living and the dead. The film makes a statement about the needs of the dead to resolve issues in their lives before they can rest peacefully. The film does not necessarily advocate a belief in the persistence of consciousness after death. Rather, *The Sixth Sense*, like Psalm 130, may be interpreted metaphorically as a film about the ghosts that plague us all and that can be laid to rest only by talking about them directly with those whom we love.

But the brief quotation of Psalm 130 leads us one step further. In the psalm, the supplicant cries out to God for help and has faith that God will hear this cry and lift him or her up from the depths. Cole's fear for his own safety and well-being made it impossible for him to hear the dead clearly, that is, to recognize their need to be heard and to be helped. He was able to conquer his fear not only by confessing his secret to Malcolm but also, primarily, by the very fact of his relationship with Malcolm. Malcom wanted to help Cole rather than hurt—or rather, Malcom's unfinished business required only that Cole be receptive to his offers of assistance, friendship, and concern. Learning to trust Malcolm brought Cole to follow Malcolm's guidance. But in a sense, Cole already knew what to do, as we see in the scene in which he advises Malcolm to speak with Anna while she is asleep; he knows that he could hear and see the dead best in the middle of the night.

Cole's ghosts are portrayed so vividly that we viewers can understand fully his initial terror. Who among us would have the wherewithall to hear and respond to the outcry of such unwelcome visitors? A metaphorical reading of the film, however, might allow us to recognize the ways in which we fear, and hence block out, those who cry out to us for help.

CONCLUSION

The Sixth Sense does not seem, at first glance at least, to be a particularly religious film. Its plots, characters, and main messages are not explicitly related to a formal piety, and they can be understood and appreciated without taking faith into account. Even the church in which Malcolm and Cole first meet, and in which Malcolm finally conveys to Cole that he believes his secret, is not for Cole a place of worship. Rather, it is a sanctuary, the only place where ghosts— aside from Malcolm—do not appear to him. As Malcolm explains to Cole at their first meeting, churches have long functioned as a place of sanctuary for those seeking to escape their pursuers. On the other hand, the brilliant red doors of the church imply the presence of the restless dead therein—perhaps Jesus, another dead man who refused to stay buried in his grave and whose business on earth remains unfinished. The fact that the church offers Cole the only place of respite may be a factor in his initial dismay at being approached by Malcolm within its walls.

The Sixth Sense can certainly be classified as a horror movie, dependent as it is on ghoulish characters, whose frightening impact on the young boy, and the viewers, is enhanced by the camera work and the use of light, color, and sound. But on second and subsequent viewing, the horror recedes as the pieces of the puzzle fit together and allow the warmth of human relationships and the drama of the human soul, coming to terms with its duties in the world, to come to the fore. The biblical quotation not only provides a key to the dynamic relationships between Cole and the dead people and between Cole and Malcolm. It also suggests that we as human beings can be agents of the divine if we would only overcome our own fears and truly listen to others.

But the subtle and very brief quotation of Psalm 130 raises an issue that has not emerged with respect to the other films discussed thus far. Viewers who are not familiar with the Psalms may not realize that the Latin words "spoken" by Cole's toy soldier and translated word for word by Malcolm with the help of his Latin dictionary are, in fact, a biblical quotation. In contrast to *Cape Fear*, in which Sam and the viewer eventually learn that the book between Esther and Psalms is Job, *The Sixth Sense* never reveals the source for or literary context of the brief Latin phrase. Certainly the film is comprehensible even without such knowledge. But the ability to identify the quotation also leads to a deeper understanding of the film, its potential religious meanings, and its metaphorical message for us all.

7

Pulp Fiction and the Power of Belief (Ezekiel)

I will execute great vengeance on them with wrathful punishments. Then they shall know that I am the LORD, when I lay my vengeance on them.

Ezekiel 25:17

INTRODUCTION

The Hebrew Bible contains a number of books associated with or attributed to individuals identified as prophets. Ancient Israelite prophecy is a complex and highly varied phenomenon. In popular parlance we often define prophecy as the ability to forecast the future, but the biblical prophets did not concern themselves with divination or oracle reading so much as with warning Israel of the consequences attached to following a path that varies from the will of God. The prophets understood themselves to be divinely inspired vehicles for God's messages to Israel and its leadership; prophecies were often introduced with a formula that indicated the divine source, such as "Thus says the Lord." In transmitting God's word to Israel, the prophets addressed not only eternal verities but also the specific situations in which they and their people found themselves.

The historical context had a strong impact on prophets like Ezekiel, who lived and wrote in sixth-century B.C.E. Babylonia. In the period leading up to the Babylonian conquest of the Kingdom of Judah in 586 B.C.E., Ezekiel and others were sending a message of impending doom. But once the conquest occurred, marking the end of the Kingdom of Judah as a sovereign state and the destruction of Solomon's Temple in Jerusalem, Ezekiel also provided a message of hope for the exiled people. The book attributed to Ezekiel is concerned with the situation of the Israelites in exile, not only the tragic circumstances that led to the Babylonian conquest but also the relationship between the exiles and those who remained in Judah.[1]

One element in the message that Ezekiel imparted on God's behalf concerned vengeance. Ezekiel 25:15–17 is only one of many passages in which God threatens vengeance on the enemies of Israel.[2] Taken on their own, God's frequent threats might be seen as support for the stereotypical view that contrasts the Old Testament God of vengeance with the New Testament God of love.[3] In its immediate context, in the literary context of the book as a whole, and in the historical context of the prophet Ezekiel, however, the meaning of this passage is much more complex. The passage concludes a prophecy against the Philistines that reads as follows:

> Thus says the Lord GOD: Because with unending hostilities the Philistines acted in vengeance, and with malice of heart took revenge in destruction; therefore thus says the Lord GOD, I will stretch out my hand against the Philistines, cut off the Cherethites,[4] and destroy the rest of the seacoast. I will execute great vengeance on them with wrathful punishments. Then they shall know that I am the LORD, when I lay my vengeance on them.

Although we often view vengeance as a private, violent, malicious act, the origins of the biblical usage may have been in judicial language. When attributed to God, vengeance is always understood as the rectification of a misdeed, not an act based on malice but the just consequences for crimes against the entire people. But when applied to an individual, the usage may be positive or negative. Excessive vengeance was forbidden under the *lex talionis* (law of retribution, Exod. 21:23–25), and its negative effects were illustrated by the story of Samson (Judges 14–16), which describes the terrible violence that ensued from the vengeful behavior that characterized the relationship of Samson and the Philistines.[5]

In the prophecy in Ezekiel 25:15–17, God warns the Philistines that they will be punished for their destructive actions towards Israel. This warning, in turn, provides hope for the nation in exile that eventually God will step in to punish their enemies for the suffering inflicted on Israel. If the defeat and exile of Israel implies God's absence or (temporary) loss of cosmic power, prophecies of vengeance provide hope and reassurance that God is merely waiting for an opportune moment to step back into history on behalf of God's people and to usher in a time when all peoples will recognize God's supremacy.

The book of Ezekiel is not common fodder for Hollywood movies, with the exception of one film. In *Pulp Fiction*, directed by Quentin Tarantino, a monologue identified as Ezekiel 25:17 has a prominent and unexpected role in the film and in the lives of several of its characters.

FILM SUMMARY

In the film's opening frames, a dictionary definition of the term "pulp" scrolls down the screen. The text, attributed to the *American Heritage Dictionary*, College Edition, highlights two meanings of the word, one referring to texture, as in the "pulp" of an apple, or the consequence of being beaten "to a pulp," the other referring to a genre of writing that often features gratuitous sex and violence and often printed on rough paper.

These definitions capture the several forms in which *Pulp Fiction* serves up the "pulp" to its viewing audience. The film certainly contains "soft, moist, shapeless mass or matter," mostly in the form of people's ruined faces and bodies, mashed or shot to a pulp (though, as some reviewers have pointed out, the film feels more violent than it actually is; a mere six individuals are killed in this film, a relatively low body count given its subject matter).[6] The occasional reference to a fictional brand of cigarettes, "Red Apples," brings to mind the soft and mushy pulp that is left over when apples are processed for juice.[7] The film's structure is also pulpy. Rather than the linear and chronological progression that we generally expect in Hollywood films,[8] *Pulp Fiction* initially appears to be a formless, even haphazard, narrative.

The second definition is also apt. The subject matter of the film is certainly lurid, including as it does vivid portrayals of sodomy, substance abuse, and murder. The film, of course, is not printed on rough, unfinished paper, but the elusive narrative structure may be an approximate cinematic equivalent to the physical appearance of printed pulp. The narrative structure makes it difficult to summarize the film's plot and to figure out the chronology. Indeed, the overall plan and order emerge only after several viewings and, even then, only by paying close attention to what are normally incidental details, such as location and clothing. Tarantino himself likens the fragmentary and interrupted nature of the film to the pulp fiction genre and the casual forms of consumption that it encourages.[9]

The film begins with a two-part narrative frame. In contrast to films such as *Fried Green Tomatoes* and *Cape Fear*, in which the frame clearly provides a context for the rest of the film, *Pulp Fiction* leaves one guessing at the chronological and logical place of the frame until the very end of the movie. The first part of the narrative frame features two petty criminals, a man and a woman who are partners in love as well as in crime. They call each other "Pumpkin" (Tim Roth) and "Honey Bunny" (Amanda Plummer), pet names that are at odds with their violent lifestyle. Over breakfast at a coffee shop, the two are having an intense discussion. Pumpkin wants to retire from the business of robbing liquor stores. "It ain't the giggle it usta be," he says. "Too many foreigners own liquor stores. Vietnamese, Koreans, they can't fuckin' speak

English. You tell 'em, 'Empty out the register,' and they don't know what it fuckin' means. They make it too personal. We keep on, one of those gook motherfuckers' gonna make us kill 'em." Honey Bunny immediately reacts to this last statement: "I'm not gonna kill anybody." Pumpkin answers, "I don't wanna kill anybody either. But they'll probably put us in a situation where it's us or them." Suddenly they see a solution to their professional dilemma: rob the coffee shop! No likely martyrs here, just workers and patrons anxious to avoid trouble. They kiss passionately and launch into action. Honey Bunny stands on the table, points her gun at the other patrons, and screeches, "Any of you fuckin' pricks move and I'll execute every motherfuckin' last one of you!"[10]

But before we can learn how events in the coffee shop will unfold, the opening credits begin to roll. When they are done, we are no longer with Pumpkin and Honey Bunny but with another pair of partners in crime: Vince (John Travolta) and Jules (Samuel Jackson). They are driving to an apartment where they will confront a group of young men that has double-crossed Marsellus (Ving Rhames), the crime boss. On the way they chat about matters small and large. Vince describes his trip to Amsterdam, speaking with particular enthusiasm about the exciting Dutch drug scene. Jules fills Vince in on a recent incident in which their boss, Marsellus, threw a buddy named Antwan out of a fourth-story window for massaging his wife's feet, and they discuss the question of whether a foot massage is an intimate act that warrants such dire consequences. Still pondering this ethical question, they arrive at their destination, and, like Pumpkin and Honey Bunny, they switch immediately into their cool, and cruel, professional personas. Jules toys sadistically with the four terrified young men in the apartment and helps himself ostentatiously to their breakfast of hamburgers and soft drinks. A few moments later, three of them are dead. Before killing Brett, the apparent head of this unfortunate group, Jules asks him if he reads the Bible. Jules then recites, with fury, a long speech that he identifies as Ezekiel 25:17.

> The path of the righteous man is beset on all sides by the inequities of the selfish and the tyranny of evil men. Blessed is he who, in the name of charity and good will, shepherds the weak through the valley of the darkness. For he is truly his brother's keeper and the finder of lost children. And I will strike down upon thee with great vengeance and furious anger those who attempt to poison and destroy my brothers. And you will know I am the Lord when I lay my vengeance upon you.

He then pumps several bullets into Brett's head at point-blank range.[11] We do not know in what way these young men "fucked" with Marsellus, though they admit to doing so. The incident has something to do with a briefcase that Vince locates in the kitchen. The contents are never divulged, but the golden glow that suffuses Vince's face when he opens the briefcase and the awe with which he gazes at it arouse both curiosity and wonder.[12]

The coffee shop and Brett episodes frame the film but only retrospectively do they help us to make sense of its main themes. The body of the film comprises three interrelated stories. In contrast to the frame stories, these are told in full, though out of chronological sequence. The first is called "Vincent Vega & Marsellus Wallace's wife." We learn from Vince's conversation with Jules that their boss, Marsellus, has asked Vince to take his wife Mia (Uma Thurman) out on the town while he is away. Naturally, Vince is somewhat nervous at the prospect; if, as he believes, Marsellus threw Antwan out of a fourth-floor window for giving Mia a foot massage, what would he do to Vince if he does not measure up to the task, or, worse, if he does something that sparks Marsellus's jealousy? To gather his courage, Vince visits his heroin dealer for some extra-special, very expensive heroin. Then he goes to pick up Mia. She seems to be equally nervous; she snorts cocaine before emerging from her dressing room. She also takes periodic cocaine breaks throughout their evening together. They go off to Jack Rabbit Slim's, a 50s retro restaurant, where the waiters impersonate classical Hollywood personalities (Ed Sullivan, Buddy Holly, Marilyn Monroe) and the menu is also appropriately 50s in name, if not in price range. After some initial uneasiness, they have a marvelous—and innocuous—time together. At the end of the evening, Vince takes her back home and she invites him in for a drink. While he is in the bathroom, she rummages through his pockets and finds the heroin. Thinking it is cocaine, she snorts it all and immediately falls into a coma. Vince panics, takes her back to the dealer, and eventually revives her by sticking an adrenaline needle directly into her chest.

The next section, entitled "The Gold Watch," features a boxer named Butch (Bruce Willis) and his lover Fabienne (Maria de Medeiros). It begins with a nightmare about an incident from his childhood, when his father's comrade in arms came to give him his father's watch, now the only memento he has of his father, who died in Vietnam.[13] He wakes up in a sweat. Later that day, Butch fights his last boxing match. Marsellus has paid him handsomely to lose this match, but Butch reneges on his part of the bargain and knocks his opponent out so powerfully that he dies.[14] Immediately after the fight, Butch puts his escape plan into high gear. He returns to the motel where his lover, Fabienne, is waiting for him, and they prepare to leave the next morning. But then Butch realizes that Fabienne, who had moved their belongings from the apartment to the motel, has forgotten to bring his keepsake watch. Butch returns to the apartment, finds the watch, and then sees a gun on the counter. It is Vince's gun, carelessly left there while Vince is in the bathroom (again). Vince has no doubt come looking for Butch at Marsellus's behest. We have already seen in the Brett sequence that Marsellus has a zero tolerance policy for double-crossers. As Vince opens the bathroom door, Butch shoots him with his own gun, carefully wipes off the prints, and leaves.

On his way back to the motel, Butch sees Marsellus, the very man he is trying to avoid. He deliberately hits him with his car, and then his car, in turn, is hit by another car. No longer able to flee quickly, Butch runs into the nearest available store, which happens to be a pawnshop. Marsellus charges in after him. Their violent struggle is stopped abruptly by the pawnshop owner, "Zed," who has other, even more violent, plans for them: to tie them up and sodomize them. Marsellus is the first victim, but Butch manages to free himself. He is then faced with a difficult moral dilemma: should he simply leave and let Zed finish Marsellus off (an outcome that would benefit Butch), or should he try to save his erstwhile enemy? He decides on the latter course and returns to battle it out with Zed using a Samurai sword that he has found in the pawnshop. Marsellus is saved. All is now forgiven on condition that Butch leave town immediately. Butch takes Zed's motorcycle, picks up Fabienne, and escapes for good.

The third story is called "The Bonnie Situation." The camera returns us briefly to the frame narrative and shows us that while Jules is delivering his impassioned rendition of Ezekiel 25:17 to the ill-fated Brett, an armed man is hiding in the washroom directly behind Jules's back. When the man hears shots, he opens the door and comes out shooting. Miraculously or coincidentally—it is a matter of opinion—Jules and Vince are not hurt. They leave Brett's place with Marvin, the fourth man in the apartment, as a hostage. As they ride along in the car, Vince accidentally shoots Marvin in the head, making a huge mess in the car. In a panic, the two drive to the suburban home of a friend named Jimmy (Quentin Tarantino). Jules calls Marsellus, who sends over "the Wolf" (Harvey Keitel) to help fix the situation. The major complicating factor, as Jimmy explains at length and with some distress, is Jimmy's wife, Bonnie (Vanessa Valentino), who works "the graveyard shift" at a hospital and is due back at any minute. Jimmy is afraid that she will divorce him immediately, no questions asked, if she comes home to find a dead body in the garage and several bloodied gangsters in her living room. The Wolf tells them what to do: clean up the car, and clean up themselves. He hoses them down, and they exchange their dark gangster uniforms for Jimmy's tennis shorts and T-shirts, looking like anything but the gangsters that they are. He then drives the car to someone who will dispose of it for them. The fact of Marvin's death is eclipsed completely by the process of cleaning up.

Jules and Vince repair to a coffeeshop for breakfast to mull over the events of that unusual morning, a few tables away from where Pumpkin and Honey Bunny are discussing their lives. In doing so, they return us to the frame story of the coffee shop robbery. The film replays Pumpkin and Honey Bunny's good-luck kiss, followed by Honey Bunny's transformation from playful little-girl lover to robber.[15]

The chronology is confusing, to say the least. That the sequences are not shown in the order in which they take place is signaled by several elements: first, the return at the end to the frame narratives implies that the intermediate stories do not bring us to the end of the story, chronologically speaking. Second, the clothing worn by Jules and Vince in the sequences they are in together suggests discontinuity. In the first story, they are in gangster suits. In the third story, we learn how they sullied their clothing and so had to change into Jimmy's shorts and T-shirts; this is how they are also dressed in the epilogue in the coffee shop. But earlier on, there is a brief scene in which they come into Marsellus's bar and Vince meets Butch. In this sequence they are also, and at the time inexplicably, dressed in what we later learn are Jimmy's castoffs. Third is the question of why Vince is on his own in Butch's apartment when otherwise he and Jules are an inseparable team. Finally, and most puzzling, is Vince's reappearance in the "Bonnie Situation" after he has been killed by Butch at point-blank range in the "Gold Watch" sequence.

From these clues we can piece together a rough chronology. The story begins at approximately seven A.M. as Jules and Vince advance on Brett's apartment. Jules kills Brett and friends, and Jules and Vince survive Marvin's attempt to kill them. They take Marvin hostage, perhaps to bring him back to Marsellus, but they inadvertently shoot him. They then have to clean up the car lest they get stopped by the police. After the cleanup, Jules and Vince go to a coffee shop for breakfast, which is where they are sitting when Pumpkin and Honey Bunny stage their holdup. Jules decides to quit the life of crime. That night, Vince and Mia go out on a date, and she nearly dies from an inadvertent heroin overdose. That same night, Butch wins the fight that Marsellus had paid him to lose. The next morning, Butch returns to the apartment to retrieve his watch and kills Vince. He meets up with Marsellus outside the pawnshop; Butch saves his life and leaves town with Fabienne.

USE OF THE BIBLE

Plot and Character

The pivotal event in this film is Jules's "miraculous" experience in Brett's apartment. As we have noted, Marvin is hiding in the bathroom of Brett's apartment when Jules and Vince come in to avenge their duplicitous treatment of Marsellus. When he hears Jules's gun go off, Marvin comes out of the bathroom shooting. Despite the fact that he is only inches away from Jules and Vince, his shots miss them both. Vince chalks up their escape to coincidence and gives it no further thought. Jules, on the other hand, is shaken to the core and begins from this point on to reevaluate his life.

> **Jules:** (to himself) Did you see the size of that gun he fired at us? It was bigger than him. . . . We should be fuckin' dead, man!
>
> **Vincent:** I know, we was lucky.
>
> **Jules:** No, no, no no. That shit wasn't luck.
>
> **Vincent:** Yeah, maybe.
>
> **Jules:** This was divine intervention. You know what divine intervention is?
>
> **Vincent:** I think so. That means that God came down from Heaven and stopped the bullets.
>
> **Jules:** That's right. That's exactly what it means! God came down from Heaven and stopped these motherfuckin' bullets. . . . What happened here was a miracle, and I want you to fuckin' acknowledge it!
>
> **Vincent:** Okay, man, it was a miracle, can we go now?

They continue the discussion in the car, into which they have bundled Marvin.

> **Vincent:** . . . you ever seen that show *Cops?* I was watchin' it one time and there was this cop and he was talkin' about this gun fight he had in a hallway with this guy, right. And he just unloaded on this guy and nothin' happened, he didn't hit nothin', o.k. It was just him and this guy. I mean, you know, it's freaky, but it happens.

Vincent tries to persuade Jules that, unusual as it may be, such things can happen. But Jules doesn't buy it.

> **Jules:** If you wanna play blind man, then go walk with a Shepherd. But me, my eyes are wide fuckin' open. . . . That's it for me. For here on in, you can consider my ass retired.
>
> **Vincent:** (shocked) Jesus Christ!
>
> **Jules:** (suddenly pious) Don't blaspheme!
>
> **Vincent:** (still shocked) Goddammit, Jules—
>
> **Jules:** I said don't do that—

Jules says he will tell Marsellus that very day; Vincent predicts that Marsellus will just laugh. At this point Vince's gun inadvertently goes off, shooting Marvin in the head and instigating the entire "Bonnie situation."

The tension between coincidence and the miraculous calls *Magnolia* to mind for two reasons: the role of television and the media (including the television show *Cops*) in forming people's sense of reality, and the struggle of the characters to interpret particular events: are they one-time coincidences that "just happen" or do they reflect some sort of divine plan? In *Pulp Fiction*, Vince argues the former position, and Jules, the latter. But Jules takes it one step further: not only was his survival that morning a miracle; it was also intended to convey a divine message: that Jules should go straight.

After delivering the now-clean car to the wrecking shop, Jules and Vince retire to the coffee shop for breakfast to talk things over. The events of that morning have persuaded Jules to quit "the life." Vincent asks, "What are you gonna do, then?" Jules is working out a plan:

> **Jules:** First, I'm gonna deliver this case to Marsellus. Then, basically, I'm just gonna walk the earth.
>
> **Vincent:** What do you mean, walk the earth?
>
> **Jules:** You know, like Caine in *Kung Fu*. Walk from place to place, meet people, get in adventures.
>
> **Vincent:** How long do you intend to walk the earth?
>
> **Jules:** Until God puts me where he wants me to be.

Jules has been transformed into a pious, born-again Christian, just waiting for God's personal word. Vincent cannot get his mind around this. As he sees it, Jules has simply decided to become a bum, "just like all those pieces of shit out there who beg for change, who sleep in garbage bins, eat what I throw away. They got a name for that, Jules, a bum. And without a job, residence, or legal tender, that's what you're gonna be, man—a fuckin' bum!" Jules wants to stop arguing. "Look my friend, this is just where you and I differ—" But Vincent can't let go: "What happened this morning, man, I agree, was peculiar but it wasn't water into wine" (cf. John 2:1–11).

This is not just a philosophical discussion for Vince. It is true that he cannot begin to understand what Jules is going through at this moment and he cannot imagine trading their financial and "career" security for a life on the streets. But Vincent is also struggling to hang on to Jules for the sake of their friendship, and perhaps also for the sake of Jules's level-headed savvy. In "The Gold Watch" sequence, would Vince have left his gun out for Butch to find had Jules been along with him?

In his decision to walk the earth, Jules models himself after two different figures, one biblical and one pop-cultural. The screenplay makes it clear that the primary reference is to Caine, the hero of the *Kung Fu* movies, who does indeed wander from town to town much as the heroes of the westerns *Pale Rider* and *Shane* did. The Caine parallel is apt. Caine is wanted for murder in China, but he has repented of his crime and has come to America to help others. But in watching the film itself, the double entendre is obvious, for it evokes the biblical Cain, the first murderer, whom God sentenced to a lifetime of wandering the earth in punishment for killing his brother: "When you till the ground, it will no longer yield to you its strength; you will be a fugitive and a wanderer on the earth" (Gen. 4:12).

Jules's decision to quit the "life" echoes the decision made in that very same coffee shop by Pumpkin and Honey Bunny earlier that morning. The couple does not yet contemplate quitting the life of crime altogether, though they are clearly toying with this idea. Just as these two could not resist holding up the coffee shop, so perhaps Jules will find it difficult to maintain his resolve. In the first place, as Vince points out, he does not have any ideas other than wandering the world until God shows him what to do. This could get tiresome in a very short time. Second, given Marsellus's response to Butch's double cross, will he let Jules, who has seen and done so much, get away? There is abundant evidence that leaving now would be a dangerous move. Vince's fear of meeting Antwan's fate should he look at Mia the wrong way as well as Jules's and Vince's own roles as Marsellus's hit men suggest that Marsellus is not likely to meet Jules's change of heart with equanimity. But unless *Pulp Fiction II* comes along, we will never know whether Jules succeeded or not.

The depth of Jules's transformation is signaled by the two scenes in which he recites Ezekiel 25:17. In the first, he is a majestic and awe-inspiring figure, proclaiming the prophecy with fury and self-righteousness, and then carrying out Marsellus's vengeance with several shots to Brett's skull. In the second scene, at the coffee shop, he appears to be a different sort of man altogether. Vince excuses himself to go to the bathroom (again), and at that moment Pumpkin and Honey Bunny stage their holdup. Jules stays seated and tosses his wallet into the green garbage bag that Pumpkin is carrying from table to table. But Jules is not done with Pumpkin quite yet. Pulling out his own gun, he forces Pumpkin, whom he dubs "Ringo," to sit down at the table across from him. He then treats Pumpkin to the same Bible lesson that he had taught to Brett, all the while pointing his gun directly into the terrified man's face.

> **Jules:** You read the Bible, Ringo?
>
> **Pumpkin:** Not regularly, no.
>
> **Jules:** There's a passage I got memorized. Ezekiel 25:17.

Jules then recites the same passage that he had earlier proclaimed to Brett, but in a much flatter, quieter, and less emphatic tone:

> The path of the righteous man is beset on all sides by the inequities of the selfish and the tyranny of evil men. Blessed is he who, in the name of charity and good will, shepherds the weak through the valley of the darkness. For he is truly his brother's keeper and the finder of lost children. And I will strike down upon thee with great vengeance and furious anger those who attempt to poison and destroy my brothers. And you will know I am the Lord when I lay my vengeance upon you.

This time, however, the speech is not followed by shots. Instead, Jules, in true postmodern fashion, reflects on the meaning of his speech and provides several different ways that it might pertain to his current situation. He tells "Ringo:"

> I been sayin' that shit for years. And if you heard it, that meant your ass. I never gave much thought to what it meant. I just thought it was some cold-blooded shit to say to a motherfucker 'fore I popped a cap into his ass. But I saw some shit this mornin' made me think twice. See, I'm thinkin', maybe it means *you're* the evil man. And *I'm* the righteous man. And Mr. 9 Millimeter here [the gun], he's the shepherd protecting my righteous ass in the valley of darkness. Or it could be *you're* the righteous man and *I'm* the shepherd and it's the world that's evil and selfish. I'd like that. But that shit ain't the truth. The truth is *you're* the weak. And *I'm* the tyranny of evil men. But I'm tryin', Ringo, I'm tryin' real hard to be the shepherd.

Jules slowly lowers his gun and lays it on the table. He tells "Ringo": "Now here's the situation. Normally both of your asses would be dead as fuckin' fried chicken. But you happened to pull this shit while I'm in a transitional period. I don't wanna kill ya, I wanna help ya." This help does not extend to handing over the briefcase found in Brett's apartment, as "Ringo" had demanded, but he does allow him a peek. "Ringo," now reflecting the glow of the case's contents, marvels at it as Vince did; we viewers, however, are still in the dark, and remain so.

Ezekiel 25:17 does not effect Jules's transformation from "the tyranny of evil men" to "the shepherd," but it provides a vocabulary with which he can reflect on his own experiences and on the choices he wants to make for the future. But in a real sense, this passage does contribute to Pumpkin's redemption. If he and Honey Bunny really meant what they said in the opening scene of the movie about leaving the life of crime, Jules has given them a golden opportunity, both by saving their lives and by being a role model for change. Were it not for the experience that Jules had had earlier that morning, they would have been dead by now. As it is, they have the chance to walk away and start again.

Ezekiel 25:17 thus becomes the marker of life and death. Just as it was Jules's signature speech in his role as hit man, it is now the mantra that he can recite in order to figure out his new place in the world. Nevertheless, it must be noted the Ezekiel 25:17 that Jules has memorized is not in the biblical book of Ezekiel or anywhere else in the Bible.[16] To be sure, the final lines of Jules's version echo the canonical passage, and several other phrases recall other biblical passages. For example, "the path of the righteous man is beset on all sides by the iniquities . . ." recalls Ezekiel 18:26 ("When the righteous turn away from their righteousness and commit iniquity, they shall die for it"). The shepherd who guides the weak through the valley of darkness recalls Psalm 23:4, in which the shepherd is the Lord, who leads the psalmist through the valley of the shadow of death.[17] The "brother's keeper" is a reference to Genesis 4:9 in which Cain, when asked for the whereabouts of his brother, responds, "Am I my brother's keeper?" Finally, the theme of vengeance is surely present. However, rather than viewing God as the one who exacts and carries out vengeance, the passage is degraded by its application to Marsellus and the various illegal and lethal schemes in which he is involved. The recitation of the passage to Brett and his friends marks Jules as a prophet of Marsellus, just as Ezekiel is a prophet of God. Jules comes to announce Marsellus's vengeance just as Ezekiel came to announce God's.

Themes

Pulp Fiction is not for the squeamish. Between Mia's graphic overdose, Jules's executions of Brett and his friends, the accidental shooting of Marvin, and the rape of Marsellus, there is more than enough blood and gore. Nevertheless, the film is a treat—amusing and engaging, and ultimately uplifting rather than depressing. The key to enjoying and appreciating *Pulp Fiction* is to recognize it for what it is—not a realistic exploration of the underworld but a parody of "pulp fiction" and a celebration of pop culture.

The primary reference point of the film is not the reality of organized crime and drug use but the corpus of "B" movies, rock and roll music, and television to which the characters, the mise-en-scène, the dialogue, the music, and virtually all elements of the film allude.[18] Although the Bible receives less attention than these other elements, scripture, or at least *Pulp Fiction*'s version thereof, is pivotal to the plot and the worldview of one of its main characters, just as the frog rain in *Magnolia* functions as the turning point in the lives of its central figures. Biblical and other religious elements also help to develop some of the main themes in this film.

The film's stance towards pulp fiction and pop culture emerges not only in its complex web of allusions but also through the depictions of the characters and the ways in which the major themes are developed. In all cases, the film plays with the stereotypes that abound in its cinematic sources. The main characters, for example, first establish these stereotypes and then subvert them. They are gangsters, involved in the underworld of organized (and disorganized) crime. There are three pairs of main characters: Pumpkin and Honey Bunny represent the gangster and his moll, who work independently. As a black man and an Italian, Jules and Vince represent the quintessential bad guys, taken from the cinema stereotypes of the inner-city streets (in the case of Jules) and the Mafia (Vince).[19] Butch and Fabienne represent the ultra macho and his ultra-feminine girlfriend. We also encounter two pairs of minor characters. One is the drug dealer and his wife, who supply heroin to Vince and help Vince to revive the unconscious Mia. The second is Jimmy and his wife. Jimmy is the friend who is peripherally but not directly involved in organized crime; his wife, Bonnie, is completely straight and has no knowledge of what her husband and his friends are up to.

Not surprisingly, given their professions, most of these characters are involved with violence in one way or another. Pumpkin and Honey Bunny rob banks and liquor stores; Jules and Vince do the killing required by Marsellus's operation, and Butch, as a professional boxer, regularly knocks people unconscious for a living. Drugs, supplied by the drug dealer and his wife, are an almost natural and inevitable part of their daily routines. Jimmy helps Jules and Vince clean up. Jimmy's wife, Bonnie, represents another aspect of urban violence. As a nurse on the "graveyard" shift, she reminds us of the professionals who often have to patch up the victims of violence such as those depicted in the film.

Thus far *Pulp Fiction* presents the stock characters that we might expect in real pulp fiction and in film noir. But from the first moment of the film, these characters also challenge and subvert the stereotypes on which they are based. This subversion occurs primarily through the ways in which they speak and interact with one another. Expletives roll easily off the tongues of many of them, yet the lengthy conversations between the characters reveal the more ordinary sides of their personalities. The opening dialogue between Jules and Vince, for example, is preoccupied with the trivial. Vince tells Jules about the Dutch habit of eating French fries with mayonnaise rather than ketchup and informs him that in France a McDonalds' "quarter-pounder" is called a "royale" because "quarter-pounder" is meaningless in the metric system. Similar conversations take place between Vince and his drug supplier and between Butch and Fabienne.

Vince and Mia, on the other hand, combine the trivial with the elevated while getting to know each other at the restaurant. They are both drugged to the hilt but manage to carry on a stilted, yet affectionate conversation using vocabulary and sentence structures that are amusingly inappropriate to their public personae. At one point, Vince builds up the courage to ask her about Antwan. Is it true that Marsellus threw him out the window because he gave Mia a foot massage? Before asking her, however, he wants her to promise not to get offended. She objects: "You can't promise something like that. I have no idea what you're gonna ask. You could ask me what you're gonna ask me, and my natural response could be to be offended. Then, through no fault of my own, I woulda broken my promise." Vince backs off: "Then let's just forget it." Mia answers, "That is an impossibility. Trying to forget anything as intriguing as this would be an exercise in futility." One hardly expects such language from someone whose every other word is a curse.

Second, in contrast to what one expects of gangster films, there is very little sex in *Pulp Fiction*. The male-female couples are playful, even childlike with each other. The two robbers in the coffee-shop sequence call each other only by their pet names and talk about their lives with an easy and affectionate intimacy. With the crucial exception of the brutal pawnshop scene, the sex that is shown—between Butch and Fabienne—is of the most loving sort. It is amusing to see a macho man like Butch, who has just killed a man in the ring, albeit inadvertently, and double-crossed a major crime boss, come home to the innocent and naive Fabienne, whose only desires are for a baby and a plateful of blueberry pancakes. Butch is very tender with her and even talks himself out of being angry when she forgets to bring his most treasured possession, his father's watch, from the apartment they have just left.

Another source of interest in the film is its appeal to morality. Almost all of the characters in the film, with the notable exceptions of Fabienne, and Jimmy's wife, Bonnie, are involved in underworld activities. The fact that the main characters do not question their involvement in these activities leads us to view them not only as immoral but perhaps also as amoral. They rarely acknowledge that their acts deviate from the acceptable norm. Yet their conversations frequently touch on moral issues and explore the fine line between morality and immorality. For example, when Jules explains to Vince what Marsellus allegedly did to Antwan for massaging Mia's feet, he comments, "That shit ain't right." These conversations allow us to extrapolate some of the details of their code of behavior and morality.

Because courtesy is important to Vince, he calls the Wolf to task during the cleanup at Jimmy's place. After rattling off a list of instructions for cleaning the car, the Wolf orders, "Boys, get to work."

> **Vince:** A "please" would be nice.
>
> **The Wolf:** Come again?

Vince: I said a "please" would be nice.

The Wolf: Get it straight, Buster. I'm not here to say "please." I'm here to tell you what to do. And if self-preservation is an instinct you possess, you better fuckin' do it and do it quick. I'm here to help. If my help's not appreciated, lotsa luck, gentlemen.

Vince: I don't mean any disrespect. I just don't like people barkin' orders at me.

The Wolf : (showing remarkable patience) If I'm curt with you, it's because time is a factor. I think fast, I talk fast, and I need you guys to act fast if you want to get out of this. So pretty please, with sugar on top, clean the fuckin' car.

A second set of values focuses on loyalty. Butch's loyalty to his father's memory is expressed in his attachment to his father's watch; he is willing to risk his freedom and his life in order to retrieve it. Vince, too, values loyalty, or so he tells himself. After returning to Mia's house from the restaurant, Vince retreats to the bathroom and gives himself a pep talk, apparently to keep himself from having sex with her. He tells his image in the bathroom mirror, "You see: this is a moral test of oneself whether or not you can maintain loyalty, because being loyal is very important."[20]

Finally, these gangsters do ascribe value to human life, despite the nature of their daily activities. On the one hand, they advocate a rough justice. Vince and his drug dealer, Lance, agree that the person who "keyed" Vince's Malibu should be killed. "No trial, no jury, straight to execution." On the other hand, Vince, Lance, and Lance's wife go to great measures to ensure Mia's survival. This may be just because she is the boss's wife, but their concern seems to go beyond this fact. Similarly, Butch risks his own life in order to save Marsellus, despite the fact that he does not yet know whether doing so will prompt Marsellus to let him off the hook.

Where morality reigns, religion cannot be far behind, at least in Hollywood. The presence of religious themes is introduced playfully, allusively, and superficially by some of the characters. This too, of course, may simply be an aspect of popular culture; movies and television shows imply that gangsters wear crosses around their necks or have crosses tattooed on their bodies.[21] Nevertheless, *Pulp Fiction* projects a metaphysical framework through its use of religious language and symbols. For example, the "chopper" on which Butch makes his getaway from the pawnshop is called "Grace." This could be a reference to the fact that it was simply there, free for the taking. It could simply be a nod to the woman whom Tarantino was dating at the time that he wrote the screenplay.[22] It could also be a commentary, however, on the free act that Butch performed in the shop of saving Marsellus.

Many of the characters swear, using "I'll be damned" and "Jesus Christ" and "Oh God." Again, these are elements of common parlance that may have no real significance other than to express surprise or dismay, but in the context of the film they may also hint at a larger religious or theological theme. Many similar elements are present in the screenplay but were not included in the final cut of the movie. In the screenplay, Vince accidentally shoots Marvin in the neck but does not kill him. Vincent then decides that the only decent thing to do is to put him out of his misery. Jules objects, but Vincent insists. To cover the noise, he says to Jules, "Okay, Pontius Pilate, when I count three, honk your horn." Jules's response is "Jesus Christ Almighty." This sequence does not draw a deep parallel between Marvin, Vincent, and Jules, on the one hand, and Jesus, the high priest, and Pilate, on the other, but simply evokes a religious element by using commonly known names and expressions.[23]

In addition to these humorous references, the film refers to more serious religious themes. As they clean up the bits and pieces of Marvin's brain and skull, Jules and Vince engage in a theological conversation of sorts. Jules declares that he will never forgive Vincent for getting them into this mess (though he is not so much lamenting the death of Marvin as protesting the hassle of the cleanup). Vincent responds, "Did you ever hear the philosophy that once a man admits he's wrong, he's immediately forgiven for all wrong-doings?" Jules doesn't buy it. Some sins simply cannot be forgiven: "The motherfucker who said that never had to pick up itty-bitty pieces of skull with his fingers on account of your dumb ass." This dialogue brings to the fore the notion of sin, which is implicit throughout the entire film, filled as it is with issues pertaining to murder, theft, coveting one's neighbor's wife, and myriad other transgressions.

The main theme, however, is the question of coincidence versus intentionality, particularly when it comes to violence and death. Jules and Vince are professional killers and, as such, certainly intend to kill Brett and his friends. Similarly, Pumpkin and Honey Bunny intend to rob the coffee shop, as they have done before in other settings, and Butch intends to knock out his opponent in the boxing match. But other violent events owe more to coincidence and bad luck than they do to human intention. Butch's boxing opponent dies inadvertently. Mia overdoses because she believes that the heroin that she has taken from Vince's pocket is cocaine. Marsellus and Butch are assaulted because they happened to enter a pawnshop operated by a group of depraved men. Marvin is shot and killed accidentally when Jules and Vince's car hits a bump in the road. Vince himself is killed due to a coincidence, because Fabienne forgets Butch's watch.

Indeed, *Pulp Fiction* warns of the danger of spending too much time in the bathroom. Several calamities occur when Vince leaves the scene to go to the bathroom: Mia rummages through his pockets and finds a bag of drugs that she takes to be cocaine, and she nearly dies; Pumpkin and Honey Bunny hold up the coffee shop while Vince is in the bathroom; and because Vince is in the bathroom, he does not hear Butch enter the apartment. Dana Polan suggests that like the spectator who leaves a movie for a moment to visit the restroom or have a cigarette, Vince discovers that the narrative is always one step ahead of him.[24]

This theme returns us once more to the miracle—or is it a coincidence?—that Jules and Vince experience in Brett's apartment. In contrast to *Magnolia*, which playfully implies the presence of a divine hand behind events that look to us like chance, *Pulp Fiction* refrains from taking a direct stand in the argument between Jules and Vince. Instead, the film suggests that it is all a matter of interpretation. There is no objective or absolute way to determine whether Jules's reading of the situation is correct or whether it is preferable to Vince's rationalist position. Despite itself, however, the film betrays a tentative preference for Jules's version of the truth. Had Vince, like Jules, left Marsellus's employ to wander the earth like Cain or Caine, he would not have been in Butch's apartment to exact retribution for Butch's betrayal of Marsellus and would not have died as he did.

CONCLUSION

Pulp Fiction is a paean to popular culture. It draws on film, television, and popular music for almost all of its cultural references and echoes. By drawing on the Bible, even in this attenuated and ultimately false form, it also tells us that the Bible, or at least an approximation of it, is a central element in popular culture. It can be called on to justify even those acts that transgress its most fundamental laws. Furthermore, it serves this purpose whether or not it is quoted correctly. Finally, the Bible serves as a resource for everyone, even the reformed criminal, to try to understand him or herself, find a paradigm for his or her own situation, and try to figure out where he or she stands in the world.

8

The Apostle and the Power of the Book (John)

In the beginning was the Word, and the Word was with God, and the Word was God.

John 1:1

Now Jesus did many other signs in the presence of his disciples, which are not written in this book. But these are written so that you may come to believe that Jesus is the Messiah, the Son of God, and that through believing you may have life in his name.

John 20:30–31

All things work together for good for those who love God, who are called according to his purpose.

Romans 8:28

INTRODUCTION

The Gospel of John begins with a prologue (1:1–18) that provides the cosmic context for the specific narrative of Jesus' life and mission that follows. Echoing the language of Genesis and the first account of God's creation of the world, John's prologue describes Jesus as the Word that originated with God, existed before the creation of the world itself, and took an active role in the creative process. In this context, Jesus' arrival in the human world was not so much a birth, as it is in the Gospels of Matthew and Luke, but an "enfleshment" of the preexistent, divinely created Word: "And the Word became flesh and lived among us" (1:14). The Gospel reminds us repeatedly throughout its narrative that the Jesus who lived, spoke, and performed signs (the Johannine term for Jesus' miracles) is the Son of God, who was sent by his Father into the world to provide a road to salvation (3:16) and who will return to his Father when he has accomplished his Father's will in the world (14:2).

At the conclusion of the body of the book (20:30–31),[1] the Gospel addresses its readers directly with a statement that emphasizes the intended role of this book in the lives of its audience. In recording these signs, the Gospel hopes to deepen the faith of its readers and in so doing to lead them to everlasting "life in his name." Just as the historical Jesus embodied the divine Word, so also does the Gospel embody not only Jesus' words and deeds but the Son of God himself. The readers of the Gospel, who live after Jesus' human lifetime, cannot encounter Jesus in person, hear his discourses, and experience his signs firsthand. But the Gospel is a medium through which believers can encounter Jesus directly and personally and be transformed by that encounter. Hence Jesus' message to Doubting Thomas: "Have you believed because you have seen me? Blessed are those who have not seen and yet have come to believe" (20:29). Those who read the signs written in this book, understand their significance, and believe in their testimony to Jesus' identity as the Christ and Son of God will have life in his name; they will be born anew of the water and the spirit (3:5–7).

Thus the Gospel writer would have us see this book as a key element in the dynamic relationship between the believer and God. Although John 20:30–31 is perhaps the most explicit inner-scriptural statement about the role that scripture can and should have in the lives of its readers, the same is implied in various books of the Hebrew Bible. In Jewish liturgy the Torah—not only its words but the actual Torah scroll written on parchment, read in the synagogue, and carried ceremoniously throughout the sanctuary—is the "tree of life" mentioned in Proverbs 3, where it is associated with wisdom:

> Happy are those who find wisdom,
>   and those who get understanding,
> . . . .
> She is more precious than jewels,
>   and nothing you can desire can compare with her.
> . . . .
> Her ways are ways of pleasantness,
>   and all her paths are peace.
> She is a tree of life to those who lay hold of her;
>   those who hold her fast are called happy.
>   (Prov. 3:13–18)

Thus not only the words of scripture and the possible historical realities to which they point but the very books of scripture themselves are charged with a holiness that can have a profound impact on the lives of those who believe them to be vehicles for the divine.

FILM SUMMARY

The 1997 film *The Apostle* is the portrait of a man whose life is shaped by his intimate relationship with the Book, not just the Gospel of John but the entire Bible from Genesis through Revelation. The Apostle of the film, played by Robert Duvall, who also directed the movie, is Sonny Dewey, who has been an evangelist in the southern Holiness movement (Holy Rollers) since the age of twelve. This evangelical movement has four pillars: belief in evangelism, belief that the entire Bible is divinely inspired, belief in the second coming of Christ, and belief in apostolic power and healing.[2] Sonny exemplifies all of these traits and has parlayed them into a highly successful and wealthy church in Texas. Like Sam Bowden in *Cape Fear*, Sonny has it all: a beautiful wife, Jessie (Farrah Fawcett); two beautiful children; and a mother (June Carter Cash) who has believed in and supported his work from childhood on. He also has, or believes that he has, the Spirit of the Lord. He is profoundly convinced that the Holy Spirit has empowered his endeavors throughout his entire life and has given him the ability to gather converts as he travels around the region holding revival meetings.

During one such trip, as he lies alone in a motel bed, he has a sudden thought that propels him out of bed and into his car. He races home to find his house and bed cold and empty. Acting on a hunch, he drives to the home of Horace (Todd Allen), the youth minister at his church, with whom, as it turns out, his wife Jessie has spent many a night, including this one. Jessie and Horace are not the only ones guilty of adultery, however. From Sonny and Jessie's emotional confrontation the next day, we learn that Sonny is something of a womanizer. Jessie is fed up with him and refuses to consider reconciliation. In short order she divorces Sonny, takes the children, and ousts him from the leadership of his church. Without Jessie, his children, or his church, Sonny's life falls apart.

Sonny himself delivers the final blow to his life as Sonny Dewey when he clobbers Horace over the head with a baseball bat at a children's baseball game. With Horace lying unconscious on the ground and a crowd of spectators, including Jessie and their children, gathering around, Sonny drives off. When he has gone some distance, he stops his car on a bridge, gets out, and pushes his vehicle into the river. He then tears up his pieces of identification and throws them in after the car. When Sonny continues across the bridge on foot, he is also metaphorically crossing over from his old life to a new and as yet undetermined identity.

Uncertain about his new direction, he camps out for a few days near the banks of the river on the property of an old fisherman. Lying in his tent, he reads the Bible and prays for guidance. After a few days, he makes a decision, or, as he might say, receives a divine sign. Sonny formally rebaptizes himself in the river and emerges as the Apostle E. F. The fisherman tells him about a retired preacher, the Reverend C. Charles Blackwell (John Beasley), in the town of Bayou Boutté, Louisiana. E. F. resolves to seek out this man and to propose that they found a church together.

E. F. travels to this town, where he works several jobs, preaches on the radio, and befriends a young man named Sam. After some initial hesitation, the Reverend Blackwell decides to trust E. F and to help him found a small church. With the help of Sam and others, they fix up the Reverend's old church building and create a new community called "One Way to Heaven." Week by week the membership grows. E. F. touches the lives of many people, not only those who attend his church but also those who listen to him preach on the radio and those who receive his donations of food. Meanwhile, back home, Horace dies, and so does E. F.'s beloved momma; E. F. is now an orphan and wanted for murder. One day, when Jessie is in the kitchen preparing dinner for her children, her radio suddenly and inexplicably picks up the signal from Bayou Boutté. She recognizes Sonny's voice and immediately places a call to the homicide division of the Louisiana police force. State troopers pull into the yard of E. F.'s church during an evening prayer service and arrest him for first-degree murder. He is convicted and, as the closing credits roll, we see him preaching to his fellow prisoners as they work on a chain gang in a field outside the prison.

On the face of it, as this brief summary suggests, the film is about a murderer who tries to evade the long arm of the law and is eventually brought to justice. But the depth and complexity of the Apostle's character deflect attention from this plot line, as does the foregrounding of his life and missionary efforts on Bayou Boutté. The film is just as much, or more, about Sonny's own inner struggles and about the founding of an integrated Holy Roller church in rural Louisiana than it is about the legal justice system.[3]

The main character, as the title suggests, is the Apostle. But another powerful force shaping this film is the Spirit of God. Indeed, the film's principal conflict is not between Sonny and the law but between Satan and the Holy Spirit. Sonny's soul is the battleground. The visible and tangible representation of the Spirit in the film is the Bible—specifically, Sonny's own copy of this book, which is his closest companion. *The Apostle* differs from most other Hollywood films in the central role given to the Bible, which is visible, cited, and quoted in virtually every scene. It is the vehicle through which the main themes of the film are expressed and developed, and it is Sonny's constant strength and point of reference as he struggles with Satan, that is, his own impulses and desires. The Bible is also central to the plot of the film and to the portrayal and development of its protagonist.

USE OF THE BIBLE

Plot and Character

Biblical quotations, allusions, and references enliven much of *The Apostle*'s dialogue, lending it texture and contributing significantly to its overall mood and setting. No book of the Bible is too small; no detail is too insignificant. Sonny teaches his own children as well as the children in Bayou Boutté to recite the books of the Bible, rapidly and in order, ending in the raucous repetition of "Revelation, Revelation, Revelation, Revelation." This is not the rote learning of basic information that every "Holy Ghost" Christian should have at her or his fingertips. Rather, it is loving and triumphant testimony to the value attached to every single biblical book and to them all as a canon.

Throughout his preaching, the Apostle frequently quotes biblical "tags" and builds on biblical concepts. The Apostle begins his first sermon in the "One Way to Heaven" church with Psalm 150 (KJV):

> Praise ye the LORD. Praise God in his sanctuary: praise him in the firmament of his power.
> Praise him for his mighty acts: praise him according to his excellent greatness.
> Praise him with the sound of the trumpet: praise him with the psaltery and harp.
> Praise him with the timbrel and dance: praise him with stringed instruments and organs.
> Praise him upon the loud cymbals: praise him upon the high sounding cymbals.
> Let every thing that hath breath praise the LORD. Praise ye the LORD.

He invites the congregants, both young and old, to play the musical instruments they have brought along to church, and in doing so, he also calls on them to bring this ancient text into their own lives and musical idiom. The psalm expresses the essence of the believer's relationship to God: to praise God in gratitude for the goodness one has received.

Another psalm that figures prominently is Psalm 23. E. F. recites this psalm on his way from the accident scene; in his preaching he proclaims Psalm 23 alongside a woman who recites a Spanish version; and he quotes the psalm during his radio preaching. Sonny also makes use of biblical tags in his spontaneous, inspired, and almost maniacal preaching style. This can be seen clearly in his "call and response" type of preaching, whether in his own churches or in the halls, tents, and campgrounds in which he conducts his itinerant mission. "Who's the King of Kings? (Rev. 19:16)" he asks. "Jesus," responds the congregation. "Before Abraham was, who was? (John 8:58)" he cries out.

"JESUS," shouts the crowd. "Who's the First and the last? (Rev. 1:11)." "JESUS." In this manner, he whips the crowd into a fervor; they shout, cry, sway, and wave their Bibles in the air. Through this use of the Bible, Sonny hopes to bring Jesus into their lives.[4]

The Apostle practices what he preaches. Just as he encourages his audience to relate personally to God and to use the Bible to do so, he also derives his way of thinking and the vocabulary for articulating his view of the world directly from the Bible. He apparently has the Bible memorized, for he can call up at the drop of a hat an appropriate verse, verbatim from the King James Version and complete with citation. After "saving" a young couple who have been in a serious car accident, he proclaims, "'Hallelujah the Lord God omnipotent,' Revelation 19:6" (KJV). As he prepares to sink his car, and all other signs of his former life, in the river, he recites Exodus 23:20: "Behold, I send an Angel before thee, to keep thee in the way, and to bring thee into the place which I have prepared" (KJV). From now on he will go where he is led by the Lord. Hence his conviction that the fisherman's casual reference to the Reverend C. Charles Blackwell in Bayou Boutté, Louisiana, is a divine sign of where he should go and what he should do. When the church is finally refurbished and ready for business, E. F. proclaims, "Stand still, and consider the wondrous works of God" (Job 37:14, KJV), then prays his fervent prayer that God will let the church survive. He is acutely conscious of the possibility that the police may catch up with him at any time. "I don't know how long its gonna last, Lord, 'cause they could be coming for me, 'cause they coming." Biblical quotations and allusions therefore provide a commentary on the events in Sonny's life. They also testify to Sonny's profound conviction that the Bible provides the context within which his life as well as his specific experiences make some sense.

But perhaps the fundamental biblical element in this film is its use of the New Testament portrait of Paul as a paradigm for the plot. The New Testament attributes fourteen letters to Paul[5] and also devotes much of Acts of the Apostles to a version of Paul's biography.[6] According to these sources, Paul had not known Jesus during his lifetime and was not one of the "Twelve," but a revelatory experience on the road to Damascus (Acts 9:1–19; cf. Gal. 1:15–16) had convinced him that Jesus truly was the Messiah and that Jesus had called him, Paul, to preach this message to the Gentiles. Paul's personality, his conflicts, and his convictions come through clearly in all of his letters. Most of his undisputed letters were written to churches—in Galatia, Philippi, Thessalonica, and Corinth—that he had founded. He uses the letters as a substitute for his own presence in the community and as a vehicle through which to address specific problems, questions, or situations that have arisen in those churches.

His letter to the Romans is an exception. Paul had not founded the Roman church nor had he ever been there. But he had planned such a visit, and the letter was intended to serve as his introduction to his community. Paul's letter to the Romans addresses a number of key issues, such as the universality of salvation through Christ, the role of the law, the nature of the Spirit, and the relationship between law and sin. Romans 8 declares that the law of the Spirit of life in Christ Jesus has freed believers from the law of sin and of death. Paul urges his readers to live according to the Spirit in order to put to death the deeds of the body: "For all who are led by the Spirit of God are children of God" (Rom. 8:14). Paul acknowledges the gap, or the dissonance, between their present suffering and the promised redemption, so he urges hope and patience (8:25).

Though Romans 8:28–30 is phrased as a general principle, it expresses the view that Paul had of himself and his divinely given mission.

> We know that all things work together for good for those who love God, who are called according to his purpose. For those whom he foreknew he also predestined to be conformed to the image of his Son, in order that he might be the firstborn within a large family. And those whom he predestined he also called; and those whom he called he also justified; and those whom he justified he also glorified.

Like the prophet Isaiah (Isa. 6:6–8), Paul considers himself to have been called before his birth—"foreknown"—and predestined to become an apostle to the Gentiles (cf. Rom. 15:16), so that the family of Christ, who are also the children of God, might be expanded. Having been predestined and called, he is also justified and glorified, that is, destined to be saved at the second coming. Those who are called may indeed suffer in the present time, as Paul explains in Romans 8:18–25, but their actions will contribute to the greater good of humankind by bringing others to Christ. Fundamental throughout is the love of God.

Throughout Romans and indeed all of his letters, Paul uses the Jewish Scriptures, in particular the Torah and the prophets. Although these texts were written long before the coming of Jesus, Paul reads them through the lenses of a true believer. To him they provide ample proof that God intended to save the world through faith in Christ and that, from the beginning, God anticipated the inclusion of the Gentiles among his beloved children and in the new order that Christ's coming, in Paul's view, had ushered in (see Galatians 3; Romans 2, 9–11).[7]

Like Paul, the Apostle E. F. sees himself as being divinely chosen. Sonny is called by the Lord at age twelve—and then re-called to a new mission as an adult when he baptizes himself as the Apostle E. F. and, in so doing, is reborn with a new identity (see Gal. 2:19–21). His baptism is also a resurrection, and it marks Sonny's profound transformation, despite the fact that events from his "old" life ultimately undo the new life that he has created. This transformation is a casting off of his old identity, symbolized by the tearing up of his identification papers, though he cannot leave himself and the flaws of his own personality as definitively as he leaves his house and his family. Like Paul, the Apostle has wandered around the known world—in his case, the United States and foreign countries, "including Mississippi"—founding churches. He has built these churches one by one by the force of his personality and the convictions behind his gospel (see Rom. 14:21–23; 15:22–29; Acts 13–14 and throughout). Like Paul (e.g., with Barnabus and Titus; Acts 13:7), the Apostle has companions that help him in his mission and are devoted to him personally, including Joe in his "former" life, who also takes care of his mother in the Apostle's absence, and Sam, in his Louisiana mission. And the Apostle, like Paul, draws frequently and liberally from the scriptures.

Sonny's resurrection as the Apostle E. F. does not become a true rebirth to new life and release from the old simply by self-baptism. Rather, his new community facilitates this transformation; in Sonny's words, the church helps him to beat back Satan. Just as he has provided salvation and community for the people of Bayou Boutté, so the community has also healed him. In doing so, it has validated his identity and role as a preacher and apostolic leader, in keeping with the Holiness tradition to which Sonny adheres.[8]

Eventually Sonny/E. F. must leave, but he is able to leave some of himself behind and still provide for his ongoing presence in the community through the written word. He does so by leaving his Bible with Sam just as Paul maintained his dynamic relationship with his communities by sending them letters. The Apostle's healing and rebirth are seen in the fact that he does not run away from justice as he had done in his former life as Sonny; instead, he takes responsibility for his actions.

Not only does E. F. accept the consequences for his actions, but he also transforms these consequences—imprisonment—into an opportunity. In this, too, Sonny echoes the apostle Paul. In Romans 8:28, Paul expresses the conviction that everything works out for the best for those who are called by God. This passage does not express a passive acceptance of one's fate but rather the possibility of turning fate around for the good of one's mission. From one point of view, Sonny's arrest is a just and fitting end to the film because it shows that he is duly punished for the crime of murder that he had committed. But by the time he is arrested, we the viewing audience have come to experience a great deal of respect and sympathy for Sonny. We see him struggle with his own impulses—what he calls Satan—and we see the good that he has done in the community and the profound ways that he has been able to touch many people without regard to age, race, gender, or ideology. But Sonny's arrest is not a tragic end to the film. As the closing credits roll, we hear and see him preaching responsively to his fellow convicts, repeating the call-and-response pattern of his earlier preaching. "Before Abraham was, who was?" "JESUS!" Like Paul, Sonny maintained his ministry in prison (Philemon; Acts 16:16–40; 28:17–31).

The apostle Paul's words spread far and wide through his letters, with which he communicated with the churches he had founded and through which his words continue to be conveyed to readers during the two millenia since his death. The Apostle E. F. also has a means of mass communication: the radio station in Bayou Boutté. The station is owned and operated by one Elmo, who also owns the body shop where Sam and E. F. work. Elmo allows E. F. and his church choir a regular spot on the show, and he himself becomes deeply involved in the church. This role allows Elmo to function as the narrator and also the interpreter of significant events in the film. This role is particularly apparent in the scene involving the stranger and the bulldozer. Elmo is broadcasting that day from the church picnic, and he provides, sotto voce, a blow-by-blow description of what is happening in the encounter between the Apostle and the stranger. This is meant to be secret and confidential, but through Elmo's eyewitness report, this event is broadcast all over the country. Ironically, the radio not only functioned to spread the Apostle's word, and word about the Apostle, but also led to his arrest when his wife Jessie unexpectedly caught his broadcast, learned of his whereabouts, and called the police.

By comparing the Apostle E. F. to the apostle Paul, we get a better sense of both, particularly, their profound conviction that they have been chosen directly by God to fulfill a mission and their single-minded and wholehearted dedication to that mission. This calling is what motivates E. F., and, if his letters are any indication, this is what motivated Paul as well. *The Apostle* is unusual among movies that borrow biblical paradigms in that its principal narrative paradigm is Paul's rather than Jesus' story. But although Paul the apostle is the closest biblical model for the Apostle E. F., the film also employs some Jesus imagery in its depiction of Sonny. Like Jesus (cf. Mark 1:13), Sonny is tested by Satan, performs miracles (the resurrection of a dead church and the revivification of a stagnant reverend), and brings others to faith and salvation. Like Jesus, he has an intimate relationship with God, evident not only in his attachment to God's holy book but also during the long night of prayer and confrontation that follows Jessie's departure from his life and that keeps the neighbors, as well as his mother, awake into the wee hours of the night. Sonny relates to God as his father, a relationship perhaps signaled by the name "Sonny" itself. The "Judas" in Sonny's life is Jessie, who betrays Sonny (or brings him to justice) by calling the police. But in contrast to Jesus, Sonny's betrayal does not lead to physical death but rather to an opportunity for carrying out his mission to the prison population.

Themes

In addition to direct quotations from the Bible and the generous, if unac-knowledged, use of Paul as a paradigm for Sonny's character and life mission, the film also draws on a number of biblical motifs. The two major events that propel the plot are Jessie's adultery (and alongside it also Jessie's knowledge and Sonny's acknowledgment of his own wandering eye), and Sonny's murder of Horace. Both of these, of course, are blatant violations of the Decalogue (Ten Commandments). Both Jessie and Sonny ask for God's forgiveness for transgressing the prohibition of adultery, for example, and though the Ten Commandments themselves are not recited, they are referred to in the Apos-tle's radio preaching. For instance, he mentions Moses up on the mountain, receiving the ten commandments, that is, "ten, not eleven, twelve, thirteen and the fourteenth commandment. And the eleventh commandment, 'Thou shalt not shout' (pause) does not exist."

Although both Sonny and Jessie have transgressed, the film does not con-demn them. Jessie's adultery is understandable in light of Sonny's own unfaith-fulness. Sonny's murder of Horace, while not condoned, does not turn us against him, for we also witness Sonny's sincere evangelism, his profound sense that he is called by God to be his apostle, and the conviction and selflessness with which he carries out this mission. We also witness his struggle against Satan in the form of his own impulses, particularly in his relationship with Toosie. Here he strives and almost succeeds in holding back his own forceful personality and his strong sexual desire in the face of Toosie's obvious reluc-tance. Given his past record as an adulterer and womanizer, this small step is significant; Sonny is beginning to beat Satan back, at least in the sexual arena.

But perhaps the most striking biblical element in this film is the role of the Bible, which is valuable not only for its content but as an object in itself. Sonny's Bible accompanies him almost throughout this entire movie. He car-ries it in a deliberate, loving, and determined manner that clearly conveys not only its personal importance but, even more, its sacredness or holiness for him. The Bible is a vehicle for the Holy Spirit; it is Sonny's channel for communi-cating with God, his most effective tool for evangelical ministry, and his most lethal weapon in a perpetual battle with Satan. Three scenes in particular illus-trate the power of the Bible, both in Sonny's life and in the lives of others.

The first episode occurs immediately after the opening credits. While dri-ving along the highway with his mother, Sonny comes upon the scene of a seri-ous car accident. He pulls over to the side of the road and asks his mother to remain in the car. He leaves the car, taking his Bible with him. Looking around to make sure that the state troopers have not noticed him, he runs across the road and into the field where one of the cars involved in the collision has come to a stop. Inside are a young man and woman, unconscious though still breathing. Sonny places his Bible on the roof of the car and gives it a careful pat. He then reaches into the car through the open window and places the young woman's hand on the young man's arm. He speaks quickly, quietly, fervently, and urgently to the man, whose eyes are open but nonresponsive. He prays for their lives and then asks the young man if he is ready to accept Jesus Christ at this very instant. "There are angels even in this automobile at this precise moment," he tells the young man. He tells him that if he accepts Jesus Christ right now he will surely go to heaven, whether he "is called home" now or at some later point. The young man stirs, nods yes, and then whispers, "Thank you." The interaction is interrupted by a police officer, who has noticed Sonny and orders him to leave the scene. Sonny takes his Bible and begins to walk away; the camera lingers on the car as we watch the young woman move her hand slightly as it rests on the young man's arm. They will both live.[9]

The policeman says to Sonny, skeptically but not quite derisively, "I guess you think you accomplished something in there." Sonny is convinced that he has, and as he strides away, he brandishes his Bible like a sword, pumps his arms up and down, and breathes out deeply. It is as if he has experienced a great surge of both adrenalin and power in talking to the young man that must now be exhaled in order for him to return to his normal self and to the mundane activity of driving his car along the highway. The scene shows us a man who is deeply engaged in the evangelism not only of communities but of individual souls. He feels tremendous satisfaction at what he has accomplished, and he exudes charisma and power that have an impact on the lives of others. Most important, his mission and his power are inextricably connected to his Bible. By placing his book on the roof of the car, Sonny transformed the vehicle into a sanctuary, a sacred space in which the angels dwell and in which God's word of salvation can go forth through his minister Sonny. The book itself is not a mere object comprised of printed pages but a dynamic, living vehicle for the Spirit and for the divine power that can confer God's own holiness on the space that it graces.

Sonny's Bible has a similar function in another scene, one of the most powerful in the film. In the early weeks of the new church that the Apostle E. F. and the Reverend Blackwell have established, a stranger (Billy Bob Thornton) enters the sanctuary during the evening service and remains standing by the door. When the Apostle acknowledges him, the man asks belligerently about the meaning of the initials "E. F." The Apostle refuses to answer the question but invites him to sit down and to participate in the service. The stranger persists, and the Apostle "invites" him to continue the discussion outside. There the stranger adds racial slurs to his impudent questions, and their confrontation culminates in a fist fight outside the church. The congregants, watching through the church's windows, are amazed, both at the fact that the Apostle resorts to violence and by his strength and fighting skills. Both of these hint at E. F.'s violent temper, as well as at the depth of his street experience. The stranger is defeated for now, but he vows to return. The Apostle, on the other hand, is somewhat sheepish and feels that he has to explain himself. He says, "I know it's not the Christian thing to do; you're supposed to turn the other cheek. But if you do that somebody's gonna take your church and nobody's gonna take any church of mine . . . 'cause I love this church." Although Sonny has escaped his home state and evaded the law, for now at any rate, he has not yet overcome some of the impulses and experiences that informed his former life. He is still prone to violence, and he is still devoted, above all else, to his church.

In just a few short weeks, the church has grown quickly and impressively from a handful of worshipers on the first Sunday, all of whom fit easily into the small school bus in which E. F. drives them to services, to a crowd of people of all colors and ages. To mark this success, the community holds a Sunday picnic and bake sale. Suddenly the stranger reappears, this time in the cab of a bulldozer and in the company of two other young men. He intends to raze the church, he announces. The Apostle cannot countenance the thought, and, urged on by his congregation, stands his ground in front of the bulldozer. A mere verbal refusal does not seem enough, however. The Apostle opens up his Bible and reads the first verse of Psalm 91, then puts the open Bible down in front of the bulldozer. One other congregant also lays down her Bible near the bulldozer.

The stranger now has three choices: to pick up the Bibles, to run over them, or to reconsider. The scene is dramatic and suspenseful. The crowd holds its breath as the young man ponders the situation. Initially he demands that the Apostle pick up the Bibles; then he steps down from the cab to remove them himself. He picks up the second, closed Bible and then bends down before the Apostle's open book. But instead of picking it up, he breaks down. The Apostle immediately crouches down beside him and supports him with his arms and with his words: "If you reach out, the Lord will accept you here today." E. F. then places the man's hand on the Bible. He offers him divine salvation and all the help he needs from himself and his congregation.

In this scene, as in the accident sequence, the Apostle's Bible is accorded a special, divine power in and of itself, separable from though intertwined with its divinely inspired content. The closed Bible of the congregant is not quite so powerful and therefore it can be picked up and removed. The Apostle's open Bible, on the other hand, constitutes a formidable obstacle to the bulldozer because the stranger, despite his belligerence, at some level shares E. F.'s view of the open Bible as a sacred vehicle for the divine Spirit. The Bible marks an impassable boundary between the profanity of the bulldozer, intended as a weapon of destruction, and the church, with its mission of salvation.

Not only the Bible itself but also its content is meaningful in this situation. Psalm 91, to which E. F. opens the book, is a commentary of sorts on the scene as a whole. Although E. F. reads only the first line aloud, the entire psalm offers to its readers the divine protection and solace that the Apostle offers to the man:

> He that dwelleth in the secret place of the most High shall abide under the shadow of the Almighty.
> I will say of the LORD, [He is] my refuge and my fortress: my God; in him will I trust.
> Surely he shall deliver thee from the snare of the fowler, [and] from the noisome pestilence.
> He shall cover thee with his feathers, and under his wings shalt thou trust: his truth [shall be thy] shield and buckler.
> Thou shalt not be afraid for the terror by night; [nor] for the arrow [that] flieth by day;
> [Nor] for the pestilence [that] walketh in darkness; [nor] for the destruction [that] wasteth at noonday.
> A thousand shall fall at thy side, and ten thousand at thy right hand; [but] it shall not come nigh thee.
> Only with thine eyes shalt thou behold and see the reward of the wicked.
> Because thou hast made the LORD, [which is] my refuge, [even] the most High, thy habitation;
> There shall no evil befall thee, neither shall any plague come nigh thy dwelling.
> For he shall give his angels charge over thee, to keep thee in all thy ways.
> They shall bear thee up in [their] hands, lest thou dash thy foot against a stone.
> Thou shalt tread upon the lion and adder: the young lion and the dragon shalt thou trample under feet.
> Because he hath set his love upon me, therefore will I deliver him: I will set him on high, because he hath known my name.
> He shall call upon me, and I will answer him: I [will be] with him in trouble; I will deliver him, and honour him.
> With long life will I satisfy him, and shew him my salvation.
>
> (Psalm 91, KJV)

Through the reference to and partial recitation of this text, this scene promises that by accepting the Apostle's message, the man will be delivered from fear of pestilence, disease, wild beasts, and all other predators, whether physical or metaphysical.

The power of the Apostle's Bible can also be seen at the climax of the film, when the Apostle is arrested for Horace's murder. The arrest takes place at the end of a powerful evening service. As always, the Apostle's Bible lies open on the lectern. The state trooper who has come to arrest the Apostle stands respectfully at the entrance; the flashing lights of the many police cars waiting outside create a strobe-like effect on the large windows that flank the entrance. The Apostle outdoes himself in fervor and eloquence, and he is matched every step of the way by his congregation, who bear witness to the success of his mission and thereby also to the Spirit that moves him. After his lengthy and passionate sermon, the Apostle calls on anyone who feels so moved to accept the Lord this very night. His young protégé Sam steps forward. Sam was fully involved in every stage of refurbishing the church and the school bus and was present at every single service. Yet until this moment he had never made a public commitment of faith. The Apostle hugs him, welcomes him as his son, and is now finally ready to bring the service to an end, having achieved his goals not only with respect to the community but with respect also to this individual young man.

E. F. knows full well that he faces imminent arrest and imprisonment. As he moves to the back of the church and out the door, escorted by the state trooper, he tells his congregation that it seems Satan is not done with him yet. The state trooper mechanically reads out the charge of first-degree murder and searches him. The Apostle removes his jewelry and places it on the hood of the trooper's car, much as he had done with his Bible on the accident victims' car in the opening scene. Meanwhile Sam, greatly distressed, has emerged from the church to catch his final glimpse of the Apostle. The Apostle calls out to him and instructs him to take the jewelry into the church to give to Reverend Blackwell; it is to be sold, and the proceeds used to support the church. The Apostle then tells Sam to take his Bible from the lectern and to keep it. By giving the Bible to Sam, E. F. gives him the gift of the Holy Spirit. Through his Bible he will leave a bit of himself behind with his friend, and through Sam, with the congregation. E. F. can now battle Satan on his own, but Sam, still a child in the Lord, will need it not only as the divine word but also as a token of the Apostle's essence, strength, and faith.

CONCLUSION

In contrast to films such as *Fried Green Tomatoes, The Apostle* portrays the southern evangelical preacher in a positive light. Although we are only too aware of the flaws in his personality, we are also deeply drawn into Sonny's story, his way of looking at the world, and his understanding of his own place within it. The film makes palpable Sonny's sense of direct connection to God and to the Bible, and in doing so largely frees him from the Bible-thumping stereotype to which such a role might fall prey. As some commentators note, Duvall took on the negative Hollywood stereotype of the evangelical preacher and humanized it.[10] Others note that the film is both a critique and celebration of a religious tradition.[11] Just as the Gospel of John testifies to the embodiment of the divine Word in the flesh of Jesus and the words of the Gospel, so the film offers us a powerful figure who lives by the power that inheres in the Holy Word, in the book in which that Word is written, and in his own persuasive words.[12]

9

The Shawshank Redemption and the Salvation That Lies Within (1 Corinthians)

And now faith, hope, and love abide, these three; and the greatest of these is love.

1 Corinthians 13:13

INTRODUCTION

Some time in the mid–first century, Paul founded a church in Corinth.[1] After the church was well established, he continued on his missionary journeys but kept in touch with the community through letters. In his first letter to the Corinthian church, Paul addresses a number of issues that have been brought to his attention by reports from "Chloe's people" (1:11) as well as from a letter that he received from the Corinthians themselves. Chloe reported on the presence of factions within the community, each laying claim to the authority of one leader or another. The Corinthians' letter apparently did not refer to this factionalism directly, but it did provide some insight into the issues that were dividing the community and the questions that were at stake, including marriage (7:1), the eating of food offered to idols (8:1), the nature of spiritual gifts (12:1), and collecting money for the "saints" in Jerusalem (16:1). The tone and content of the letter shows that Paul felt threatened by the situation in Corinth. He repeatedly defends himself and the authority of his apostleship, as in 9:1–2: "Am I not free? Am I not an apostle? Have I not seen Jesus our Lord? Are you not my work in the Lord? If I am not an apostle to others, at least I am to you; for you are the seal of my apostleship in the Lord." His answers to the Corinthians' specific questions underscore his role as their apostolic leader but also provide detailed explanations for the positions that he proposes.

The most famous section of 1 Corinthians is chapter 13:

> If I speak in the tongues of mortals and of angels, but do not have love, I am a noisy gong or a clanging cymbal. And if I have prophetic powers, and understand all mysteries and all knowledge, and if I have all faith, so as to remove mountains, but do not have love, I am nothing. If I give away all my possessions, and if I hand over my body so that I may boast, but do not have love, I gain nothing.
>
> Love is patient; love is kind; love is not envious or boastful or arrogant or rude. It does not insist on its own way; it is not irritable or resentful; it does not rejoice in wrongdoing, but rejoices in the truth. It bears all things, believes all things, hopes all things, endures all things.
>
> Love never ends. But as for prophecies, they will come to an end; as for tongues, they will cease; as for knowledge, it will come to an end. For we know only in part, and we prophesy only in part; but when the complete comes, the partial will come to an end. When I was a child, I spoke like a child, I thought like a child, I reasoned like a child; when I became an adult, I put an end to childish ways. For now we see in a mirror, dimly, but then we will see face to face. Now I know only in part; then I will know fully, even as I have been fully known. And now faith, hope, and love abide, these three; and the greatest of these is love.

Taken out of its context in First Corinthians, this passage is a paean to love, which no doubt accounts for its frequent use as part of Christian wedding services. In the context of the letter as a whole, however, this chapter makes some pointed comments on the situation in Corinth. Apparently many in the Corinthian church boasted of impressive abilities—spiritual gifts—in particular, the ability to speak in tongues. Paul criticizes such boasting. He provides a hierarchy of gifts of which glossalalia is at the bottom and urges the Corinthians to recognize that strength lies not in a specific gift but in a diversity of gifts. All of these gifts are needed in the corporate body of the church just as eyes, ears, arms, legs, and so on are all needed in order for the physical body to thrive. The key is love: any ability is a spiritual gift if it is used for the good of the community and motivated by love of God, Christ, and fellow believers. Gifts that are used to create divisiveness, on the other hand, are like noisy gongs; they have no meaning and merely fall harshly on the ears. First Corinthians 13 places this argument into an eschatological context. Paul refers to a future time when all of these specific gifts will be meaningful because the truth will be known face to face. In that future time, only three gifts will remain: faith in Christ, hope in the future perfect era, and love between God and the believer.

The passage thus prescribes a strategy that was no doubt essential in the early Christian communities, namely to live in the difficult and oppressive present time in anticipation of a better, future era. Faith, hope, and love are the essential tools that make living in the present more bearable and that assure one's place in that future world.

FILM SUMMARY

A film that brings this Pauline perspective to life is *The Shawshank Redemption* (1994), directed by Frank Darabont and based on a short story by Stephen King entitled "Rita Hayworth and the Shawshank Redemption."[2] Andy Dufresne (Tim Robbins) is serving a life sentence at Shawshank Prison for killing his wife and her lover. Viewers know from the outset that Andy is innocent. We have watched Andy, a young, handsome, clean-cut, but extremely drunk man, sitting in his car outside the home where his wife is making love with her golf pro lover. He thoughtfully handles the gun that he has taken from the glove compartment and discards it. The camera cuts abruptly to the courtroom where Andy is on trial for murder and continues cutting back and forth between the car, the lovers, and the courtroom. By the time Andy enters Shawshank Prison, we know two things: that he is innocent and that he is extraordinarily self-contained. It is this quality, as much as the circumstantial evidence against him, that causes the judge to hand down two life sentences back to back. The judge's assessment is damning: "You strike me as a particularly icy and remorseless man, Mr. Dufresne. It chills my blood just to look at you."[3]

Once he reaches Shawshank, Andy's story is told by Red (Morgan Freeman). A convicted murderer, Red is a "man who knows how to get things" and an important man in prison society. He has his eyes on Andy from the moment Andy steps out of the prison bus in 1947. Andy stands out from the crowd insofar as he is wearing a three-piece suit and tie and carries himself like the young and uptight banking executive he was until his conviction. Thin and clean cut, he does not look like he will take well to prison. Red bets that he will crack that very first night, but not so. In the morning Andy may be wearing prison garb like everyone else, but he has by no means lost his air of self-contained distance.

As Red notes, "Andy kept pretty much to himself at first. . . . It wasn't until a month went by that he finally opened his mouth to say more than two words to somebody." But one day he saunters over to Red in the yard and introduces himself. He wants Red to get him something: a rock hammer. Red hesitates; he is far from believing in Andy's self-declared innocence. As he puts it, every one in Shawshank—with the exception of Red—is innocent. A rock hammer sounds uncomfortably close to a weapon to Red; Andy's description of the tool as a small pickax is not exactly reassuring. If he does not want the hammer as a weapon, perhaps he plans to use it for digging his way out of Shawshank, Red suggests mockingly. Andy just smiles. He was a "rock hound" on the outside, Andy tells Red, and he hopes to continue, in a limited way, in prison. A rock hammer will help him to shape the rocks that he may find in the prison yard. When Red finally sets eyes on the rock hammer, he understands why Andy smiles: it is less than foot long, small and thin. Red realizes that "it would take a man about 600 years to tunnel under the wall with one of these."

Over the course of almost twenty years, Andy lives the usual Shawshank life. He works in the laundry and other areas; he makes friends with Red and a few other men; he is beaten and raped by "the sisters." After a lengthy letter-writing campaign, he receives money and books to build a proper library and fill it with books and music. He teaches young convicts how to read and helps them to pass their high school equivalency examinations. He shapes rocks with the rock hammer that Red had procured for him and then polishes them with a rock blanket. He remains a very serious man; his one frivolous indulgence is the movie-star poster that he has on his wall, which he exchanges periodically for a larger and more current movie star. Because he had been a banker outside, he provides free help at tax time for prison employees, and he runs a complex money-laundering scheme on behalf of the brutal and Bible-thumping prison warden. Then one day, after nineteen years, he escapes.

USE OF THE BIBLE

The Bible is prominent in this film—through frequent quotation, reference, and allusion; as a paradigm for plot and characterization; and as a prop on the screen. The film plays with at least two levels of meaning in its use of the Bible: a narrow, mundane meaning and a broader, more existential sense.

Plot and Character

The Shawshank Redemption quotes the Bible both visually and verbally. In both cases the Bible is a means of expressing and developing the relationship, as well as the contrast, between Andy and the warden, Mr. Norton. The visual quotation is the embroidered text that hangs on the wall of the warden's office, covering up the warden's safe. The text reads, "His judgment cometh and that right soon" (paraphrase of Rev. 14:7). When Andy first comes into his office, he notices and admires the picture; the warden tells him that his wife embroidered it. In its context in Revelation, the text refers to the eschatological judgment that Christ will carry out on his expected return. The text is a fitting one for a prison warden, who oversees the punishment of those on whom the judgment of the state has already come. But when his money laundering scheme collapses, the warden himself stands condemned by the same text. As the police car sirens scream on their way to arrest the warden for fraud, the camera flashes on this text and thereby announces to the viewers that the warden's own judgment is imminent; it "cometh right soon," sooner, indeed, than he had expected. But he cheats the justice system itself by taking his own life, thereby, in effect, visiting judgment on himself.

Like this wall hanging, the verbal quotations in the film also demonstrate the interplay between the literal and metaphorical meanings of the Bible. They occur during a dramatic scene in which the warden and his henchmen conduct a random inspection for contraband. Andy's cell is chosen, either because he has no cell mate or, more likely, because the warden is checking him out in preparation for "hiring" him for the financial scheme he has in mind. As the men enter Andy's cell, he is sitting on his bed reading his Bible. The Warden is pleased to see this. After all, he is a strong believer in the Bible. The warden takes the Bible from Andy and asks, "Any favorite passages?" Andy replies immediately, "Watch ye therefore: for ye know not when the master of the house cometh."[4] The warden immediately identifies the passage: "Mark 13:35. Always liked that one. But I prefer 'I am the light of the world: he that followeth me shall not walk in darkness, but shall have the light of life.'" Without missing a beat, Andy says, "John 8:12."

This brief dialogue shows the warden that Andy is not merely reading the Bible "for show" but that he also knows its content and can see its applicability to his own life. Of course, for Andy and any prison inmate, Mark 13:35 resonates in a very literal way. The warden is the master of the house and is likely to surprise them with a visit at any time. Within its context in Mark, this verse has a figurative meaning. Jesus is the Master of the house—the world—and believers are to be prepared at any point for his return. Norton's small and self-satisfied smile suggests that he enjoys the opportunity to see himself in the role of Jesus in relationship to the men under his control. The second passage, John 8:12, is similarly subject to two levels of interpretation: Norton may simply be promoting the idea that his prison's inmates, including Andy, should see Jesus—the speaker of these words in the Gospel of John—as the light of the world and seek salvation through faith in Jesus as the Christ and Son of God. Given the relationship that develops between the warden and Andy, however, it is possibly, indeed likely, that he intends to offer Andy a deal: if you live by my rules, that is, "by *my* light," you will survive here in Shawshank.

Inside and Outside

The film expresses a number of themes that link it with the Bible. Underlying all of them is the contrast between two worlds—the world inside

Shawshank Prison and the world outside it. In the Bible, this contrast emerges most strikingly in the narratives of creation and redemption. In the creation story, God creates a perfect world from which humankind emerges into a less than perfect mundane world; stories of redemption, whether the prophets' visions of a future perfect time or the Christian Gospels, hold out hope for a return to a more perfect existence. In *The Shawshank Redemption* this contrast initially appears to be limited to a critique of the injustice of the prison system and its impact on human beings: Shawshank is a damp, dark, brutal, oppressive all-male world that takes men convicted of violating the laws of the "real" world and turns them into "institutional" men, incapable of living in the "real" world even after they are released. But as we shall see, the explicit use of Christian and other biblical images suggests that this gritty contrast also may be read metaphorically and, indeed, eschatologically.

The oppressiveness of the world inside Shawshank is illustrated most graphically by the fate of Tommy, a young punk who has been in and out of most of the prisons in New England. Tommy is illiterate when he enters Shawshank; he works hard with Andy in preparing for the high school equivalency examination. One day, Tommy inquires about the crime that placed Andy in jail and then tells a remarkable story about a former cell mate in another prison, Elmo Blatch. Blatch bragged incessantly about the jobs he had pulled. He was particularly proud of his murder of a rich golf pro and his lover, whom he had killed in the course of robbing the pro's house. Not only did he not get caught, but the woman's big-shot husband was tried and convicted for the crime.

This story finally convinces Red that Andy is indeed innocent, as he has insisted all along. But it also spurs Andy to make his only big mistake during the years at Shawshank. He tells the warden and is shocked and then enraged when Norton fails to be sympathetic, let alone supportive. Norton chides Andy for falling for Tommy's story; even if it were true, Norton says, it would be impossible to find Blatch and succeed in a retrial. Andy loses his temper: "How can you be so obtuse? . . . Is it deliberate?" To punish him for this impudence and to remind Andy just who is in charge, Norton throws Andy into solitary confinement for a month. A kindly old guard passes along the news that Tommy has passed his high school equivalency. But Tommy does not live to benefit, for he is taken aside by Hadley and Norton and killed. Norton visits Andy at the conclusion of his confinement. Andy declares to the warden that he is pulling out of all the schemes. Norton warns, "Nothing stops, nothing, or you will do the hardest time there is. No protection from the guards. I'll pull you out of that one-bunk Hilton and cast you down with the Sodomites. . . . And the library? Gone. Sealed off brick by brick. We'll have us a little book barbeque in the yard. . . . Catching my drift? Or am I being obtuse?" Norton then gives Andy another month in solitary to think it over.

This scene reveals the true face of Shawshank. Norton is completely uninterested in justice. Evoking the tropes of religious persecution, the warden promises to remove any shred of human dignity and comfort if Andy does anything—including seeking justice—that jeopardizes the business he has been conducting on the warden's behalf. The warden's language brands him as a diabolical figure who has the power to cast Andy down to the nether realms of the jail (both literally and morally) and to burn the books in the fires of hell.

The institutional man is someone who has lost all hope, all sense of his own humanity, and all ability to live productively on the outside. The movie graphically illustrates the fate of the institutional man in a sequence featuring Brooks Hatten, the old convict who took care of the meager library at Shawshank in the days before Andy came along. Brooks was not enthusiastic about leaving Shawshank after so many decades, but having served his entire time, he had no choice. He took a job in a supermarket and a room in a boarding house. After a short time, he carved his initials on the window frame and hung himself. The Shawshank experience had killed his spirit.

Andy's friend Red knows full well that he, too, has become an institutional man. One day as they are sitting in the prison yard, Andy asks Red, "You think you'll ever get out of here?" "Yeah, one day when I gotta long white beard and two or three marbles rollin' around upstairs," says Red. Andy then shares his dream, to go to Zihuatanejo, a small town in Mexico on the Pacific coast, "a warm place with no memory." He would like to open up a little hotel right on the beach, buy a worthless old boat, fix it up, and take his guests out charter fishing. Andy invites Red to join him in this venture when he gets out. "In a place like that I could use a man that knows how to get things," he says. But Red rejects the idea: "I don't think I could make it on the outside, Andy, I been in here most of my life; I'm an institutional man now. . . . In here I'm the guy who can get things for you but outside all you need is the yellow pages. . . . Pacific Ocean . . . scare me to death, something that big." Andy shakes his head: "Not me, I didn't shoot my wife and I didn't shoot her lover. Whatever mistakes I made I paid for them. . . . I guess it comes down to a simple choice, really, get busy living or get busy dying." He walks off, then turns around for a final word with Red. Despite Red's negative response to what Red calls Andy's "shitty pipe dreams," Andy gives him a set of very explicit instructions to follow should he ever leave Shawshank and decide to follow Andy to Mexico: Red is to look for a particular rock in a long, rock wall in a hay field in Buston, New England, dig up a box that is buried there, and follow the instructions inside.

From the moment that he enters Shawshank, Andy resists the powerful forces that would turn him into an institutional man. And as he gets to know some of the other men, he makes some efforts to reawaken in them the pleasures and sensations of the life outside. Despite, or perhaps even because of, his air of distance and dignity, Andy attracts the unwanted attention of the "sisters," "bull queers" who take their pleasure in raping newcomers and anyone else who plays "hard to get." The "sisters" pursue him relentlessly, stalk him in the laundry where he works, and send him to the infirmary on a number of occasions, though not without a stalwart fight.

All this changes after Red, Andy, and some other buddies spent a few glorious May days tarring the roof of the prison's license-plate factory. As the convicts worked, the guards wandered around on the roof, shooting the breeze. As always, the conversation was dominated by the meanest, most sadistic, and most talkative guard: Warden Norton's henchman, Hadley. Hadley has unexpectedly inherited $35,000 but complains bitterly that the "tax man" will seriously deplete this amount. To the horror of his buddies, Andy approaches Hadley, risking life and limb when he not only reveals that he has been listening in but also has an opinion on the matter. "Mr. Hadley, do you trust your wife?" Andy asks. "Do you think she'd go behind your back to try to hamstring you?" As Hadley showers Andy with verbal abuse and threatens to throw him over the side of the building, Andy quickly explains that the IRS allows a one-time gift of $60,000 to a family member, tax-free. "If you want to keep all that money, give it to your wife. . . ." No doubt, Andy continues quickly as he dangles over the roof's edge, Hadley already knew about this perfectly legal loophole, but, adds Andy, "You do need someone to set up the tax-free gift. I suppose I could set it up. Nearly free of charge. I'd only ask three beers apiece for each of my coworkers. I think a man working outdoors feels more like a man if he can have a bottle of suds." To Red's surprise, Hadley not only lets Andy go but provides due payment:

> And that's how it came to pass that on the second to last day of the job . . . [we were] sitting in a row at ten o'clock in the morning drinking icy cold bohemian style beer. . . . We sat and drank with the sun on our shoulders and felt like free men . . . we were the lords of all creation. As for Andy, he spent that break hunkered in the shade. You could argue he'd done it to curry favour with the guards, or maybe make a few friends among us cons . . . me: I think he did it just to feel normal again.

Andy provides other humanizing experiences for his fellow convicts. When the first shipment of books and records arrive at Shawshank, Andy takes the opportunity of a guard's bathroom break to play disk jockey. First he chooses a Mozart aria; then he locks the door of the bathroom, thereby trapping the guard inside. He places the recording on the turntable, turns up the volume, and allows the glorious music to soar above the walls of Shawshank. Here is Red's impression: "I tell you those voices soared higher and farther than anybody dares to dream. . . . It was like . . . some beautiful bird flapped into our drab little cage and made those walls dissolve away. And, for the briefest of moments, every last man at Shawshank felt free. It pissed the warden off something awful. Andy got two weeks in the hole for that little stunt."[5]

On Andy's return from "the hole," his friends greet him with some good-natured teasing: "Hello, Maestro! You couldn't play something good, Hank Williams or something?" Andy says it was the "easiest time I ever did. I had Mr. Mozart to keep me company . . . it was in here [he taps his forehead and his heart]. That's the beauty of music. They can't get that from you. Haven't you ever felt that way about music?" The men look at him uncomprehendingly. The gap between Andy's sensibilities and their own is brought home to the viewer by Red, who says, "I played a mean harmonica. Doesn't make much sense in here." But in Andy's view, it is precisely in Shawshank that music does make sense. "You need it so you don't forget . . . that there are places in the world that are not made out of stone, that there is something inside that they can't get to that they can't touch that's yours . . . HOPE." Red comments that "hope is a dangerous thing. Hope can drive a man insane. It's got no use on the inside. You better get used to that idea." But Andy does not get used to the idea, for without hope there is only despair.

It is not that Andy remains unaffected by the prison experience. As he tells Red, Andy was highly professional in his business dealings, "straight as an arrow," when he was on the outside. He became a crook only in prison. It could be said that he had no choice but to launder the warden's dirty money if he wanted to survive; the warden made it quite clear that refusal to do so would be tantamount to suicide. On the other hand, we also know that after his escape, his new identity and life on the outside are financed by his "take" from the warden's ill-gotten gains. We may see this theft as morally justified, but it is nonetheless theft and ultimately derived from bribery, fraud, and the exploitation of legitimate businesses. Because we tend to see Andy's liberation from Shawshank as just and to rejoice in the fulfillment of his dream, we may also ignore the ethical implications of the ways in which he extracts financial retribution from the warden. Or we may think that—given the injustice that ran rampant under the warden's reign at Shawshank—Andy was merely reaping his just desserts.

Themes

Hope

Some time after Andy's escape, Red is paroled. Like Brooks Hatten, he takes a job at the supermarket and a room—the same room—at the boarding house. He seems lost and unsure of himself, and we fear that he will take Brooks's way out as well. But one day he walks away from his room and his job and goes searching for the box that Andy has hidden for him under a volcanic rock in a wall in a field in Buxton. In that box, he finds money and a note:

> Dear Red. If you're reading this you've gotten out. And if you've come this far maybe you're willing to come a little further. You remember the name of the town, don't you? I could use a good man to help me get my project on wheels. I'll keep an eye out for you and the chess board ready. Remember Red, hope is a good thing, maybe the best of things and no good thing ever dies. I will be hoping that this letter finds you and finds you well, your friend, Andy.

Red gets on a bus, crosses the border, and, at the end of the film, meets Andy on the pristine Pacific beach in Mexico. The final lines of Red's voice-over narration emphasize the main theme of the movie: "I hope I can make it across the border. I hope to see my friend and shake his hand. I hope the Pacific is as blue as it has been in my dreams. I *hope*."

The qualities that Paul in 1 Corinthians 13 attributes to love are those that Andy attributes to hope and that he himself exemplifies throughout the film. Indeed, if we substitute "hope" for "love" throughout Paul's chapter, we will have a fairly good description of Andy; he has certainly endured all things, and as for patience, he must set a record of sorts. He patiently writes letters to the State requesting funds for his library over a period of six years and more. He executes his escape plan over nineteen years. He not only patiently keeps his own hope alive but also nurtures hope in the lives of others, most particularly Red. Initially, as we have seen, Red resists the notion that there is some value to hoping and dreaming about a small enterprise in Mexico, but by the end Andy has helped him to hope and has shown him that sometimes hopes can come to fruition.

Granted, the hope that Andy and Red share is not the eschatological hope to which Paul refers in 1 Corinthians 13. Rather, it is a more mundane, this-worldly, and limited hope. But it nevertheless has a broader role and application than the anticipation of the good life on a Pacific beach. The very ability to hope, to nurture a dream, to envisage a life after Shawshank allows Andy to endure prison and to retain a sense of his own worth and individuality in an institutional setting that aims to erode its prisoners' innate personhood. The question that the film does not answer is whether there are situations in which, as Red says, hope can be a dangerous thing. Perhaps Andy could hope because he was doing something that could eventually result in his freedom.[6]

Redemption

During their final prison-yard conversation, Red agrees halfheartedly that he will be Andy's partner in his post-prison venture, but he is clearly humoring Andy. Red is deeply disturbed by Andy's words and his mood. At mealtime he shares his concerns with his buddies. Can it be that Andy is planning to commit suicide? These concerns are heightened when another friend relates that

Andy has asked him for, and has duly received, a six-foot length of rope. Red stays up all night and worries. His worst fears seem to be confirmed at morning roll call, when he hears the guards' frantic announcement: "Man missing on Tier 2 245." Andy has disappeared. The guards skitter around, but it is finally the warden who discovers the escape route when, in a rage, he throws a rock at the poster and hears it resonate through the building as it falls far below. He rips the poster off the wall and reveals what Andy's movie actresses have been hiding: a growing hole in the cell wall. With nineteen years of patience and his little rock hammer, Andy has chiseled a hole in the porous cement large enough for him to slip through. After crawling through 500 yards of sewage he literally fulfills his "shitty pipe dream" and is safely on the outside. Once outside, he changes into the business suit and shoes that he has "borrowed" from the warden and calmly walks into the various banks in which his paper alter ego, Randall Stephens, has been depositing and investing money for years. He walks out with $370,000 of the warden's ill-gotten fortune—fitting payment, perhaps, for the nineteen years Andy has spent serving a life sentence for two murders that he did not commit. In the process, he also posts a full accounting of the warden's activities to the local paper, thereby ensuring that judgment comes, "and that right soon," to the warden and his henchmen.

The prison break itself evokes the crucifixion/resurrection event, both in verbal images (Red's voice-over narration) and in visual detail. As Red puts it, "Andy crawled to freedom through 500 yards of shit-smelling foulness I just can't imagine, or maybe I just don't want to. That's the length of five football fields, just shy of half a mile."[7] Andy emerges on the other side, into clean water, rips off his prison garb and stretches out his arms in triumph. The camera moves up and away from him; we gaze down at his rapturous face from above, as his cruciform position, the cleansing rain storm, and the majestic orchestral score evoke the triumphal crucifixion scene in *Ben Hur*. He has shed his prison identity, and indeed, the next morning, as he walks into bank after bank and reclaims the fortune he has salted away, we know that "Andy Dufresne" has died and been reborn as "Randall Stephens."

Jesus imagery occurs in other scenes as well. Andy is "baptized" twice. The first time occurs upon entry into the prison, when all the new prisoners are doused with water and a lice-killing solution. This "baptism" marks their entry into the prison system, their "death" to "old" lives on the outside and "rebirth" (if one can call it that) as institutional men. The second time occurs during his escape, when he must swim through the equivalent of the River Jordan in order to get to the other side. Again this marks his death to his institutional self and his rebirth not only to freedom but to a new identity.

Like Jesus, Andy gathers disciples around him. This group is formed by the appropriate number of men—twelve—men who were chosen for roof-tarring detail. By the time they finish the three beers apiece that Andy secures for them—risking life and limb in the process—they are transformed into Andy's disciples and remain devoted to him and, later, to their memories of him. Like Jesus, Andy teaches his disciples about salvation and shows them how to preserve their human dignity in this world while hoping for a better life to come. The main venue for such teachings is meal time, during which Andy's quiet yet authoritative voice contrasts with the brash tones of some of his "coworkers." After he escapes, his friends continue to talk about him and to reminisce about "the things he'd pulled." Red, his most faithful disciple, follows him into freedom, reenacting a conversation in John 13:36 in which Simon Peter asks Jesus, "Lord, where are you going?" Jesus answers, "Where I am going, you cannot follow me now; but you will follow afterward." Finally, Andy, like Jesus, is associated with the sea and the simple life of the fisherman.

In the final analysis, this film, as the title suggests, is about redemption: Andy's own redemption and the redemption that he offers to Shawshank. The cornerstone of this redemption is hope, as we have already noted, but also transformation. If the movement from entirely straight to somewhat crooked (with respect to his business dealings) indicates an ethical slide, his development on the emotional plane moves in the opposite direction. Andy tells Red that he was a "closed book" to his wife, unable to show his love for her, so, indirectly, he feels responsible for driving her into the arms of her lover and hence, inadvertently, to her death. Over the years in Shawshank he has not developed into an open book, but at least he is now someone capable of expressing warmth, compassion, concern, and interest. These qualities emerge most clearly in his relationship with Red, with whom a close friendship develops, and also to some extent with Tommy. The care he takes to prepare Red's way to Mexico, both financially and emotionally, and the warmth of their greeting when Red finally arrives, suggest that Andy's time in Shawshank, a waste of time in most respects, served at least to open Andy to the gift of friendship.

The redemption that Andy experiences is paralleled and perhaps symbolized by his actual escape. He also offers a new life to Red. However, it is not clear what he ultimately offers to the other inmates of Shawshank. While he was there, he provided some experiences and some benefits to them, particularly with respect to the library. But ultimately he leaves, and it does not seem that there is a similar leader to step into his shoes.[8] Perhaps the point is that he has released the prison from the grip of Warden Norton, though there is no guarantee that the next warden will be more ethical and less brutal than Norton was.

But the message of the film goes beyond the specific history and prospects for Shawshank Prison. The Jesus imagery implies a metaphorical meaning to the prison and the contrast between its intense, hierarchical and flawed world and the new world of sun, beach, and water to which Andy and then Red escape. Upon leaving Shawshank, neither Andy nor Red returns to the "real" world from which they had come. The Mexican beach represents an eschatological vision as foreign to the realities of modern North American life as it is to Shawshank Prison. From the perspective of its final scenes, Shawshank may well be a metaphor for our own flawed world, where justice is habitually perverted and human beings have lost their hope in a better life to come.

"Salvation Lies Within"

The visual presence of the Bible on the screen also has several levels of meaning and is integrated into the plot directly. The Bible first appears when Andy enters Shawshank. He, along with his fellow inmates, receives a Bible and a lecture from the warden: "I believe in two things, discipline and the Bible. Here you'll receive both. Put your trust in the Lord. Your ass belongs to me." Most important is the biblical law against blasphemy. "I will not have the Lord's name taken in vain in my prison," he declares. This may be the only law, secular or divine, that Mr. Norton does take seriously.

This scene immediately creates a moral ambivalence around the Bible. Devotion to the Bible should theoretically be the hallmark of a decent human being, which Norton decidedly is not. This ambivalence has led Robert Jewett to argue that the film is overtly hostile to religion.[9] But other elements suggest that Jewett's judgment may be too harsh.

After the Bible-quoting exchange during the warden's search of Andy's cell, Norton comments, in a seemingly nonchalant way, "I hear you're good with numbers. How nice. A man should have a skill." He expresses his disapproval of the Rita Hayworth poster on Andy's wall but says that "exceptions can be made." He then leaves the cell, still carrying Andy's Bible. As the cell locks behind him, he turns around and hands the Bible back to Andy, saying, "Almost forgot. I'd hate to deprive you of this. Salvation lies within." Andy, who looked slightly stricken when the warden began to walk off with his Bible, simply says, "Yes, sir."

The phrase "Salvation lies within" is not so much a biblical quotation as it is a statement about the Bible. At first viewing, the meaning appears to be straightforward. The scriptures contain the key to salvation; reading them and accepting and believing whole heartedly in the message they contain will lead to salvation. This is a figurative, theological meaning, and it may be the message that the Bible-thumping warden has in mind. But at the conclusion of the film, this phrase takes on a more immediate and literal meaning. After Norton discovers Andy's escape from Shawshank, he opens the safe in his office into which he regularly places the books and other documents prepared by Andy each evening. On this occasion, however, instead of his financial books, he finds Andy's Bible. He opens it and reads Andy's inscription: "Dear War-den, you were right. Salvation lay within." Leafing through, the warden dis-covers a cut-out space in the shape of small hammer. Andy's salvation, that is, his rock hammer, had indeed been lying within the Bible, fittingly tucked into the book of Exodus.

But there is yet another level of meaning to the catchphrase "Salvation lies within." Indeed, this statement may be seen as a summary of the film's funda-mental message about hope and the human spirit. From the moment that Andy enters Shawshank Prison, his fellow inmates as well as the guards notice a spirit about him that puzzles and challenges them. When he learns that one of his fellow newcomers has been beaten to death by the guards for crying and car-rying on during his first night in prison, he asks the prisoner's name. In so humanizing him, he shocks his new peers, who thought of the prisoner only as "fat ass." When he requests three beers apiece for his roof-tarring coworkers he is able to pick up on the one thing that for a brief moment reminds them of what it felt like to be free. As Red says, they could have been tarring the roof of one of their own homes. Similarly, in building the library and helping men study for their high school equivalency examinations, he provides room within the prison itself for some expression of human dignity and self-development.

Finally, hope, dignity, music, and all other pleasures of the mind and soul are the salvation that lies within the human spirit while the human body is con-fined behind bars. The "redemption" in *The Shawshank Redemption* is not only Andy's patient and daring escape to freedom but also the redemption that he attempts to provide for his fellow inmates by nurturing those parts of them that the prison system and its guardians cannot touch.

CONCLUSION

Robert Jewett views *The Shawshank Redemption* as the story of an educated yup-pie with a flair for numbers, and he suggests that it reflects escapist trends in American society. He objects to the film because, in his reading, it is critical of biblical religion while continuing to use its redemptive language.[10] Jewett may be right to a degree, for it is true that Andy secularizes First Corinthians 13 by substituting hope for Paul's focus on faith and on love as the greatest gift. But ultimately this does not degrade the film. The movie can be seen as convey-ing a more positive and worthy message, not about religion but about the Bible. *The Shawshank Redemption* shows that the Bible can be a source for themes, language, and images about fundamental things, even for people who do not necessarily identify with the religious institutions and communities that hold the Bible as sacred canon.

In *The Shawshank Redemption*, as in *The Truman Show*, there is an interplay between two worlds: the "real world" in which most of us live and another world—the world inside a television set, or inside prison walls—that limits human freedom and choice in significant ways. Both of these films feature a protagonist who moves between these two worlds in one or both directions. These movements precipitate fundamental changes for these protagonists. Changes in the lives or perspectives of the protagonists also have profound and positive effects on others (the viewers, in the case of Truman; Red and the other inmates, in the case of Andy). Whether these changes bring people closer to religion in the institutional sense is not necessarily a measure of their redemptive and transformative value.

10

Pleasantville and the Nostalgia for Eden (Revelation)

"Let anyone who has an ear listen to what the Spirit is saying to the churches. To everyone who conquers [evil], I will give permission to eat from the tree of life that is in the paradise of God."

Revelation 2:7

Then I saw a new heaven and a new earth; for the first heaven and the first earth had passed away, and the sea was no more.

Revelation 21:1

INTRODUCTION

The book of Revelation, also known as the Apocalypse of John, is the final book in the canon of the Christian Bible. It claims to record prophecies of God, delivered by an angel to a visionary named John who is living in exile on the Island of Patmos. The book begins with a series of letters to seven churches. The promise of permission to eat from the tree of life, quoted in the epigraph, is from the letter to the church in Ephesus. But the body of the work is a series of visions about the final days of the present world order, when God, like the general of an army, will do battle with the forces of evil, reinstate the perfection of the world created in Genesis, and, along with it, perfect harmony between God and humankind. Humankind will not return to Eden in retreat from the present world; rather, the world as a whole will cast off the forces of evil and oppression and will be God's new creation.

Many scholars believe that Revelation was written toward the end of the reign of the Emperor Domitian (81–96 C.E.) during which the churches in Asia, and perhaps more broadly throughout the Roman Empire, were facing persecution and death. The book warns that those who worship "the beast"—the Roman Emperor—will ultimately suffer defeat (13:10), and it encourages believers to "hold fast to the faith of Jesus" (14:12), which is the only true victory.[1] The promise of a new creation also assures believers that there will ultimately be respite from their current persecutions; though the situation looks bleak right now, the future will see a return to an ideal and peaceful world created and ruled directly by God. In the new creation believers will have no enemies and will live in perfect harmony with nature and with the Creator. Susan Niditch notes that while few biblical writers "expect a return to paradise with its lack of hierarchy, its absolute harmony, and its de-emphasis on certain kinds of distinctions which mark human existence in real time," some "do imagine the coming about of a new creation" in which the ideal state does not take on the structures and strictures of reality.[2] Such thoughts are not limited to biblical writers such as Paul and the author of Revelation; they are evident in contemporary film as well.

FILM SUMMARY

The longing for a kinder, gentler past is acted out in the humorous 1998 film *Pleasantville*, directed by Gary Ross. Like *The Truman Show*, this film is set primarily inside the set of a television program. In contrast to *The Truman Show*, which it followed by less than a year, it does not feature an entrapped hero who is longing to escape but rather an ordinary guy who, along with his twin sister, is mysteriously transported to a 1950s sitcom also entitled *Pleasantville*. The film is an enjoyable mixture of genres, a combination "coming of age" film and romantic comedy, with a few science fiction touches for good measure.

Jennifer (Reese Witherspoon) and David (Toby Maguire) are the urban, 1990s twin children of divorced parents. David is a studious "nerd" who fantasizes about dating one of the popular girls but cannot work up the courage to ask her out. He is a maven of the *Pleasantville* TV series, who knows every detail about every episode. Not only does he intend to watch the entire *Pleasantville* marathon (staying up all night to do so) but also to compete in the trivia contest, which he has some hope of winning. From 6:30 P.M. on Friday until the same time on Saturday, David plans to be immersed in *Pleasantville*'s world. Jennifer could not be more different than her brother, as her friends never tire of pointing out. Hardly a nerd, she smokes, dresses provocatively, and is sexually experienced. She has little patience for her brother, and he seems to have little connection with her. David and Jennifer thus represent the two realms—the TV world of *Pleasantville* and the confusing and complex world of 1996 America—whose contrast is at the center of this film.

The complexity of life in the late twentieth century is brought home to Jennifer and David on a daily basis. Day after day, hour after hour, their school teaches them that the world that awaits them after graduation is one of uncertainty and crisis. The college counselor warns that they will have trouble landing a job: "For those of you going on to college next year, the chance of finding a good job will actually decrease by the time you graduate. Entry-level jobs will drop from thirty-one to twenty-six percent, and the median income for those jobs will go down as well." The health teacher declares that "the chance of contracting HIV from a promiscuous lifestyle will climb to one in one hundred and fifty. The odds of dying in an auto accident are only one in twenty-five hundred. Now this marks a drastic increase. . . ." The science teacher explains about the depletion of the ozone layer and its impact on global warming: "By the time you are twenty years old, average global temperature will have risen two and a half degrees. Even a shift of one degree can cause such catastrophic consequences as typhoons, floods, widespread drought, and famine."

Things are just as complicated on the home front. David overhears his mother on the phone with his father, trying to make arrangements: "No, you have custody the first weekend of every month and this is the first weekend. . . . No, I am not going to bail you out. I'm going out of town this weekend. . . ." She later continues, angrily, "No, that's not the point. The point is you're supposed to see them. (pause). Fine, fine, fine—see them another time."

While this conversation is going on, David is engrossed in an episode of *Pleasantville*, a 1950s family sitcom in which the parents, unlike his own, live in the same home and speak politely to each other. As the television father, George Warner (William H. Macy), walks in the front door after work, he neatly hangs up his hat and calls out, "Honey, I'm home." His wife, Betty (Joan Allen), responds from the kitchen, "Hello, darling." She comes to greet him at the door, as she unties her apron, hands George a fresh martini, and kisses him on the cheek. Their conversation goes as follows:

> **Betty:** How was your day?
>
> **George:** Oh, swell. You know, Mr. Connel said that if things keep going the way they are, I might be seeing that promotion sooner than I thought.
>
> **Betty:** Oh darling, that's wonderful! (an adoring gaze) I always knew you could do it.

Yes, life in Pleasantville, where roles are clearly defined and everything always works out for the best, is much easier and, well, more pleasant, than David and Jennifer's complicated existence.

That night, in the midst of a terrible thunderstorm, something extraordinary occurs. Their mother has left for the weekend, and David is about to settle down to the long-anticipated twenty-four hour *Pleasantville* marathon when Jennifer grabs the remote control. Jennifer's "hot date" is expected to arrive at any moment ostensibly in order to watch an MTV special. Jennifer and David tussle over the remote until it falls and breaks. Almost immediately, the doorbell rings, and there, to their amazement, is a wizened TV repairman (Don Knotts). The man largely ignores Jennifer but engages in friendly banter with David and then quizzes him on the minutiae of *Pleasantville*.

TV repairman: Remember the one where Bud lost his cousin when he was s'posed to be watching him?

David: Yeah . . .

TV repairman: What department store did they go to?

David: McIntire's.

TV repairman: McGinty's.

David: No. McIntire's. Remember: (sings) "For the very best in men's attire, Head right down to McIntire's."

TV repairman: (stunned) That's right.

David's expertise has a peculiar affect on the TV repairman. He stares at David, speechless, for a moment, then smiles fondly and reaches beside him for his tool kit. He offers David a rather strange-looking remote control that manages to look both "old-fashioned" and futuristic at the same time. With their big beautiful set, he tells them, "You want something that'll put you right in the show."

These words are prescient. As soon as the repairman leaves, the teens resume their fight while the opening scenes of the *Pleasantville* marathon play in the background. As they struggle, the television screen depicts the Warner children, Bud and Mary Sue, similarly arguing over possession of Mary Sue's transistor radio. Suddenly "a huge white light emanates from the contraption, like their own atomic blast wave. The entire room is filled with a BLINDING AURA for a second or two, before it actually gets sucked into the TV. WIDE ANGLE. LIVING ROOM. It is suddenly empty, illuminated only by the soft glow of the picture tube. David and Jennifer are nowhere in sight." But when we look at the TV set, we see that "David and Jennifer are standing in the middle of the 1950s' living room, dressed in Bud and Mary Sue's clothing. They still clutch the remote control in the exact same position that was occupied by their fictional counterparts. David and Jennifer glance at one another, then look horrified around the room. THE WORLD HAS TURNED TO BLACK AND WHITE. . . ."[3]

Despite his shock and disbelief, David is thrilled to be an actor in this familiar and well-loved environment. His only concern is to play his role properly without upsetting the status quo. Jennifer, on the other hand, is both repelled and intrigued. She sets out to make some waves. Little does she know what a storm she will cause by doing so.

The town of Pleasantville is oblivious to the fact that David and Jennifer are now standing in for Bud and Mary Sue. But gradually the entire population is affected. As she had promised, "Mary Sue" changes things, principally by introducing the young and the not-so-young to the joys of sex. And despite himself, "Bud," too, makes changes, bringing knowledge of history, geography, culture, and everyday life to his friends. These changes are welcomed by some and condemned by others, but their overall effect is to transform the black and white of Pleasantville into blazing color. Bud and Mary Sue are also transformed. In Pleasantville, in contrast to his "real" life, David tastes love and sex while Jennifer learns to value books and knowledge and discovers that the intellectual life is more satisfying than the "slutty" life she led back "home." At the end, contrary to what we might have expected at the outset, it is David who decides to return to his messy 1990s life and Jennifer who opts to stay, to finish high school, go to college, marry, and have children of her own.

The film *Pleasantville* has an overt message articulated by David in his Pleasantville persona as "Bud." At the film's climax, the mayor of Pleasantville, Big Bob, has put "Bud" and his friend Mr. Johnson on trial for painting a mural on the wall of Mr. Johnson's soda shop. The mayor sees this mural as symbolic of all of the unwanted changes that have occurred in his town. Before a packed courtroom, "Bud" tells the mayor, "I know you want it to stay 'Pleasant' around here, but there are so many things that are so much better: like Silly . . . or Sexy . . . or Dangerous . . . or Brief. . . . And every one of those things is in you all the time if you just have the guts to look for them. . . ." Mayor Bob angrily demands that this behavior stop at once. But "Bud" calmly points out, "See that's just the point. It can't stop at once. Because it's in you. And you can't stop something that's in you."

Entertaining as the premise and its execution might be, "Bud's" message is no more than that trite and tired truism that we must be true to our own inner selves—our wants, needs, and deepest desires. But there is much more going on in this movie than the plea for personal actualization that "Bud" expresses. The film warns its viewers that problematic, complicated, and unsatisfactory as our own world might seem to us, it is folly to long for a past era when life was simpler, more orderly, and less fraught with ambiguity. The film develops this theme in two ways: by emphasizing that change, while threatening, is not only inevitable but enriching; and by exposing the perfection of the past as an illusion that covers a dark and oppressive core.

The contrast between the "real world" of the late 1990s and the television world of the 1950s is illustrated through the use of color. Pleasantville is a black-and-white world, both visually and socially. Our world, on the other hand, is portrayed in technicolor. This contrast is employed at both the literal and the figurative level. The contrast itself is developed in three spheres: the personal, the societal, and the cosmic. A subtle interplay among all of these elements is developed through dialogue, plot, editing, sound track, and visual images.

USE OF THE BIBLE

Plot and Character

The Bible is not quoted directly in *Pleasantville*, but a number of scenes contain explicit allusions to biblical images from the books of Genesis and Exodus. A luscious red apple is picked off a tree by a beautiful young woman and fed to an obliging and smitten young man. A tree bursts into flames and is not consumed, and a rainbow magically appears after a lengthy rainstorm. There is a reference or two to a flood or deluge, and, for a moment, Massacio's "Expulsion of Adam and Eve" appears on the screen. Finally, there is a brief glimpse of "Bud" as Christ crucified, standing triumphantly in the rain with arms outstretched and looking up to the heavens, as did Andy in *The Shawshank Redemption* and Jesus in *Ben Hur*.

These allusions are not explored directly or in depth in the film, but together they constitute a commentary of sorts on the changes that David and Jennifer bring to Pleasantville. The Genesis and other Pentateuchal allusions associate Pleasantville with the garden of Eden in its popular guise as paradise; the adventures of "Bud" and "Mary Sue" follow the Christian "fall of man" story line, albeit with some inversions and diversions along the way. "Bud" and "Mary Sue" are the vehicles of transformation and perhaps even redemption for themselves and for others. The plot follows the general pattern of paradise and the fall as it has appeared in Christian tradition.

Pleasantville as Paradise

Genesis presents two creation stories: in one, the world is created in seven days, with humankind, male and female, created simultaneously on the sixth day (Gen. 1:1–2:4a); in the other, a man is created before the garden is planted, and a woman is created from his body (Gen. 2:4b–3:24).[4] *Pleasantville*, like *The Truman Show*, draws images, words, and motifs freely from both stories as suits

its purpose, with no attempt to differentiate them. The analogy between the town of Pleasantville and the primordial garden is expressed explicitly by the TV repairman, who himself refers to Pleasantville as paradise when he angrily shouts at the recalcitrant David, "YOU DON'T DESERVE TO LIVE IN THIS PARADISE!" Eden stands in for the 1950s, not as this era was in reality but as it is represented in the media and as it is recalled in both popular imagination and political rhetoric. On this level, the 1950s represent perfection: family values, safe sex, everything pleasant, and everyone happy. All human needs are taken care of, as in the first creation story in which God gives everything to the first human beings. The world is static, predictable, and unchanging, and everything works out in the best way possible. In contrast to the garden of Eden, in which the roles of the first man and woman were not differentiated, social and gender roles in Pleasantville are clearly defined and follow the same basic pattern that is set out for Adam and Eve when they are expelled from the garden: Adam will work, and Eve will bear children. In Pleasantville, as in the 1950s society that it mirrors, the woman's role also entails caring for the house and preparing meals in addition to bearing and raising the requisite boy and girl.

The "Fall" of Pleasantville

The arrival of David and Jennifer had as profound an impact on Pleasantville as the creation of the two primordial people had on the garden of Eden. Not only do they instigate specific changes, but they also introduce the very notion of change, an idea that even in small doses proves to be much more problematic in Pleasantville than in the world of the 1990s. The changes are marked by allusions to biblical images that are deeply embedded in our culture.

The problem of change is apparent from the early days of David and Jennifer's sojourn in Pleasantville. "Mary Sue" has learned that the star basketball player, a good-looking fellow named Skip, is "sweet" on her. Skip approaches "Bud" on the basketball court and asks his advice on whether to ask "Mary Sue" out on a date. David is terrified at the thought of his sexually experienced twin sister going out with this 1950s innocent and tries to put Skip off, saying, "Look, Skip . . . I don't think it's a real good time for that right now. . . . What I mean is . . . Mary Sue's a little 'different' lately. . . ." Skip is stunned: "She won't go out with me? . . . I don't know what I'd do if she wouldn't go out with me. . . ." Suddenly, Skip takes the basketball he's been holding and hurls it toward the hoop. The ball pops out of the basket, the first time in the history of Pleasantville that a player has missed the hoop. This amazing event makes David realize that in tampering with the script (in which Mary Sue is thrilled to date Skip), he is shaking the Pleasantville world order to its very core.

David is now convinced that he and Jennifer must cause absolutely no change to the *Pleasantville* scripts. He seeks out his sister and tries to convince her to go out with Skip. "No way," says Jennifer. David pleads with her. "One date, Jen, please—that's all I'm asking. If you don't go out with this guy we could throw their whole universe out of whack. . . . I will get us out of here. I really will. But if we don't play along we could alter their whole existence. And then we may never get home."

David initially resists change: he sees why everything must remain the same. Given that this episode, like all others in the *Pleasantville* marathon, is a rerun, how is any change to the script imaginable? But he cannot tolerate Pleasantville's static nature for long. Pleasantville's inability to absorb change is exemplified by Mr. Johnson, who, even more than Skip, is the proverbial canary in the mines. When David, as "Bud," arrives slightly late for work on his first day in Pleasantville, he finds Mr. Johnson wiping down the counters, in an agitated state. "I didn't know what to do," he says. "I always wipe down the counter and then you set out the napkins and glasses and then I make the french fries. . . . But you didn't come so I kept on wiping." David approaches Mr. Johnson, who has polished one section of the counter right down to the wood. Taking the towel out of Mr. Johnson's hand and folding it neatly in front of him, David gently tells him, "You know, if this ever happens again, you can make the fries even if I haven't put out the napkins yet."

It has clearly never occurred to Mr. Johnson, or indeed to anyone in Pleasantville, that things could happen differently than they always do. It takes him a few tries, but eventually Mr. Johnson learns that he can indeed vary his routine, and he is so proud of himself that he has to come to "Bud's" house to tell him so. "You know how when we close up, I close the register, then you lower the blinds, then I turn out the lights, then we both lock the doors. . . . Well you weren't around this time so I did the whole thing by myself. . . . Not only that, I didn't even do it in the same order. First I lowered the blinds, then I closed the register." The shooting script notes that "Mr. Johnson has a strange look of 'manly pride' on his face. His shoulders square back. His chest puffs out a little. There is a sudden sparkle in his eye."

This is just the beginning. Through casual conversation David learns that Mr. Johnson looks forward all year long to the Christmas season because he can paint pictures on his soda shop windows. It has never occurred to him that he can paint at other times or use other media, perhaps because he has never seen color before. He shows David his windows, and David becomes convinced that Mr. Johnson has real talent, in addition to a passion for painting that Mr. Johnson has never fully realized himself. He brings him an art book, in full color, and thereby changes Mr. Johnson's life. David's recognition that changing anything in Pleasantville is liable to wreak havoc on their entire universe cannot restrain his natural impulse to introduce basic knowledge and skills that will help Mr. Johnson satisfy his longing for color and art.

Jennifer, on the other hand, does not hesitate at all to shake things up in Pleasantville. After David insists, she agrees to go out with Skip, and, to Skip's shock and surprise, she takes him to Lovers' Lane, where she does exactly what David feared she would do: she introduces him to sex. After dropping her off at home, a stunned and ecstatic Skip sees a sight never before possible in Pleasantville's black-and-white world, a pink rose just opening on the bush. It is not long before all the young couples catch on, and Lovers' Lane is clothed in vibrant color. The young people themselves also begin to take on color, especially their lips and tongues, a development that alarms their mothers and mystifies the town physician.

David, too, is drawn into this fervor. Back home, he had been too timid to approach the girl he liked; in Pleasantville, however, he is pursued by a lovely and lively young woman named Margaret. Margaret and "Bud" also visit Lovers' Lane. There Margaret provocatively plucks a ripe red apple and lovingly shares it with "Bud." This scene obviously evokes the image of temptation in Genesis 3, when the primordial woman succumbs to the snake's tempting offer of the fruit of the tree of knowledge of good and evil, takes a bite of the delicious fruit, and offers some to the primordial man, who also takes a bite. This act of disobedience results in the man and woman's expulsion from the garden, the onset of mortality, and initiation of human life and history as we know it. The scene as a whole plays on the connection between knowledge and sexuality, as embodied in the popular phrase "to know in the biblical sense."

But it is not only the young people who are awakened to their own sexuality. In Pleasantville, as it turns out, even the adults do not have sex nor do they know what it is all about. Apparently children just happen, through the magic of studio casting, perhaps. As a show committed to the 1950s version of the ideal family, sexuality is not portrayed, nor is it even hinted at. Twin beds in the master bedroom evoke the style of the 1950s but also imply that George and Betty have never slept together, either literally or figuratively. A touching and humorous scene portrays a role reversal, in which Jennifer ("Mary Sue") gives her mother Betty the sort of sex education lesson that Jennifer's real mother may have given her.

Betty: Mary Sue.

Jennifer: Yeah? (pause)

Betty: What goes on up at Lover's Lane?

Jennifer: What do you mean?

Betty: Well, you hear these things lately . . . kids spending so much time up there. . . . Is it holding hands? That kind of thing?

Jennifer: Yeah. . . . That, and . . .

Betty: What?

Jennifer: It doesn't matter.

Betty: No. I want to know.

Jennifer: (glances toward the living room [where the others are watching televison]/ lowers her voice) well . . . Sex.

Betty: Ah. . . . What's sex?

Jennifer stares at her stunned, but Betty just looks at her with a blank, curious expression. Jennifer hesitates.

Jennifer: You sure you want to know this?

Betty: Yes.

Jennifer: Okay.

She crosses to the kitchen door and closes it. The sounds of the TV in the living room disappear. Jennifer crosses back to the kitchen counter and turns to her.

Jennifer: You see, Mom . . . (softer and with understanding), when two people really love each other very much . . .

The camera leaves the rest of the conversation to our imagination, but returns us to Jennifer and Betty at its conclusion:

Jennifer: Are you okay?

Betty: (nods, shaken but "fine." She stares long and hard at the plate of chocolate chip cookies. She's far away.) Yes. . . . (softly) It's just that. . . . Well . . . (looking up) . . . your father would never do anything like that.

Betty seems wistful. She cannot see a way that she will experience what Mary Sue has described—until Mary Sue suggests that "there's ways to 'enjoy' yourself without Dad." After receiving instruction from Mary Sue, Betty draws and experiences the most sensual and pleasurable bath she has ever had.

ALL AT ONCE, EVERYTHING AROUND STARTS TO TURN FROM BLACK AND WHITE TO COLOR. A BIRD OUT THE WINDOW BECOMES A RED-BREASTED ROBIN. THE TILE

ON THE TUB TURNS OUT TO BE PURPLE. GREEN
TOWEL . . . PINK ROBE . . . BRIGHT YELLOW DAISIES ON
THE PLASTIC SHOWER CURTAIN. CLOSE UP. BETTY'S
FACE. She stares in amazment. Beads of sweat form on Betty's fore-
head as the world goes to TECHNICOLOR. The THUNDERING
WATER POUNDS IN THE BACKGROUND, but beneath can be
heard the beginnings of a faint, low, MOAN. Her eyes dart around the
room. Her breathing quickens: Faster . . . Harder . . . More intense . . .
THEN SUDDENLY . . . (Camera moves to the exterior of the house)
NIGHT. The HUGE ELM TREE across the street suddenly
BURSTS INTO FLAMES. Fire shoots straight up into the sky as bil-
lowing clouds of black smoke fill the air. BRIGHT ORANGE
FLAMES LIGHT UP THE NIGHT.

Like the burning bush of Exodus 3, the elm tree burns and burns without
being consumed. Not only the absence of ashes but the very fact that it is burning is surprising to the denizens of Pleasantville, for the town is constructed
entirely of inflammable materials. As Jennifer learned on her first day as "Mary
Sue," even the matches do not burn. The fire department exists for the sole
purpose of rescuing cats from trees. When the elm tree in front of the Warn-
ers' house erupts into flame, "Bud" must not only summon the fire fighters but
also show them that there is water in their hoses and teach them that this water
will extinguish the flames.

In the biblical context, the bush is the first locus of God's revelation to and
communication with Moses. In the film, it is a spectacular and vaguely divine
acknowledgment of Betty's new-found knowledge, revealed to her by Jennifer.
Betty's sexual awakening paves the way for a major change to the Pleasantville
script: Betty and Mr. Johnson, the soda shop owner and Bud's boss, finally
acknowledge the love between them. In a number of tender scenes, they dis-
cover each other as full adults rather than the two-dimensional television characters they have been until now. But this relationship also shows that personal
change affects society as a whole. One day George returns home to find that
Betty is not there to welcome him as she always does. Even worse, she has not
prepared him any dinner. (We viewers know that she is with Mr. Johnson, but
George does not.) When he recounts this astounding event to his bowling
buddies, George learns that she is not the only wife who is neglecting her
duties. One woman has burnt her husband's shirt because she was thinking
while ironing. Yet another woman has been campaigning for—horror of
horrors—a double bed to replace the twin models that are de rigueur in Pleasantville. Although the changes seem to pertain to two individuals only, they
are altering the entire social fabric of Pleasantville and threatening the practices and social structures on which it had depended. Can it be that "family
values" are gone forever? This is the fear that lies at the heart of the mayor's

harsh reactions to the changes in Pleasantville. As "Bud" tells him at his own trial for public mischief (he and Mr. Johnson painted a mural on the outside wall of the soda shop), "Everyone's turning colors. Kids are making out in the street. No one's getting their dinner—hell, you could have a flood any minute. . . . Pretty soon the women could be going off to work while the men stayed at home and cooked. . . ." The mayor reacts to this scenario with horror: "That's not going to happen!" "Bud" persists: "But it could happen."

The changes that the twins bring to Pleasantville are not limited to sex. As we have already seen, "Bud" teaches the firefighters the basic facts about fire and water and demonstrates to Mr. Johnson that variation in routine can be useful. "Bud" becomes the medium through whom the residents of Pleasantville, principally its young people, learn about the world outside Pleasantville as well as the world of books.

All of these issues come to a head on the day after Bud helps the fire fighters put out Pleasantville's first fire. "Bud" enters the soda shop for his work shift to confront a room full of intent stares. His sister explains, under her breath: "Um. . . . They wanna ask you a question. . . . I didn't know how to handle it. So. . . ." "Bud" crosses to the booth where several young people look up at him. Glances are exchanged. Finally, a boy asks, "How'd you know about the fire?"

> **David:** What?
>
> **Boy:** How'd you know how to put it out and all?

David hesitates, weighing his words.

> **David:** Well, where I used to live. . . . That's just what firemen did.

This sends a MURMUR through the shop. The boy leans forward.

> **Boy:** And where's that?
>
> **David:** (carefully) Um. . . . Outside of Pleasantville.

This sends a much LOUDER MURMUR rifling through the kids. It's like electricity. They glance excited at one another. A hush descends.

> **Boy:** What's outside of Pleasantville?
>
> **David:** It doesn't matter. It's not important.
>
> **Girl:** What's outside Pleasantville?

David stops and looks out at the kids who are hanging on every word.

Finally, David explains: "Well . . . there are some places where the road doesn't go in a circle. There are some places where it keeps on going. . . . it all just keeps going. Roads . . . rivers . . .

2nd Boy: (from the back) Like the "Mighty Mississippi."

David: . . . What?

He moves forward extending a book. The cover reads, *The Adventures of Huckleberry Finn.* David opens the first page. There is printing inside.

Boy: (quoting) "It was big 'n brown 'n kept goin' an' goin' as far you could see."

Jennifer: (quickly) Okay this was not my fault. When they asked me what it was about I didn't remember because I read it like back in tenth grade. When I told them what I DID remember, that's when the pages filled in.

David: The pages filled in?

Jennifer: But only up to the part about the raft, cause that's as far as I read.

David flips through the book and sure enough only the first chapter has print. The pages are blank after that.

2nd Boy: Do you know how it ends?

David: (hesitating) Yeah . . . I do.

Margaret: (breathless) So how does it end?

She has moved closer and is gazing at him from a couple of feet away. It is silent in the soda shop.

David: Well, um, OK, let's see . . . they were running away, Huck and the slave. . . . And . . . they were going up the river. . . . But, in trying to get free they see that they're free already.

David looks down at the book. Its pages are no longer blank.

This development instantly creates a new craze among Pleasantville's youth for reading. They line up in front of the library for hours and emerge excitedly with their books. The couples go to Lovers' Lane not only, or not even primarily, for sex, but in order to read to one another as they sit on the newly green and pleasant banks of the river. David and Jennifer have unleashed their natural, human curiosity about the world, and they cannot get enough.

Bud also teaches his peers to accept the variety that the real world of nature has to offer, not just color on the trees and all around them, but the basic elements of fire and rain. On the day that Margaret and "Bud" pay their momentous visit to Lovers' Lane, they and all the other young lovers, who are not making love but reading together on the banks of the river, see the skies open up. The thunderstorm scares and shocks the young people, who have never experienced rain, let alone a storm. But "Bud" shows them there is nothing to worry about: he stands out in the rain, arms outstretched, looking up at the sky and laughing. This Christ image is Christ triumphant, unvanquished by all the violence that the world has unleashed against him. "Bud," on the other hand, is simply showing them that rain, like other natural phenomena, can not only be endured but celebrated. This, as the Christ allusion suggests, is both redemptive and transformative. The event and Bud's acceptance of it has redeemed the young people from the monotony of sameness and transformed them into individuals who can handle change.

After the storm, a brilliant rainbow appears in the sky, an obvious allusion to the rainbow that God sent as his pledge that the destruction he had wrought on the world and humankind through his grand storm and flood would never again be repeated (Genesis 6–9). The scene in the film does not necessarily carry with it the covenantal context of the biblical text, but it does imply the fittingness of both the rain and the rainbow, as if God is responding to the changes that have been occurring in Pleasantville with the biblical refrain "And God saw that it was good" (cf. Gen. 1:10). In this film, rain heralds moments of change. The TV repairman arrives in the midst of a thunderstorm; George's shocked realization that Betty is not at home to serve him dinner occurs during a rainstorm, the same one that the teens out on Lovers' Lane experience with fright and then amazement. The rain thus symbolizes events beyond one's control that can be both disturbing and destructive but also necessary for growth—the growth of vegetation in the natural world and the growth of ourselves.

Thus David and Jennifer bring knowledge and color to this black-and-white world. In doing so, they act out the parts of Adam and Eve, who acquire knowledge when they eat the fruit of the forbidden tree and disseminate that knowledge to their descendants. Just as Adam and Eve's eating of the fruit did not have divine approval and resulted in some serious consequences for them both, David and Jennifer's activities raise the ire of the powers that be and have consequences that are felt by them and all of Pleasantville. A subtle warning of these troubles comes in a visual image. In the course of encouraging Mr. Johnson to take up painting, "Bud" gives his friend an art book of masterpieces of the Western world that he has borrowed from the library. The first page that Mr. Johnson turns to reproduces Massacio's "Expulsion of Adam and

Eve," which, according to the screenplay, "leaps off the pages in vibrant, tortured color. The beauty of the garden is offset by their agony and their shame." This painting intimates the relationship that he will have with Betty, but it also hints at the possibility of unpleasantness in Pleasantville as a punishment for the introduction of knowledge and vibrant color to this bland environment.

The "fall" of Pleasantville—that is, the introduction of knowledge, sex, books, and other elements of late-twentieth-century life—does not ultimately lead to the expulsion of the pair who initiated the change, but it does lead to the disappearance of the black-and-white, harmonious, homogeneous, and orderly society that had characterized Pleasantville until the arrival of David and Jennifer. In this film, as in *The Truman Show*, the loss of paradise is welcomed by all except those who had a vested interest in keeping change at bay. The point of the film is clear, however: who would not prefer the bright and vibrant color of the new Pleasantville to the drabness of the old?

The allusions to biblical paradigms of creation and redemption may suggest that Jennifer and David, in their Pleasantville personas of "Mary Sue" and "Bud," play the biblical roles of temptress and savior. A case can be made for these identifications, for it is "Mary Sue" who introduces the youth and adults of Pleasantville to sex, while it is "Bud" who opens their eyes to the knowledge that can save them from their narrow views of the world. But this may be over-interpreting the film and its relationship to the Bible. In contrast to *The Truman Show*, where the biblical allusions pointed to a structural similarity between the film's plot and the Genesis narrative, the allusions in *Pleasantville* serve primarily to identify the TV town as a perfect society that represents the longings of people like David, who live in complicated times, for the simplicity, orderliness, and pleasantness of an earlier era. Pleasantville, like God's garden, is always sunny, is populated by people who know their proper place, and does not deviate from the path that God—or the scriptwriter—has set. The real world has none of these features, but what it does have is complexity, eventfulness, and, above all, color.

Themes

David's longing for the ideal society that Pleasantville represents for him mirrors the nostalgia that at least some feel for the clear realities of the 1950s—if not the realities of everyday life then, at least, those that were served up in the family sitcoms of the era. But the film shows that this paradise is an illusion that plays on the surface only; it masks repressed emotions, cardboard personalities, stale and static relationships and, more insidiously, hatred of change and of difference.

This element appears most forcefully in the treatment that the black-and-white citizens of Pleasantville dish out to the "coloreds," that is, those that have engaged in new experiences and tried out their new-found knowledge, not only of sex but of reading. The mayor and his followers, including Bud and Mary Sue's father, George, initiate a campaign against "coloreds" who, by turning color, are threatening the very things that have made life in Pleasantville so pleasant. The campaign entails the very visible and obvious overtones of the civil rights strife in the United States of the 1950s as well as the Nazi persecution of Jews. "Coloreds" are forbidden from shopping in certain stores. As the stores open for morning business on Main Street, more and more "No Coloreds" signs appear in the windows: next to the donuts . . . by fishing poles . . . beside the stationery supplies. . . . Everything else looks frighteningly the same. The campaign also bans the practices that are seen as giving rise to the "colored" population, such as listening to rock-and-roll music, sleeping on double beds, borrowing books, and spending time at Lovers' Lane. Startling in their familiarity (at least to those of us who were watching the news during the American race riots of the 1950s and beyond) are scenes that show "black-and-whites" breaking in the windows of "colored" businesses like Mr. Johnson's soda shop and heaping books upon huge bonfires.

"Colorism" affects the Warner family directly. During the book burning, "Mary Sue" struggles valiantly to prevent Skip from throwing her book on the fire. Elsewhere, "Bud" is confronted by a character named Whitey, who, in the original *Pleasantville* series, is paired up with Margaret, "Bud's" girlfriend. "Bud" is still in black and white, but Margaret has already turned into full color. Whitey inquires threateningly about why "Bud" is not at the town hall rally against coloreds, and he provides his own answer: "I thought maybe it was cause you were too busy entertaining your colored girlfriend." He leers at the girl: "You know, Margaret, you can come over and bake those oatmeal cookies for me anytime you want to."

The most terrifying scene occurs when Betty, now in living color, is assaulted by "black-and-whites" while walking alone (itself a nearly unheard of activity in the "old" Pleasantville) on her way from Mr. Johnson's soda shop. The screenplay notes,

> The ROSY HUE of her face stands out in stark relief to the black and white faces around her. Betty holds her head high with dignity (and fear) while the ugly epithets overlap one another . . . Ya, come on— why don't you show us what's under that nice blue dress? Hey, wher're you going? There's nowhere to go over there. One of the boys yanks at Betty's skirt and she quickens her pace. Just at that moment the boy is shoved to the ground.
>
> David shields his "mother" as he shoves one of the boys into the dirt. The kid gets up but David punches him hard in the side of the jaw and the rest of them just stare. (Violence is as new as anything else and it seems to freeze the moment.) David steps in front of his

"mother" with both fists clenched. He plants his back foot primed for action. The crowd of black and white thugs just stares at it. They look at him warily. The boy reaches up and feels the side of his mouth where a trickle of RED BLOOD is running down his chin. He looks at his finger in horror and starts backing away.

David: Get out of here!

They back away further and David takes a threatening step. The boys turn and run as he turns back to face his "mother."
  With this act, "Bud" finally turns into color, as he sees in his mother's pocket mirror.

The conflict comes to a head when "Bud" and Mr. Johnson are arrested and put on trial for painting a huge and colorful mural of Pleasantville on the outside wall of the soda shop—this in the face of the prohibition of using any colors but black, grey and white. At the trial, coloreds are banished to the back of the courtroom while "Bud" and Mr. Johnson are interrogated by the mayor. Mr. Johnson passionately declares his need for color but offers to submit his colors to the mayor for scrutiny. "Bud," on the other hand, stands up valiantly for what he has done. In the process, he creates a situation in which his father announces that he loves and misses Betty and promptly turns into color himself. Finally, the mayor himself turns into color when "Bud" provokes him to acknowledge how angry he was with "Bud" and "Bud's" supporters. Having become "colored" himself, the mayor flees the courtroom, but as the doors open wide, it becomes evident that all of Pleasantville is now in glorious, living technicolor, brighter than the natural world itself. Coincidentally, or perhaps not, this moment coincides with the arrival of color television—a new technology—in the appliance store window.

These changes displease not only the mayor but also the TV repairman—who, we presume, is an even higher authority. As in *The Truman Show*, the Christian allusions in *Pleasantville* imply a particular relationship between the male protagonist and an older man who is identified with the TV show itself. The relationship between David and the TV repairman parallels at least to some degree that between Truman and Christof, though the relationship is of lesser intensity and less intimacy.

In contrast to Christof, the TV repairman's precise role with respect to the television show is never made clear. But it is clear that he has a special role. He arrives at the house of David and Jennifer precisely because of David's extraordinary knowledge of *Pleasantville* trivia, and his offer of the strange and powerful remote is precisely in order to put them "in the show," as he says. The repairman calls this a miracle. "Every time I thought I'd found someone they'd turn out to disappoint me. They'd know the early episodes, but they wouldn't know the later ones. . . ." The repairman is upset that David and Jennifer don't seem to appreciate what he has done for them:

> But you don't know how long I've been looking for someone like you. . . . I'm very disappointed. . . . (deep breath) In fact . . . I'm start- ing to get a little upset. . . . You look for someone for years. . . . You pour your heart into it. . . . This is a privilege you know. (shakes his head) I don't think I better talk about this right now. . . . I don't think we should discuss this until I'm a little more composed. . . . Maybe in awhile when I'm not so emotional. . . .

With these words, he disappears from the screen. Clearly the TV repairman has some extraordinary powers: to appear and disappear from the television screen at will and to transport viewers into, and presumably back out of, Pleas- antville. But it is hard to know what he expects to gain by doing so.

Later on, when the repairman is more composed, he returns and announces to David that he has reconsidered and is now willing to bring them home again. But by this point life in Pleasantville has become interesting for David, given its promise of a relationship with Margaret. However, the real reason for the TV repairman's offer is his alarm at the changes that David and Jennifer have wrought: "I'll be honest with you, Bud. I'm getting a little concerned about what I'm seeing in some of these re-runs. . . . Like when Margaret Hen- derson makes her cookies for Whitey. . . . Those are not your cookies, Bud." By now, David has completely forgotten his own advice to Jennifer, that rock- ing the boat in one area of Pleasantville life may have cosmic consequences in another.

> **David:** Yes, I know they're not my cookies.
>
> **TV repairman:** Those are Whitey's cookies, Bud, they belong to him. Then he eats them and asks her to go to Lover's Lane.
>
> **David:** Look, I'd love to talk about all of this right now but I'm really in a hurry. Why don't we hook up tomorrow?

David then turns off the television, sending the TV repairman to "electronic limbo."

But the repairman is persistent and reappears to David in the myriad of tele- vision screens in the local appliance store. "What the hell do you think you're doing? Get in here . . . NOW." According to the shooting script, "The sound reverberates like God Himself." David ducks into the store and slams the door; fifty images of Don Knotts glare at him from every television screen.[5]

TV repairman: (still pretty loud) You think this is a toy? You think it's your own little goddamn coloring book. . . .

David: Well, it just sort of happened.

TV repairman: Deluge doesn't just happen.

A box appears in the upper right-hand corner of the screen showing Bud and
Margaret at Lover's Lane. The tape rolls as she holds out the bright red apple
to Bud, who hesitates, then takes it, then puts it to his mouth and takes a bite.
So the repairman has seen the pivotal Eve temptation scene. "YOU KNOW
YOU DON'T DESERVE THIS PLACE," he shouts, as the image of David
biting the apple plays over and over like a sports instant replay. ". . . Because
you're coming home, you little twerp and I'm gonna put this place back the
way it was. . . . You're gonna get that remote and you're gonna come home and
we're gonna make everybody HAPPY AGAIN!!!"

These dialogues imply that the TV repairman is a divine figure of sorts. He
sees everything that is happening (on his television set, of course); he has the
means to insert people into his world and remove them again, though he must
use an instrument, the remote control, to do so. He is unhappy when someone tampers with his world and is deeply concerned about its corruption.
However, in contrast to the God of the scriptures, he is not a creator but one
who maintains the status quo.[6]

This portrayal combines with the biblical allusions identified earlier, however, to express a distinctly theological message about human nature and the
world that God created. Whereas the TV repairman, along with his represen-
tatives within the television series (such as the Mayor), deplores change and
views it as a corruption of his pristine world, the "real" God views the changes
that David and Jennifer have wrought with joy and delight. He expresses this
joy by erupting into spectacular miracles: the rainstorm, the rainbow, the burning bush, and, most spectacularly, the color. God is called on to sanction the
essential message of the film—to celebrate change, human self-actualization,
and the confusion and complexity of the here and now.

At the movie's conclusion, we return to the story of the twins, David
and Jennifer. Not only have they brought knowledge, change, complexity,
and, above all, color, to Pleasantville, but they have changed themselves,
become more complex, more rounded, and more fulfilled. Jennifer finishes
high school in Pleasantville then heads off to college, a barely recognizable,
mature, demure, and attractively nerdy version of her former self. The film
concludes with a brief and tender scene between David and his mother. It turns
out that David has been away for only one hour of the Pleasantville marathon, but he turns off the television, no longer in need of the escape that this

show had provided him. He finds his mother in the kitchen, crying. She, like David, has returned from her trip, and she is in tears over the conflicts in her own role and self-image. David comforts her gently by wiping her tears and her oppressive makeup, thereby revealing, symbolically and literally, her true face and her true self. She marvels at the wisdom and understanding that he has suddenly gained, but we viewers recall the scene in which "Bud" comforted Betty, and we know that his maturity is a result of his experiences in Pleasantville.

The film, then, has two messages in addition to that of personal fulfillment. First, change is inevitable and should be welcomed rather than feared. Second, the longing for a "kinder, gentler" time gone by, when men worked and women stayed home, is misplaced. This form of "family values" required both women and men to suppress their curiosity, their sexuality, and their innate talents, interests, and emotions. Further, and more important perhaps, is that these kinder, gentler times were so only on the surface; the effort to maintain order and the pleasant life masked the fear, hatred, and suppression of difference. The movie functions as a warning not to return to the 1950s, with its racism, its sexism, and its narrow understanding of the world.

CONCLUSION

Pleasantville appeals to David for its order and, well, its pleasantness. But just as the Genesis stories present a selective and highly constructed depiction of this ideal world, so the TV series *Pleasantville* presents a highly idealized version of the homogeneous suburban lifestyle of the 1950s. It is no more a real place than is paradise. Hence the longing for the paradise of Pleasantville is a longing for a fantasy that has been constructed and served up by the media of the 1950s to entertain, to sell products, and to reinforce a particular set of values.[7]

The notion of longing for the past is not new; it is present in prophetic and apocalyptic literature of the Hebrew Bible and New Testament. The movie does not make explicit reference to these passages but expresses a similar longing for an idealized past that is free of the problems, suffering, and complexities of the present. The longing for the past in biblical literature is expressed in two ways: through a longing for the world to return to the primordial and perfect relationship with God that was present at the time of creation, and through a longing for the simple and powerful relationship between Israel and God at the time of the exodus.

The longing for Eden is apparent in Isaiah's message of comfort to exiled Israel:

"The LORD will comfort Zion;
   he will comfort all her waste places,
and will make her wilderness like Eden,
   her desert like the garden of the LORD;
joy and gladness will be found in her,
   thanksgiving and the voice of song."
(Isa. 51:3)

The prophet Jeremiah, on the other hand, idealizes the period of wandering in the desert. Jeremiah portrays God as reminiscing with nostalgia:

"I remember the devotion of your youth,
   your love as a bride,
how you followed me in the wilderness,
   in a land not sown."
(Jer. 2:2)

Similarly in Hosea, God looks forward to a future time when he will

"allure her [Israel],
   and bring her into the wilderness,
   and speak tenderly to her.
From there I will give her her vineyards,
   and make the Valley of Achor a door of hope.
There she shall respond as in the days of her youth,
   as at the time when she came out of the land of Egypt."
(Hos. 2:14–15)

But God's longing for the simplicity and intensity of the wilderness period is difficult to reconcile with the detailed accounts of that period provided in the books of Exodus through Deuteronomy. In Exodus 16:1–3, for example, the Israelites complain bitterly against Moses and Aaron: "If only we had died by the hand of the LORD in the land of Egypt, when we sat by the fleshpots and ate our fill of bread; for you have brought us out into this wilderness to kill this whole assembly with hunger" (cf. Num. 11:4–6). Later, they complain about not having enough water to drink: "Why did you bring us out of Egypt, to kill us and our children and livestock with thirst?" (Exod. 17:3). The Golden Calf and numerous other incidents imply a degree of tension in the relationship between God and Israel that the passages in Jeremiah and Hosea overlook.

The book of Revelation takes the longing for a simpler and more secure past one step further by building a return to the ideal conditions of Eden into its vision of the future messianic era. In this regard it brings the Christian scriptures full circle, from God's creation of the ideal world in Genesis 1–2 to the promise of a new creation, indeed, a new heaven and a new earth. Like the prophets Isaiah and Jeremiah, the author of Revelation was likely addressing his work to an audience experiencing very hard times, including active persecution by the Roman Emperor Domitian. The author's promise of God's victory over the powers of evil and the onset of God's new creation may have been the only way of offering hope and a promise of better times, even in some distant future, in the face of intractable hostility and suffering.

These observations suggest that the longing for and idealization of a long ago time and place are not unique to films such as *Pleasantville* or indeed to our complex era. The books of Exodus, Numbers, Isaiah, Jeremiah, and Revelation all imply that tough and complicated times may quite naturally lead us to look back to a time when life seemed simpler; it may also be natural to overlook the negative elements of that previous era. The book of Revelation—with its focus on the future and a new heaven and earth (new creation)—draws attention both to the antiquity of the impulse that the film addresses and also to the point that the film is trying to make: that the desire for Eden is misguided. It is neither possible nor desirable to return to the *past* as it was; even God says so!

11

Pale Rider, *Nell*, and the Misuse of Scripture

"Beware that no one leads you astray. For many will come in my name, saying, 'I am the Messiah!' and they will lead many astray."

Matthew 24:4–5

INTRODUCTION

As we have seen in the previous chapters, there are many films in which biblical quotations or other direct references or allusions to the Bible contribute to plot, characterization, and theme. In these cases, knowledge of the reference, its content, and its context will deepen the viewers' understanding of and appreciation for the film. But such is not the case for all films in which the Bible plays an explicit role. In this chapter we will discuss briefly two films, *Pale Rider* (1985) and *Nell* (1994), that explicitly draw on the Bible, but in a way that does not illuminate the film but may in fact lead us astray.

FILM SUMMARY (*PALE RIDER*)

This 1985 western, directed by Clint Eastwood, has all the hallmarks of the genre: big sky, rugged landscape, and a social world marked by the battle between good and evil, with tough-talking, tough-looking, gun-toting men on each side. Throw in the requisite romance and close-ups of Clint Eastwood, and you get the full picture. What makes this film stand out in its genre (though it is not entirely unique in this regard) is the aura of the superhuman, or even supernatural, that surrounds the figure played by its star, the Pale Rider of the movie's title. This aura is accentuated by the quotation of biblical passages at crucial points in the narrative, and it is complicated by the omission of other biblical passages that may, in fact, have been a more appropriate guide to the significance of the Pale Rider to the people into whose lives he rode.

The film begins with men on horseback, riding purposefully, relentlessly, ominously; pounding hoof-beats dominate the sound track. The camera cuts back and forth between these riders and a ramshackle, peaceful, small mining community. As the riders move forward, the mining men, women, and children carry on with their daily activities—panning for gold, doing the laundry, preparing food, fixing equipment. The town looks vulnerable, open, and almost ephemeral. As the horsemen approach the encampment, their horses' hooves pound more insistently and their speed increases. Finally, inevitably, they enter the community, shooting, terrorizing, and destroying. They ride off as suddenly as they came. When the dust settles, viewers see that some men are injured, the buildings are in ruins, and the entire community is shaken. Some townspeople decide to leave, then and there; most stay but are fearful.

This introduction firmly identifies the two parties to the conflict that stands at the center of this film. Though we do not yet know the motivation for their raid, the riders are obviously the "bad guys"; they have might and power; they do not hesitate to destroy and to terrorize. Their victims are the "good guys." They are peaceful, mind their own business, and are in dire financial and emotional straits. Without outside intervention, these victims will share the fate of the small dog that is killed during the raid. They will be trampled by these powerful adversaries and left for dead.

The dog had belonged to a beautiful teen-aged girl named Megan (Sydney Penny). As she buries her dog in the woods, she recites an abridged version of Psalm 23; her own annotations articulate the fears, hopes, and needs of this beleaguered community:

> The LORD is my shepherd; I shall not want. (But I *do* want). He leadeth me beside still waters. He restoreth my soul (but they killed my dog). Yea, though I walk through the valley of the shadow of death, I shall fear no evil (but I *am* afraid): for thou art with me; thy rod and thy staff they comfort me. (We need a miracle). Thy lovingkindness and mercy shall follow me all the days of my life (if you exist). And I shall dwell in the house of the LORD for ever. (I'd like to get more of this life first. If you don't help us, we're all going to die. Please, just one miracle.) Amen.[1]

Megan's despair is palpable. She does not find the prescribed words powerful enough, nor do they resonate well enough with her own situation.

As she talks, the camera cuts back and forth to a solitary rider. At first he is almost transparent, perhaps a figment of Megan's imagination. But as she proceeds in her words, the rider's image becomes clearer and clearer. The cutting back and forth between the rider and the girl implies that he may indeed be the answer to her prayers.

At the same time as Megan is burying her dog, Hull Barrett (Michael Moriarty), Megan's mother's fiancé and the informal leader of this community, is heading for town in order to purchase the supplies needed to clean up the mess left behind by the riders. The shopkeepers warn him that his credit is running out; he promises to pay his debts with the next gold nugget that he finds. As he steps outside with his goods, Hull is brutally assaulted by a group of men. They taunt him and beat him with wooden clubs. Suddenly, out of nowhere, the solitary rider who had appeared during Megan's prayer reappears. He, too, picks up a club. Effortlessly and wordlessly, he pounds all the attackers until they surrender and then heads out of town.

Hull catches up with him and invites him home. When they arrive, Hull finds one of his men preparing to leave and others thinking about doing so. Meanwhile, Megan is inside Hull's house, reading to her mother, Sarah (Carrie Snodgrass), from the Bible, while Sarah prepares a hot meal. Megan's text is Revelation 6:4–8: "The power was given to him that sat thereon to take peace from the earth, and that they should kill one another and there was given unto him a great sword, and when he opened the third seal I heard the third beast say, 'Come and see.'" (Sarah interjects, "Megan, fetch me some butter and some syrup.") "I beheld and lo a black horse! And he that sat on him had a pair of balances in his hand. And I heard a voice in the midst of the fourth beast say, 'A measure of wheat for a penny and three measures of barley for a penny and see thou hurt not the oil and the wine!'" (At this point the background music becomes ominous and suspenseful.) "And when he had opened the fourth seal, I heard the voice of the fourth beast say, 'Come and see!' And I looked" (we now see Sarah looking out the window; the camera follows her eyes as she gazes at Hull and the stranger as they approach the house) "and behold a pale horse" (the stranger on his pale horse is viewed in full screen through the window) "and his name that sat on him was Death." (Now both women are looking out the window and staring at the stranger, riding a pale horse). They are astounded and awestruck. Almost as an afterthought, Megan completes the verse: "and Hell followed with him."

Megan reads the first few lines in a rather mechanical way, creating the impression that such readings are a required part of her education. For her part, Sarah is barely listening as she bustles about the kitchen, occasionally interrupting Megan to ask her to fetch one ingredient or another. But as Megan reaches the last two verses, the women's interest is sharpened; when the passage bids them to "come and see" they look out the window and see

Hull's stranger—clearly identified by the passage and by the film editing as the "Pale Rider" of Revelation 6:8.

Hull enters the house and introduces the stranger to the women. The stranger goes into a bedroom to change. Sarah worries about their houseguest: "What is he, a gunman? A hired killer?" She begs, or orders, Hull to get rid of him that very day. Suddenly the stranger emerges from the bedroom dressed in clean clothing and a preacher's collar. They all stare at him in surprise; Sarah is disarmed. He breaks the ice by helping himself to whiskey and admiring the dinner spread. Megan looks at him adoringly and asks him to say grace. He complies: "For what we are about to receive, may we be truly thankful." Majestic music is heard in the background. The stranger, henceforth referred to as the Preacher, is now accepted as an ally, without fear or suspicion.

What follows is a series of confrontations between the LaHood family, which controls the town and owns a large industrialized mining operation, and the tiny community in Carbon Canyon. The LaHoods are attempting to force Hull and his fellow "tinpan" miners out of the canyon so that they can expand their operation. The conflict becomes increasingly violent when the small group rejects LaHood's offer to buy them out for $1000 apiece. It ends in a spectacular gunbattle between the lone Preacher, who represents the community, and the seven men—the marshal named Stockburn (John Russell) and his six deputies—hired by the LaHoods. Not surprisingly, the Preacher dispatches the deputies, one after another, and then does the same to Stockburn—but not before the marshal recognizes him, astonished at his presence. He then rides off into the mountains, his work in the town completed.

Several themes emerge. One is the contemporary ecological message. The tinpanners, despised by the LaHoods (who use hydraulic technology) are better stewards of the earth. The former are not out to get rich but simply to support themselves and build up their families. The LaHoods, on the other hand, blast the mountain with water, dam up the creek, and erode the soil. This last point is shown clearly when a tree simply topples over because the soil has eroded away from under its roots. The senior LaHood, whose sons have been terrorizing the Carbon Canyon community, complains that some politicians want to do away with hydraulic mining. "Raping the land, they call it." This ecological theme was no doubt intended to appeal to the sensibilities of its 1985 audience, though there may be some irony in the presence of an anti-industry theme in a Hollywood, big-business film.

A second theme concerns the "old-fashioned" or "pioneering" values of community, whose members help each other out and set down roots. The people of Carbon Canyon value an honest day's physical labor, as does the Preacher, who works alongside the others and opines that there are "few problems that can't be solved with a little sweat and hard work."

USE OF THE BIBLE (*PALE RIDER*)

The film contains a number of biblical allusions. The Preacher reminds LaHood that one cannot serve both God and mammon (Matt. 6:24, KJV); LaHood, in turn, tells the Preacher that he will have the blood of his friends on his own hands if they turn down his financial offer (echoing Pilate's washing his hands of Jesus' blood; Matt. 27:25). More significant are the film's two explicit biblical quotations. Psalm 23 is the basic text of Megan's soliloquy as she is burying her dog and praying for a miracle. She later reads Revelation 6:3–8 aloud to her mother, just as the Preacher arrives at their doorstep. Both of these have a prophetic function. As we have seen, Megan's recitation of Psalm 23 is a prayer for deliverance that is connected in some mysterious way to the appearance of the Pale Rider.

The role of Revelation 6:3–8 is more complex. The title of the film as well as the camera work and editing in this latter scene explicitly draw our attention to this passage as the key to the identity of the mysterious Preacher and his mission in Carbon Canyon. Certainly the Preacher has some elements in common with the horseman in Revelation 6:3–8. He rides a "pale horse." Like a ghost, he appears and disappears mysteriously and suddenly. He may even be a ghost, or, alternatively, he may have experienced resurrection. A "back-story" in which Stockburn had previously shot and killed him is supported by the bullet scars in the Preacher's back.

Another element of Revelation 6:3–8 is the repetition of terms pertaining to vision: "come and see" and "behold." Vision is also an important structural element in the film—most obvious perhaps when Megan reads the Revelation passage as she and her mother, and the viewers along with them, gaze out the window of the house to see the stranger riding towards them. But many other scenes portray characters viewing the action through windows. Most prominent are two sets of characters. The storekeepers are shown gazing at the violence that is enacted repeatedly outside their shop windows: Hull being beaten up by the LaHood boys and rescued by the stranger; a friend of Hull's being killed by the marshal and deputies; the final showdown between the marshal and the Preacher. The senior LaHood observes the same scenes through another window until he is killed by Hull and, fittingly, falls through the window, shattering the glass. Hence the terms pertaining to vision in the verse connect to the images of characters who gaze through windows and observe the surprising events being enacted before them.

Thus far, Revelation 6:3–8 coheres relatively well with the film's plot and characterization. More puzzling is the passage's conclusion that Hell followed after him. Certainly the Pale Rider was no stranger to violence and death, but the Hell that the tinpan miners were experiencing predated his arrival on the scene. The continuation of the text, which Megan did not read, is similarly ambiguous: "And power was given unto them [the rider and Hell] over the fourth part of the earth, to kill with sword, and with hunger, and with death, and with the beasts of the earth." The Preacher has extraordinary powers and does not hesitate to use whatever weapons are available to him (though he has no sword), and he exerts power, both with his weapons and by his very being. Yet his main mission is not to kill but to save this small community from destruction. The broader context of Revelation 6:3–8 identifies this rider as one of the elements unleashed when the Lamb opens up the seven seals—these forces are part of the divinely orchestrated apocalyptic plan of salvation. Nevertheless, it is not easy to see how the events in Carbon Canyon fit into a grand apocalyptic scheme. The tinpan miners experience ultimate redemption: the freedom to carry on as they have been doing without fear.

On closer scrutiny Revelation 6:3–8 does not do much more than identify the Preacher as a divine agent of justice or judgment. Although this passage is explicitly put forward as an interpretive key to the film, the book of Revelation contains another passage that seems far more fitting than the one that Megan reads to her mother. This is Revelation 19:11–16 (KJV):

> And I saw heaven opened, and behold a white horse; and he that sat upon him [was] called Faithful and True, and in righteousness he doth judge and make war.
>
> His eyes [were] as a flame of fire, and on his head [were] many crowns; and he had a name written, that no man knew, but he himself.
>
> And he [was] clothed with a vesture dipped in blood: and his name is called The Word of God.
>
> And the armies [which were] in heaven followed him upon white horses, clothed in fine linen, white and clean.
>
> And out of his mouth goeth a sharp sword, that with it he should smite the nations: and he shall rule them with a rod of iron: and he treadeth the winepress of the fierceness and wrath of Almighty God.
>
> And he hath on [his] vesture and on his thigh a name written, KING OF KINGS, AND LORD OF LORDS.

This passage also is not a perfect fit, but some of its details are far more descriptive of our Preacher than are those of the earlier passage. Here, too, is a white horse; the Preacher's horse is white though with some markings. Second, the Preacher showed himself to be faithful and true to the people of Carbon Canyon; he was there when needed and ultimately acted as the instrument through which they were forever freed from the threat to their lives, livelihood, and community. Third, the Preacher, like the rider of Revelation 19, judged and made war. He assessed the situation, made a judgment on the integrity of the LaHoods, chose his sides, and made war accordingly. Fourth, his eyes are remarkable, as the senior LaHood and Stockburn remark. Fifth, he no doubt had a name but no one knew it. Indeed, he deflected all attempts to draw him out about his past or his true identity. His wish to hide his identity is apparent even with those whom he helps the most and who love him: Hull, when he first makes his acquaintance, and, in an even more pointed way, Sarah, who has fallen in love with him but knows that there is no hope of a stable relationship with him. "Who are you? Who are you really?" she asks. He answers, "Really doesn't matter, does it?" She says, "No," but then again, why did she ask in the first place? Sixth, the Preacher is clothed in a vesture or uniform of sorts. The uniform refers not only to his clerical collar but to his overall outfit, which looks identical to that worn by the marshal and his deputies: dress shirt; pants; long, tailored overcoat; scarf or tie; and hat. It is no doubt meaningful that the marshal and the deputies number seven. Finally, while the Preacher is not followed by armies, he does "smite the nations," meaning those who are out to rape the land and exploit the people who work it with their own hands and sweat rather than with hydraulic machines.

The passage associates this "white rider" with Christ, resurrected, as he comes to prepare the world for the final incursion of God. The film implies the Preacher's own resurrection and shows that he, like the sword-toting Christ of Revelation 19, is on the side of right, but not afraid to fight. He is aware that the salvation of "his" people, his friends, can come about only by violence and by destroying the evil that the "bad guys" have created.

The Preacher is Christ-like in one other respect: his asceticism when it comes to women. Like Jesus, the Preacher is shown enjoying food, drink, and the company of others around the dinner table. He deals gently yet firmly with the love that Megan declares for him. He overlooks the childish way in which she meets his rejection, for after all, she is but a child. His feelings for Sarah are harder to fathom. When Megan accuses him of loving her mother instead of her, he neither accepts nor denies it. Later, when Sarah declares her love for him, she also acknowledges that there is no future to their relationship, as if she had assumed his love for her. Again, he neither accepts nor denies it, but he agrees that he cannot offer the sort of stability that Hull can.

Finally, his body is marked by wounds of an earlier time that should have killed him but did not. At the same time, the wounds that he inflicts on others often mark their hands, their feet or the middle of their foreheads, reminiscent of the wounds suffered by Christ. These are not meant to label them as Christ-like but rather to identify the Preacher as an avenging Christ figure. In this context, his killing of Stockburn not only settles an old score but possibly symbolizes Christ's final destruction of evil in the world in the eschatological times to come, as described in the book of Revelation.

Yet the question of the Preacher's identity is still not fully resolved at the end. Indeed, we may even wonder whether he has been completely conjured up by Megan herself. After all, he appears in the mist, and then more solidly, while she is praying, and perhaps even in answer to her prayer. He rides to their house at the very moment that she is reading the passage that describes him as a "Pale Rider," whether or not we see that designation as being entirely appropriate to his actions and role in the film. At the end of the film, her good-byes echo throughout the mountains as he is on his way back to wherever it is that he came from. The preacher is thus presented as God's answer to Megan's prayers. Indeed, Megan is the only character who seems to have a personal relationship with God.

The ephemeral nature of the Preacher's existence, suggested by the camera work, the strength of Megan's own desires, his tendency to appear and disappear unexpectedly, his fighting abilities, and the strong reaction that his presence provokes both from his friends and his enemies indicate that he is real enough, for now at least. Whether he is a "preacher" is another question. He seems oddly reluctant to do the sorts of things that people expect preachers to do: say grace, give a sermon, engage in "spiritual" labor. Further, he does not seem to hanker for a church, nor does he desire to expand his mission, as LaHood has offered. He often wears his clerical collar, but not always. It is missing, for example, from the scene in which Sarah declares her love for him, and it is also absent from view during the final shootout. He is never shown carrying or reading a Bible, nor does he invoke God at any time, even when he does say grace: "For what we are about to receive, may we be truly thankful." Yet the music that plays in the background of these and other scenes is distinctly religious, even "churchy"—and the big sky, big mountains, and breathtaking natural surroundings do imply a divine role in the entire story.

In the final analysis, we are left with a sense both of salvation and of mystery. The large landscape and the larger-than-life character of the Preacher are a fitting vehicle for portraying the eternal conflict between Good and Evil, here presented without the nuances that often complicate simple moral evaluation in our own lives. The use of Revelation is natural in this context, as this biblical book, too, is preoccupied with the conflict between Good and Evil. In addition, Revelation, like *Pale Rider*, accepts the necessity of violence as way of resolving the struggle. But ultimately the film's use of Revelation is superficial; exploration of either passage does not lead to deeper or unexpected insights into plot, character, or theme. The possible association of the mysterious stranger with supernatural or even divinely given powers is made amply clear by the vistas, the music, and his appearance during Megan's recitation of Psalm 23.

FILM SUMMARY (*NELL*)

Nell (1994) is another film that uses the biblical quotation in a way that does not add insight to the plot, characters, or theme of the film. *Nell* (directed by Michael Apted) tells the story of a young woman, Nell Kelty (Jodie Foster), who has grown up in a shack in the woods in rural North Carolina. Her existence is discovered only after the local doctor, Jerry Lovell (Liam Neeson), and the sheriff, Todd (Nick Searcy), come to the shack to register the death of her mother, whose body had been found by the local boy who used to deliver the groceries. Nell is hiding in a corner of the shack, but once they spot her she lashes out at them so suddenly and so violently that Todd is not even sure what he has seen. From a note found in an old family Bible, Jerry learns her name but nothing else. The young woman seems deranged. She mutters to herself in an indiscernible language; she shows no desire to communicate; indeed, she is utterly lacking in social skills.

Jerry is intrigued and puzzled enough to seek help. Perhaps he also feels a sense of responsibility, as a doctor and as a human being, simply because he is the one who found her. He arranges a meeting with a psychologist, Dr. Paula Olson (Natasha Richardson), at Charlotte University. In doing so, he inadvertently instigates a struggle over Nell's fate and her very soul. Paula, her colleagues, and her superiors at Charlotte University are intent on bringing Nell in for psychiatric examination, ostensibly for Nell's own good. But, as Jerry quickly notes, their altruism is seasoned by curiosity and ambition. A genuine "wild child" has not been found in many years; Nell affords a golden opportunity not only for study but also for academic publication, recognition, and promotion. Jerry, on the other hand, believes that Nell is capable of taking care of herself and of thriving on her own as long as she is left to her own devices.

Once knowledge of Nell is out, the events that Jerry set in motion by going to consult with Paula cannot be halted. In the process, Nell's personhood is violated in numerous ways. Paula insists on taking a blood sample from Nell; the act of forcefully putting the needle in her arm is akin to assault. When Paula produces a court order requiring that Nell be taken to the Charlotte University Hospital psychiatric facility, Jerry retaliates with a counter order stipulating that Nell give her consent. The situation is at an impasse; because no one can communicate the situation to Nell, she is unable to give her consent. The matter is taken to court, where the judge postpones his decision until three months hence. At that time, Nell's fate—whether to remain in the woods on her own or to enter the psychiatric facility for treatment and study—will be decided.

The key to Nell's fate is communication. Can she be taught to speak English, or, alternatively, can others learn her language? Or are her utterances merely gibberish and symptomatic of a fundamental lack of intelligence and competence? Jerry and Paula set up camp near Nell's house to observe her behavior and to attempt to decipher her speech. Paula establishes a high-tech home away from home, in a comfortable houseboat complete with a modern kitchen as well as audio and video surveillance equipment. This way, Paula can minimize her direct contact with both nature and with Nell. She can cook her store-bought food, observe Nell on videotape, and listen to her on audiotape. Jerry, on the other hand, camps on the property and cooks his food over an open fire. He spends time with Nell in her cabin and attempts to interact with her directly. He not only tries to get Nell to communicate with him, but he talks to her, unself-consciously and freely, about himself and his childhood. These self-revelations have an effect on Nell, who communicates with him in her own special language and in pantomime.

As time goes on, Jerry and Paula move from being competitors to being colleagues. Though there are some tensions, they share information and work together to try to figure out Nell's language. Ultimately Paula comes to share Jerry's sincere affection for Nell and to put aside her own career interests in favor of what is best for Nell. Paula gradually emerges from her houseboat, spends more time outdoors, and interacts with Nell directly and warmly. Soon Jerry and Paula come to realize that Nell speaks a form of English influenced by both the speech patterns of her aphasic mother (who could only speak out of one side of her mouth due to one or more strokes) and the linguistic patterns of the King James Version of the Bible, "the Word of the Lord," which her mother apparently read aloud to her on a regular basis. An additional factor is "twin speak;" Nell had had a twin sister, May, who had died sometime between the ages of 6 and 10 and whom Nell still missed terribly.

Not only does Nell speak an intelligible language, but she has both social and physical skills that allow her to function among people as well as in her environment. Nell has a special ability to sense when people are troubled or in pain, and she is able to comfort them with words and with touch. This gift is first evident in her brief contacts with the troubled wife of the Sheriff. Furthermore, Nell has the life skills needed to fend for herself. She splits wood and stacks it carefully for the winter; she carves bowls out of wood; and she can prepare food, play, swim, and live a full if simple and solitary life. Nell learns not only to tolerate but also to enjoy the presence of Jerry and Paula. The three form emotional bonds, and Nell recognizes the love that is developing between Jerry and Paula before they recognize it themselves. She does have fears, however. She distrusts all men except for Jerry, and she is afraid of stepping outdoors in the daytime.

For nearly three months, Jerry, Paula, and Nell live a life of peace, harmony, and daily discovery. But several days before the end of this period, they suffer a serious intrusion. A local journalist from Charlotte learns of Nell's existence and comes out to investigate. After a front-page article in the *Charlotte Tribune*, the place is surrounded by helicopters, TV crews, and journalists. Jerry and Paula spirit Nell away to the only place they can think of, namely, the hospital in Charlotte. Once there, Nell enters into a profound depression. She will not talk to anyone; even after Jerry smuggles her out of the hospital to a local motel, she is entirely uncommunicative.

The next day is the court hearing. Jerry and Paula hold out no hope that the judge will allow Nell to return to her own home in the woods. Al, Paula's autocratic superior at the hospital, is almost gloating in anticipation. But Nell surprises them all. At the hearing she rises and makes a brief but moving speech that shows her to be not only competent but insightful. She tells the court, "You have big things. You know big things. [She looks around at the people in the courtroom]. But you don't look into each other's eyes. And you are hungry for quietness. I've lived a small life; I know small things. I know loved ones [she turns to Jerry] Jerry, and Paula, and Ma and May. I know everyone goes. Everyone goes away. . . . [she turns to Jerry] Don't be frightened for Nell, don't weep for her. I have no greater sorrows than you."

The movie closes out with a brief scene from five years later. Nell hosts a birthday party, still in her wooded home, and invited are all those who had helped her, including, of course, Jerry and Paula, now married with a young daughter, Ruthie. The simple life lived in a shack in the woods has triumphed over the "big things" of modern city life and its many and complex institutions. Nell is no longer a fearful recluse but a capable woman who loves and is loved by her many friends.

USE OF THE BIBLE (*NELL*)

Just as Nell is a simple person, so is *Nell* a simple movie. The "right" side wins out in the end; all the loose ends are wrapped up. As in films such as *The Shawshank Redemption* and *Fried Green Tomatoes*, the Bible is used to develop the plot and some of the major themes. Nell's story revolves around an opposition between the natural world and "civilization." The film implicitly makes the case that most, perhaps all, people are better off resisting our society's tendency to institutionalize those who are ill or in other ways deviate from a norm defined by youth, health, and social interaction.[2] This theme is reinforced by the editing, which cuts back and forth, abruptly and quickly, between Nell's natural and beautiful landscape and the monumental and artificial structures of the big city. The camera shows us how these buildings appear to Nell, as she gazes up at them from the back seat of Paula's convertible: confining, dark, and somewhat unstable.

Emblematic of the artificiality of the institutional world is the glass picture window into which Nell crashes when Jerry and Paula bring her to the hospital. Ostensibly, the window provides an avenue to the outside world, albeit only a visual one, just as the hospital is ostensibly a place where Nell will be protected from those who want to exploit her for their own benefit. But the window, like the hospital, proves deceptive; both function as a barrier between Nell and the home she longs for. Nell is used to experiencing the world directly, not through a glass barrier; she is used to fending for herself, not being treated like a helpless patient. Nell's frightened reaction to "civilization" and its monuments contrasts meaningfully with Jerry's awestruck response to the beauty of the lake, mountains, and meadows where Nell finds her home. The frequent lengthy shots of Nell's natural environment, particularly during sunrise and sunset, evoke the biblical garden of Eden, a connection accentuated when Jerry exclaims, "God, it's beautiful!" during his first visit to the area. These scenes draw attention to the notion that the natural world is divinely created and is as close to paradise as any place can be. In this indirect way, God weighs in on Jerry's side to favor the natural world over the synthetic, "civilized" world and its institutions.

Jerry also gives voice to the film's statement about human dignity. He implicitly calls into question how our society treats those who are different from the norm. Rather than allowing them their human dignity, we shut them away in institutions—for their own good, so we say, but really for our own good. Jerry treats everyone with dignity, as we can see in the following exchange between Todd and Jerry, immediately after they see Nell for the first time. "What the hell is it, Jerry?" asks Todd. Jerry deliberately uses the feminine rather than picking up on Todd's use of the neuter pronoun: "She's scared." Todd persists, "We don't even know what that thing is." Jerry responds calmly, "She's a human being and she's frightened." "Well, what are you going to do?" asks Todd. Jerry says, "I'm going to talk to her, if I can." As in *Dead Man Walking*, the theme of human dignity echoes the conviction that humankind is made in God's image (Gen. 1:27) and hence all human beings, regardless of age, gender, ability, or other differentiating characteristics, are worthy of respect.

As in *The Apostle*, Nell's own Bible plays a significant role in plot and characterization. When Jerry first finds Nell, he also finds a very large, very old family Bible. He opens it up and finds a note: "The Lord led you here stranger. Gard [sic] my Nell. Good child. The Lord care you." From this he learns Nell's name, and, reluctantly, finds himself cast in the role of her "guardian angel." The age and size of the Bible imply a time when the mother, if not her children, lived within human society instead of outside it. The Bible also appears, briefly, in the sheriff's office. The sheriff receives some faxed information about Nell's mother, including a copy of a newspaper article reporting the rape of a woman after church. From this article, Jerry surmises that Nell must be the child of this rape; her birth was never registered and officially she does not exist. Jerry places the fax inside the Bible. The information that it conveys, together with the Bible, accounts for Nell's behavior and her situation in the woods all alone and unknown to any until her mother's death. Because of the rape, her mother has taught her to be fearful of men (whom she saw as the "evildoers" of Isaiah 1:4) and to beware of going outside in the daytime, when she can be easily seen. The children born of the rape, Nell and May, need no other company than themselves, and they develop their own games and their own language. Nell's mother read to them regularly from the "Word of the Lord" and also used it as a vehicle for understanding the world and her own experiences within it.

When Jerry returns the "Word of the Lord" to Nell, she opens it and asks him to read a specific passage to her: Isaiah 1:4 (KJV): "Ah sinful nation, a people laden with iniquity, a seed of evildoers. . . ." Nell recites along with him, evidence that she knows the passage well. When he comes to the word "evildoers" she stops him; he then realizes that it is a key to a word he had trouble understanding: *evedo* . . . , apparently meaning men. She explains as best she can that "evildoers" inflict a skewer in the belly, apparently the way in which her mother warned her against men and the possibility of rape.

Nell also resembles films like *The Shawshank Redemption*, *Pleasantville*, and *The Sixth Sense* in that it ascribes Christ-like qualities to its male protagonist. Jerry's family name, Lovell, reflects the warmth and respect with which he treats others, but it is also reminiscent of Christ, as the Western figure who is most strongly associated with love. Jerry's affinity with this aspect of Jesus is accentuated by the simple silver cross that he wears; the cross catches the light and draws attention to itself at crucial points in the action. Nell considers him to be her guardian angel, as she often says, and willy-nilly, self-consciously, he does set out to save her from the machinations of the medical profession as exemplified by Paula's boss, Al.

The large, old family Bible and the Isaiah quotation help to amplify our understanding of Nell's background and the way she was raised, but they are not central to the development of the film's main themes. The allusions to biblical themes, such as the perfection of the natural world and the association of the lead male character with Christ, help to confirm the moral evaluations suggested by other elements of the film, namely, that Nell and humankind more generally thrive in the natural environment and wilt in institutional settings and that Jerry is the "good guy" who has Nell's best interests at heart.

But the most prominent and problematic biblical elements in this film are its quotations from the Song of Songs. This book, also known as the Song of

Solomon or Canticles, is surely one of the most vivid and graphic of biblical books. In form, the Song is a compendium of sensual love poems that describe in both metaphoric and graphic terms the love between a man and a woman in all of its emotional, spiritual, and physical dimensions. This frankly and joyously erotic book may seem a surprising contribution to a canon of scripture that is often viewed, correctly or not, as a foundation for a chaste view of human existence. Its inclusion was associated with, and perhaps justified by, a line of interpretation according to which the song was not to be read literally but figuratively, as a song celebrating the love between God and Israel, or, within the Christian church, between God or Christ and the church. This reading transforms the erotic images and emotions into religious ones, while still maintaining the emotional and spiritual elements that emerge from a literal reading.

The Song employs various types of imagery, including military (e.g., 3:7, 4:4) and royal (e.g., 1:4, 3:11) images, in order to describe the relationship between bride and groom. Most pervasive, however, is imagery taken from the natural world. The female lover is the rose of Sharon, a lily of the valleys (2:1). Her eyes are like doves (4:1); her cheeks, like a pomegranate (4:3); her breasts, like fawns (4:5). The male lover comes leaping upon the mountains (3:8), his arms rounded gold set with jewels, his body like ivory (5:14). The spring— when flowers appear on the earth, the voice of the turtledove is heard, the fig tree puts forth its figs, and the fragrant vines are in the blossom (2:12–13)—is the time of their meeting. The garden (5:1), the vineyard (7:12), the pasture (6:3), and the orchard (6:11), are its place. The Song thus situates the love of the man and woman in a natural setting that recalls both the primordial and divinely planted garden of Eden and the cultivated spaces that are the product of human toil after humankind's departure from the garden.

The film quotes the Song of Songs three times. The first quotation occurs during the scene in which Jerry, urged on by Paula, joins Nell for her evening swim in the buff as a way of "curing" Nell of her fear of men. Highly self-conscious and awkward, the nude Jerry eases himself into the water and smiles hesitantly at Nell, his cross gleaming in the moonlight. After a brief moment, Nell approaches him, caresses his face, puts her arms and head on his chest, and recites, "Thou art beautiful, O my love, as Tirzah" (6:4). Jerry is startled, and perhaps also sexually aroused, but he is reassured when Nell swims away and laughs with joy. He asks, "Who's Tirzah?" Clearly he does not identify the quotation, and there is nothing in the film that would allow a viewer unfamiliar with the Song of Songs to identify it.

The other two quotations occur during the period of time that Nell spends away from home. In the first instance, Nell is in the hospital and has withdrawn into herself completely. Her unresponsiveness leads some of the observers to

suspect autism, or perhaps Asperger's syndrome, though her other characteristics do not fit the usual profile.[3] In an attempt to calm her down, Paula reads
to her from the Bible, from the Song of Songs, 6:1–6 (KJV). The passage is not
identified, and the viewers may or may not recognize the words from Nell's
earlier recitation to Jerry. Nell does not respond to Paula's reading. The final
quotation is again uttered by Nell as she is standing sadly on the balcony of
her room at the Days Inn, staring at the parking lot puddle and remembering
her sister: "Thou art beautiful, O my love, as Tirzah, comely as Jerusalem,"
says Nell softly as she stares into the water.

This last scene develops a poignant motif, namely, Nell's unresolved grief
for her sister. At many points in the film we are privy to Nell's recollections of
her twin sister; she replays their games and recalls how they would brush each
other's hair and whisper secrets in the bed they shared. The viewer learns, long
before the two doctors do, that much of the behavior that they find so puzzling is Nell's solo reenactment of the games she used to play with May. Nell's
grief is bearable so long as she is in her own home, where she and May used
to live together; there she can visit the place where May died and adorn May's
tiny skeleton with flowers. Proximity, and the fantasies and memories that
proximity encourage, stave off the worst of Nell's continuing grief for her sister. So when Jerry and Paula place Nell in the hospital, she descends into a
depression from which they cannot rouse her.

The turning point comes during her brief stay at the motel. She steps out
onto the balcony and gazes out over the stagnant water, so different from the
lake that surrounds her home in the woods. Unlike the lake, the puddle cannot harbor life but only dead leaves and other debris. But it is here that Nell
finally says good bye to May. She replays in her mind the scene of May's
drowning—that same, beautiful lake in which Nell swims every evening—and
softly recites the Song of Songs passage as tears roll down her face. After some
time, she comes back into the room and falls into a deep sleep. Jerry and Paula
eventually lie down with her on the bed and caress her protectively, as parents
do their sad children. We viewers sense, though we do not know for certain,
that something has changed, both for Nell and for her two doctors *cum* parents, who finally admit their love for each other. The next day, Nell secures
her freedom with her passionate short speech to judge, jury, and Jerry.

One inference from this series of quotations is that her mother must have
read this song many times within the context of the loving relationships in her
small family, and thus the passage provided a language of love for Nell, just as
Isaiah 1:4 provided a language of fear. That Paula has picked up on the importance of the song to Nell is implied by her reading this passage to calm Nell
during her traumatic hospital stay. Paula may have chosen it, however, simply
because of its pastoral setting—though the danger exists that the poem may

serve as a painful reminder to Nell of the home from which she was separated so abruptly.

What is a viewer to make of the first quotation, uttered while swimming nude with Jerry? In this instance, identifying the passage and placing it in its fuller context does not provide insight but rather misleads. This verse, in its context within the Song of Songs, implies an erotic relationship between the male speaker of these words and his female beloved. This context in itself would imply the presence, or the promise, of a sexually charged, romantic relationship between Jerry and Nell. Jerry does not deny that he finds Nell beautiful. He admits as much in a previous scene, when he watches Nell taking her evening swim with frank enjoyment. Paula initially views Jerry's fascination with Nell with some suspicion and unacknowledged jealousy. But Jerry is not at all interested in Nell romantically, nor is Nell interested in him. In keeping with her portrayal as a simple person who has insight into the souls of others, Nell "sees" early on that Jerry and Paula should be together.

Nell's attempt to be matchmaker between Jerry and Paula is the subject of two humorous scenes. In the first, Nell comes to Paula's boat and overhears a fierce argument between Jerry and Paula over whether to bring Nell to the hospital. Nell is very distressed. She orders Jerry and Paula to speak to each other and brings their foreheads together, touching. Paula grudgingly assures Nell that "Mommy loves Daddy, really" interpreting Nell's gesture not as an expression of concern for Jerry and Paula but as a sign that she, like a child, is distressed when her two caretakers argue with each other. The second scene is more explicit. After Nell has narrowly escaped humiliation and possible rape in a pool hall during her first outing to the town, Jerry and Paula decide that she needs to learn something about human sexuality beyond what her mother may have taught her. They buy her a book of drawings that depict human sexual activity. Nell is fascinated and comes over to them with a picture, asking them to name what the man and woman are doing. Jerry responds, "Making love." Nell then points to the man and woman in the picture and calls them Jerry and Paula. "Jerry, Paula making love." This embarrasses the two doctors, but not Nell, who is satisfied that Jerry and Paula should be together, as indeed they are by the end of the movie.

An awareness of the biblical context of Nell's "love" declaration to Jerry thus creates the anticipation of an erotic motif in the relationship between Jerry and Nell that does not cohere with the rest of their characterization and that quickly reaches a dead end. As Terrence Rafferty notes, the film "doesn't have the courage of its own sentimental convictions," precisely because of its asexuality.[4] Viewers who, like Jerry, do not know who "Tirzah" is may recognize that Nell is quoting from the Bible, but they are unlikely to be perturbed at its use in the context of Nell's entirely innocent affection for her guardian angel. Viewers who do know the Song of Songs, however, and attempt to use it in their interpretation of the film will travel down a dead end.

This misleading use of the Song of Songs raises an interesting question: Why is the erotic potential in the relationship between Jerry and Nell dismissed so easily by the movie and by Nell herself? Nell's sexual innocence and her lack of interest in experiencing sexuality for herself are simply presumed, not explored. Within the story, it can be explained by the fears with which her mother raised her. Nevertheless, Nell overcomes other fears as well as the social isolation imposed by her limited upbringing. Why not this one too?

Any answer to these questions will be speculative. Nevertheless, several suggestions come to mind. One is that Nell's sexuality would have eclipsed the main themes of the film (such as the conflict between nature and civilization), which require Nell's innocence. This same theme also necessitates Jerry's moral integrity, in order that viewers might continue to identify with him and hence with his viewpoint on the contrast between the natural life and the institutional "civilized" life. He cannot be seen as disrupting the doctor/patient relationship or as exploiting Nell's innocence in any way. He becomes her guardian angel from the moment he finds her mother's note inside the Bible, and he must remain true to that role. More subtly, we may suggest that there is a taboo in Hollywood's mainstream fare against showing those who somehow deviate from the norm as having sexual feelings or erotic experiences. In fact, "retarded" or other "simple" protagonists abound in the corpus of wholesome family films that convey a "high" set of moral values. The films *Being There* (1979), *Sling Blade* (1996), and *The Green Mile* (1999), all of which have "Bible" connections of one sort or another, come to mind. In all of these films, the protagonist may be intellectually or socially "challenged," but he or she is also morally and sexually innocent, and so, in some ways, superior to those so-called "normal" people who might judge him or her to be deficient.

Perhaps the closest meeting point between Song of Songs and the film *Nell* is in their mutual emphasis on the lushness and grandeur of nature. Both are replete with gorgeous images of trees, mountains, and breathtaking vistas, and the salutary effect—of love and passion in the case of the Song and peace and healing in the case of *Nell*—that nature can have on the human soul. But even this parallel is somewhat misleading, for the dominant natural images in the Song of Songs are not those of unsullied nature but those of cultivated gardens, vineyards, and orchards.

The party at the end of the film provides the traditional happy ending we expect from this genre of Hollywood film. But there are still some questions that can be asked. The opposition between the good natural world and the evil hospital might seem to advocate the "back to nature" lifestyle of self-sufficiency as an antidote and antithesis to the commodified nature of modern and postmodern urbanized existence. But, as Joseph Ntali has noted, Nell is not really a "natural" person. She, too, has been acculturated: "She spoke a mix of twin speech and . . . aphasic speech; her head was filled with myths planted by her mother. Nell is hardly the totally natural, wild creature that anthropologists dream of finding. And yet she is wild and natural enough for us . . . sufficiently distanced from our unnatural lives."[5] The movie is thus not a critique of culture, nor even of commodities. Nell (and her mother, before her death) do not grow their own food but rely on food deliveries from the supermarket in the local town. On her visit to that town, she is utterly captivated by the array of products in the supermarket. Despite the fact that she lives without electricity and modern appliances, Nell is essentially one of us; hence what is good for her is also good for us.[6]

CONCLUSION

In both *Pale Rider* and *Nell* the use of the Bible is superficial; one senses that biblical quotations are chosen only because they contain phrases ("love") or images ("pale horse") that fit a particular moment. In both cases the relationship between the passage and the film breaks down under scrutiny. Both presume little if any biblical knowledge on the part of their viewers and may reflect little if any direct knowledge or even interest on the part of the filmmakers; however, of course, this is speculative. Yet even in such cases, knowledge of the Bible has its uses. Though it does not provide insight into the film's plots and characters, it does occasionally illuminate the flaws and problems in these films and hence provides a starting point for critique.

Conclusion

From the sample of twelve popular films discussed in this book, one might be tempted to draw some general conclusions regarding the sorts of movies in which the Bible is likely to take a starring role. Top on the list would be prison films, featuring characters who are in jail (*The Shawshank Redemption, Dead Man Walking*), on their way to jail (*The Apostle*), or just released from jail (*Cape Fear*). One might even include in this category films about people who are trapped inside a television show (*The Truman Show, Pleasantville*), though this may be stretching the prison genre beyond its natural boundaries. Alternatively, one might conclude that the Bible is most prominent in films set in the South (*The Apostle, Dead Man Walking, Cape Fear, Fried Green Tomatoes, Nell*) or in films that depict supernatural events of one sort or another (*The Sixth Sense, Magnolia, Pulp Fiction, Pleasantville*).

Such generalizations would be misguided, however. First of all, at least one of the films we have chosen does not appear in any of these categories (*Pale Rider*). Second, and more important, our sample represents a minuscule percentage of the total and ever-growing number of films in which the Bible appears. Though a rudimentary statistical analysis is impossible, our studies do permit some comments regarding the uses, and misuse, of the Bible in popular film that others may wish to test on the basis of other movies.

Despite the cautions just expressed, it is possible to distinguish several broad categories of films in which the Bible appears. The first comprises films in which the use of the Bible is realistic and unsurprising, that is, films that are set in situations in which the use of the Bible contributes to verisimilitude. The movie *Nell*, for example, falls into this category. We are not surprised that a rural North Carolina family would have passed a large family Bible down through the generations and believed that it spoke to their own particular woes and joys.

184

Similarly, it is natural that preachers—whether in *Fried Green Tomatoes* or *The Apostle*—as well as nuns and chaplains—in *Dead Man Walking*—quote the Bible.

Second, there are films in which the quotation of or reference to the Bible is justified by the overall portrayal of specific characters. *Cape Fear*'s Max Cady, illiterate at the time of his imprisonment, learned to read in jail and read the Bible thoroughly. Mr. Norton, the warden of Shawshank Prison, values the Bible, or so he says. Megan, who lives far from any school, studies the Bible at home with her mother as she awaits her Pale Rider.

Third, some films portray characters whose recourse to biblical quotations is surprising. Examples include *Pulp Fiction* (Jules) and *The Sixth Sense* (Cole or his toy soldier). The biblical utterances in these cases require us to adjust our views of these characters and to accommodate their knowledge (even if faulty, as in Jules's case) and their appeal to the Bible.

Finally, in some films the biblical references appear out of nowhere and catch our attention precisely because they are so out of context. Thus we are caught unawares by the frog rain in *Magnolia* and by the fleeting references to Exodus 8:2, if we even notice them. The occasional references in *The Truman Show* and *Pleasantville* contribute to the films' humor (for example, Christof's imperious "Cue the sun") and hint at a metaphorical interpretation of the film (the very name Christof for a television show's producer; the TV repairman's references to Pleasantville as paradise).

In most of these films, the Bible is not only quoted but it also makes an on-screen appearance. In some films, the use of the Bible as a prop reveals something about the background of the characters (e.g., *Nell*) or about their interests and convictions (e.g., *The Apostle*). In some films a Bible is integral to the plot, as in *The Shawshank Redemption*, in which Andy's escape tool resides in his copy of the Bible, and in *Dead Man Walking*, in which the Bible has an important role in Matthew's spiritual salvation. At times it serves as a commentary on the action, as in *Pale Rider*, in which Megan's citations of Psalm 23 and Revelation 6 are meant to influence our interpretation of the Preacher and his role in Carbon Canyon. Interestingly, the only films in this selection in which the Bible does not appear as a prop are *Magnolia*, *Pleasantville*, and *The Truman Show*, the same films in which biblical references occur unexpectedly.

A number of these films use biblical books or stories as a model for their plots. Many of them employ Jesus imagery and, in so doing, evoke and adapt the classic Christian story of redemption and salvation that focuses on the supreme or perhaps superhuman role of one individual. This theme is evident in *The Shawshank Redemption*, in which Andy saves himself and restores hope to others, and *Nell*, in which Jerry Lovell is instrumental in saving Nell from the clutches of the psychiatric ward. The creation stories are used to good effect in *The Truman Show* and *Pleasantville*, in which the plot entails escaping from an ideal setting (for Truman) or transforming it (for the residents of Pleasantville). While they adapt the basic pattern of creation and fall (evident in Christian interpretations of the Genesis narratives), these films also subvert this pattern by implying that escape from Eden was a good, necessary, and even blessed event in the life of humankind. Just as Truman had to escape Seahaven in order to grow up, and the inhabitants of Pleasantville had to accept change and difference in order to realize their human potential, so perhaps it was necessary for Adam and Eve to leave the garden in order to allow life, and human history, to take shape. Creation and redemption, while perhaps the most prevalent paradigms in the films that we have studied, are not the only biblical models. The books of Ruth and Job shape the narratives and characters of *Fried Green Tomatoes* and *Cape Fear*, respectively; the life, mission, and writings of the apostle Paul are evident in the stories told in *The Apostle* and *The Shawshank Redemption*. This feature of the Bible's appearance in popular film testifies to the ongoing appeal of biblical narrative, an appeal that may help to account for the Bible's status as a perennial bestseller. It also reveals the degree to which biblical narratives have shaped the ways in which Western culture tells its stories.

All of our selected films employ biblical references, quotations, citations, and allusions. In most cases, these biblical texts have been filtered through the lens of Western culture. The most obvious example is the apple, which is immediately recognizable as a symbol of temptation and an allusion to the primordial couple's act of disobedience in Genesis 3, despite the fact that the biblical text does not identify the fruit of the forbidden tree. Other images, such as crucifixion, the burning bush, the plague of frogs, and the rainbow are similarly popular images that should be recognizable to everyone, even those who have never even opened a Bible. Occasionally, however, these films draw on lesser known passages, such as Psalm 130, whose use does not necessarily derive directly from the Bible but from liturgy, as is the case with the more familiar Psalm 23. This feature suggests popular culture depends on and uses other, and often, older cultural elements, even when viewers are not aware of them specifically.

One of the most difficult questions relates to whether audience knowledge of the Bible is essential, desirable, or even helpful when viewing these films. In most cases, one would guess that filmmakers do not assume that viewers will necessarily identify the biblical references. If an allusion, quotation, or reference is essential to the film (as it is, for example, in *Cape Fear* and *Fried Green Tomatoes*), it will be identified clearly within the film. In a film like *The Sixth Sense*, the quotation of Psalm 130 is never identified as such. Although the film is comprehensible to those who do not catch the reference, knowledge of the entire psalm adds depth to one's understanding of the film as a whole, and, in particular, of Cole's own struggle to come to terms with his special gift.

In some cases, however, one suspects that the filmmakers themselves do not have thorough or complete knowledge of the passages or images they themselves draw on. P. T. Anderson admits as much in his explanation of how the frogs came to have their dramatic role in *Magnolia*. In some cases, the biblical reference is not only superficial but misleading, as we have argued with respect to *Pale Rider* and *Nell*. In such cases both viewers and filmmakers would benefit from a higher level of biblical literacy.

Just as we draw on our cultural knowledge to interpret the biblical images and references in these films, so we bring various expectations to our interpretation of the various Bible-quoting characters in films. In this regard, there are two sets of competing expectations and stereotypes. One expectation is that the character who quotes the Bible is a sincere, spiritual, religious person whose viewpoint represents the moral center of the film. This set of expectations is fulfilled in some films, such as *Dead Man Walking*, in which Sister Helen represents, with integrity and refinement, the film's stand against the death penalty. But other characters subvert these expectations, such as the Bible-quoting villain of *Cape Fear* and the hypocritical reverend of *Fried Green Tomatoes*. These films imply a second set of cultural assumptions in which a preacher, or anyone else who habitually quotes the Bible, is viewed with some suspicion. *The Apostle* self-consciously challenges both of these stereotypes by portraying a compelling character who is far from perfect but who lives his life in constant and dynamic relationship with the Bible. The negative portrayals of preachers and other characters who quote the Bible has led some critics to accuse the film industry of being antireligious (Jewett, Medved). But in my view this criticism is misplaced. These films do not criticize the Bible so much as they show how the Bible can and has been misused by misguided, psychopathological, hypocritical, or self-serving individuals. Indeed, film corresponds to real life insofar as both realms provide evidence for the notion that the Bible can be used for good (as Sister Helen did for Matthew) or for ill (as Cady did for Bowden).

Finally, these films, whether intentionally or not, attest to the role of the interpretive community in the ways in which the Bible is used and abused by individuals. Characters like Sister Helen and the Apostle E. F. may be said to use the Bible appropriately insofar as they use it to improve the spiritual lives of others and to guide their own behavior. The reverend in *Fried Green Tomatoes* as well as the chaplain in *Dead Man Walking* may be criticized precisely because of their narrow understanding of the Bible and its application to the individual. The verbal tug of war between the warden and Andy in *The Shawshank Redemption* illustrates the interplay between the literal and figurative meanings of New Testament verses. These verses also function as a commentary of sorts on the film itself, exemplified in the cryptic and multilayered statement "Salvation lies within." This usage does not diminish the value of the Bible, but rather shows that it continues to be applicable outside of religious communities and for individuals in whose lives formal religion may play a very small part.

If filmmakers occasionally misuse the Bible, then characters within films also at times abuse the Bible. Our main example of course is Max Cady, who perverted the Bible for his own purposes. His story illustrates the dangers of a solitary and idiosyncratic reading of the Bible and implicitly provides support for the position that the Bible becomes dangerous particularly when it is read in a vacuum. History may provide examples where community readings may also be dangerous, but such exceptions do not necessarily undermine the value of reading the Bible within an interpretive community. The redemptive role of community is illustrated in the experiences of Sonny (the Apostle E. F.), which make it clear that some communities can be destructive, and others, redemptive. This contrast is apparent in the differences between the large and wealthy church that his wife, Jessie, "stole" from him after his discovery of her adultery and the small, poor church that he founded along with the Reverend Blackwell.

Just as movies reflect society's symbols and values, so they also shape them. Viewers whose lives do not include a Bible, or whose biblical knowledge is only indirect and general, will not recognize that Jules's version of Ezekiel 25:17 is phoney, nor are they likely to think through the differences between a literalist and a more nuanced understanding of *lex talionis*, "an eye for an eye." While popular movies generally convey a positive view of the Bible and its role as sacred scripture, those of us who regularly read and study biblical literature should worry about those for whom popular culture is the primary vehicle for biblical knowledge. Our mission, should we choose to accept it, is to help others to an educated reading of the text against which movies and other popular representations of the Bible may be tested.

Of course, the Bible is more than a window to popular culture. It is a cultural expression in its own right that must be placed in the context of the Ancient Near Eastern, Hellenistic, and Roman civilizations that are more foreign to us than Pleasantville was to Jennifer. And for many of us, the Bible is a powerful personal resource. The movies attest to the Bible's role in shaping the ways in which we tell our stories, mold our heroes, understand our experience, imagine our future, and explain ourselves to ourselves. If Andy, Sister Helen, and Jules are able to situate themselves within the moral and symbolic universe of the Bible, so may we in our different ways find a place there for ourselves.

If we brought Jules, Sister Helen, Mr. Norton, Megan, Nell, and Max Cady all together in a room, they would be able to agree on only one thing: Read the Bible! Malcolm would teach us to look up the hard words we do not know in the dictionary; the Apostle E. F. would ask us to listen to him read from the Psalms or Revelation, and Nell would respond to every situation by quoting "The Word of the Lord." As one who has taken them at their word, I cannot say whether reading the Bible will make one a happier or better person, but I do know one thing: the more familiar one becomes with the Bible, the more fun it is to go to the movies.

Notes

Introduction

1. For discussion of the epic genre, see Derek Elley, *The Epic Film: Myth and History* (London: Routledge & Kegan Paul, 1984).
2. Larry J. Kreitzer, *The New Testament in Fiction and Film: On Reversing the Hermeneutical Flow* (The Biblical Seminar 17; Sheffield: JSOT Press, 1993); idem., *The Old Testament in Fiction and Film: On Reversing the Hermeneutical Flow* (The Biblical Seminar 24; Sheffield: Sheffield Academic Press, 1994); idem., *Pauline Images in Fiction and Film: On Reversing the Hermeneutical Flow* (The Biblical Seminar 61; Sheffield: Sheffield Academic Press, 1999).
3. Robert Jewett, *Saint Paul at the Movies: The Apostle's Dialogue with American Culture* (Louisville, Ky.: Westminster/John Knox Press, 1993) and idem., *Saint Paul Returns to the Movies: Triumph Over Shame* (Grand Rapids: Wm. B. Eerdmans Publishing Co., 1999).
4. (Harrisburg, Pa.: Trinity Press International, 2002).
5. See, in particular, Margaret Miles, *Seeing and Believing: Religion and Values in the Movies* (Boston: Beacon Press, 1996); Joel W. Martin and Conrad E. Oswalt Jr., *Screening the Sacred: Religion, Myth, and Ideology in Popular American Film* (Boulder, Col.: Westview Press, 1995); Clive Marsh and Gaye Ortiz, eds., *Explorations in Theology and Film: Movies and Meaning* (Oxford: Basil Blackwell Publishers, 1997); Lloyd Baugh, *Imaging the Divine: Jesus and Christ-Figures in Film* (Kansas City, Mo.: Sheed & Ward, 1997).

Chapter 1: *The Truman Show* (Genesis)

1. The designation 2:4a refers to the beginning part of verse 2:4; 2:4b refers to the second part of the verse.
2. The use of the masculine pronoun to refer to God is not a theological statement; strictly speaking, God is neither male nor female. Rather, the masculine usage reflects the fact that God as a character in the book of Genesis is drawn in masculine terms and referred to by means of masculine nouns and pronouns. This usage is reflected also in this film, in which the relationship between Christof and Truman reflects that between God and Adam.
3. The consequences of disobedience for the snake and the primordial man and woman, described in Genesis 3:14–19, are often referred to as curses. Some feminist scholars, however, propose a more nuanced reading. See Phyllis Trible, *God and the Rhetoric of Sexuality* (Philadelphia: Fortress Press, 1978, 122–32; Carol Meyers, *Discovering Eve: Ancient Israelite Women in Context* (New York: Oxford, 1988), 95–121.

4. Although commentators regularly speak about the primordial woman as "Eve," it is important to note that she is named only at the very end of the creation accounts, when she and the man are about to leave Eden (3:20). For discussion of the significance of this point, see Mieke Bal, *Lethal Love: Feminist Literary Readings of Biblical Love Stories* (Bloomington: Indiana University Press, 1987), and Adele Reinhartz, *"Why Ask My Name?" Anonymity and Identity in Biblical Narrative* (New York: Oxford University Press, 1998), 86–88, 143–44.

5. For an accessible introduction to the discussion of biblical sources, see Richard E. Friedman, *Who Wrote the Bible?* (New York: Summit Books, 1987).

6. In his comment to Genesis 2:8 (the creation of the first man), the medieval Jewish commentator known as Rashi (Rabbi Shlomo ben Isaac, 1040–1105) states that "He who hears [this second creation story] might think that it is a different account entirely, whereas it is nothing else but the details of the former general statement" [Genesis 1:26–28]. See M. Rosenbaum and A. M. Silberman, eds., *Pentateuch with Targum Onkelos, Haphtaroth and Rashi's Commentary* (Jerusalem: The Silberman Family by arrangement with Routledge & Kegan Paul, 1929), 10.

7. The biblical text does not specify the type of fruit. The traditional identification of the fruit as an apple likely comes from the Latin, in which the word meaning "evil" (*malus*) resembles the word for "apple" (*malum*). See Victor P. Hamilton, *The Book of Genesis, Chapters 1–17* (Grand Rapids: Wm. B. Eerdmans Publishing Co., 1990), 191. Rashi (*Pentateuch*, 13) identifies the fruit as a fig, on the grounds that this is the only fruit specifically identified in the passage; to him it made sense to think that the tree that provided the forbidden fruit would also have provided the clothing that the couple would have needed as a consequence of tasting the fruit.

8. The apple, for example, appears as the symbol of temptation and sin in dozens of works of art, including a third-century fresco in the Catacomb of St. Piretro and St. Marcellino, Rome; thirteenth-century wall paintings in Hardham Sussess and Kelmscott, Oxfordshire; Michaelangelo's *Temptation and Fall* on the ceiling of the Sistine Chapel (1508–1512); and even the 1998 works by Philip Ratner (Israel Museum). For a lengthy listing and links to photographs, see the Web site at www.textweek.com/art/garden_of_eden.htm.

9. Unless otherwise noted, all movie quotations are taken from my own transcription.

10. The film was shot in a real town, Seaside, Florida, a theme-park-like planned community in northwest Florida. The blue dome is in Universal Studios in Anaheim, California. The show, as some film reviewers have noted, is "Candid Camera" run amok. See Richard Corliss, "Smile: Your life is on TV" (*Time* [June 1, 1999]: 151/21); Rita Kempley, "Truman: The Camera Never Sleeps" (*Washington Post* [June 5, 1998]: F1).

11. For publicity's sake, Meryl, in an interview, implies that she has no other life: "Well, for me there is no . . . there is no difference between a private life and a public life. My life . . . is my life, is the Truman Show. The Truman Show is . . . a lifestyle, it's a noble life. It is . . . a truly blessed life." But the shooting script provides a "backstory," not developed in the film, in which "Hannah [the actress who plays Meryl] would carefully rehearse all of the [sexual] moves and angles with Christof weeks in advance. (Hannah often described her feelings for her director as 'complicated.')." See Andrew Niccol, *The Truman Show: The Shooting Script* (New York: Newmarket Press, 1998), photo album, page 8.

Christof's relationship with Hannah, though not evident on screen, is consistent with the image built up in the movie of an egocentric creator who seeks to dominate his creation in every possible way.

12. Omnicam is not mentioned in the film itself, but see the backstory (*The Truman Show*, xiii). See also Steve Russell and Michael J. Gilbert, "Truman's Revenge: Social Control and Corporate Crime" (*Crime, Law and Social Change* 32 [1999]: 59–82). They argue that Truman's life has a corporate purpose, to the extent that it has any meaning at all. Presumably this means that his life is primarily intended to further the economic goals of the corporation.

13. Genesis does not explicitly convey Adam's reluctance to leave Eden, but it is implied in the statement in 3:4 that God drove him out (*vayegaresh*).

14. See, for example, *The Greatest Story Ever Told* and *Pale Rider.*

15. Sylvia, a.k.a. Lauren, also does this; after leaving the show, she launches a "Rescue Truman" campaign. She watches the Truman show incessantly and, so the film implies, is waiting for him when he finally walks off the set.

16. For a fascinating account of the human understanding of the world and its place in the cosmos, see Vincent Cronin, *The View from Planet Earth* (New York: William Morrow, 1981).

17. *Calender Live*, Movie Review (June 5, 1998).

18. See Margaret Kim Peterson, "What Else is On? Augustine, Pelagius, and The Truman Show" (*Pro Ecclesia* 8 [1999]:270). Viewers, unlike Truman, are free to do as they please, yet they "freely choose to behave as if they are enslaved." An amusing example is the man who watches the show while soaking in the bathtub. He continues to watch even when Truman is sleeping.

19. In contrast to Christof, who is a sore loser, God, in rabbinic literature, is portrayed as exulting in his creation's ability to best him. A famous story in the Babylonian Talmud (Tractate *Baba Metzia* 59b) illustrates this point:

> One day Rabbi Eliezer was in dispute with the other sages on a matter of law. He brought all the proofs of the world in support of his opinion but the other sages would not accept them. He said to them, "If the law is according to me, let this locust tree prove it." And the locust tree moved one hundred cubits. (Some say four hundred cubits.) The sages said to him, "The locust tree cannot prove anything." Then he said to them, "If the law is according to me, let this stream of water prove it." And the stream of water turned and flowed backward. They said to him, "The stream cannot prove anything." Then he said to them, "If the law is according to me, let the walls of the house of study prove it." The walls of the house of study began to topple. Rabbi Joshua reprimanded the walls, "If scholars are disputing with one another about the law, what business is it of yours?" The walls did not fall down out of respect for Rabbi Joshua and did not straighten up out of respect for Rabbi Eliezer. They are still so inclined! Then Rabbi Eliezer said to them, "If the law is according to me, let the heavens prove it." A voice then came forth from heaven and said, "Why do you dispute with Rabbi Eliezer? The law is according to him in every case." Thereupon, Rabbi Joshua rose to his feet and said, "'It is not in heaven'" (Deut. 30:12). Torah has been given once and for all at Mount Sinai. For You have already written in the Torah at Mount Sinai: 'After the majority one must incline'" (Exod. 23:2). Later on, Rabbi Nathan came upon Elijah the Prophet. He said to him, "What was the Holy One, Blessed be He,

doing at that moment?" Elijah said to him, "He was smiling and saying: 'My children have defeated Me! My children have defeated Me!'"

20. Niccol, *The Truman Show*, xi–xviii. This backstory was created for the amusement of the cast; the idea of using it as the basis of a documentary, or, more precisely, "mockumentary," was entertained but abandoned.

21. For the television show's use of product placement, see *The Truman Show*, xii–xviii. For product placement in this film, see Maurice Yacowar's "Thirteen ways of Looking at *The Truman Show*" (*Queen's Quarterly* 105/3 [1998]: 430). Yacowar comments that ubiquitous product placement makes *The Truman Show* an unending commercial. On product placement more generally, see Mary Kuntz, "The New Hucksterism" (*Business Week* [July 1, 1996]: 76–84); Janet Wasko et al, "Hollywood meets Madison Avenue: The Commercialization of US Films" (*Media, Culture and Society* 15 [1998]: 271–93); Marc Gunther, "Now Starring in *Party of Five*—Dr. Pepper" (*Fortune* [April 17, 2000]: 88–90).

22. This detail echoes the foreshadowing technique found in some of the classic Jesus films. For example, *From the Manger to the Cross*, an early silent film (1912), shows us a young Jesus carrying a plank on his shoulder that casts the shadow of the cross on the ground behind him.

23. For a variety of views on the Father-Son relationship in the Fourth Gospel, see Adele Reinhartz, ed., *God the Father in the Gospel of John.* (*Semeia* 85 [Atlanta: Society of Biblical Literature, 1999; appeared 2001]).

24. This photograph can be viewed at the following Web site: http://www. historyplace.com/kennedy/warhero.htm.

25. The reading of Genesis 3 as a "fall" is specific to Christian interpretations of Genesis. See Elaine Pagels, *Adam, Eve, and the Serpent* (New York: Random House, 1988).

26. For a summary of this approach, see D. Andrew Kille, *Psychological Biblical Criticism* (Minneapolis: Fortress, 2001), 109–24.

27. "Genesis 2.4b–3.24: A Myth about Human Maturation," *Journal for the Study of the Old Testament* 67 (1995): 3–26, cf. especially 7–8.

28. Ibid., 12.

29. Ibid., 26.

30. See 1 Peter 3:20–21, where the salvation of Noah and his family is compared with baptism. My thanks to Benjamin Wright who drew this reference to my attention.

31. *British Columbia Christian News* ([July 1998]: 18/7). Available at www. canadianchristianity.com.

32. *British Columbia Report* 9, no. 44 (1998): 60.

Chapter 2: *Magnolia* (Exodus)

1. See Donald B. Redford, "Pharaoh," in *The Anchor Bible Dictionary*, vol. 5, ed. David Noel Freedman (New York: Doubleday, 1992), 288–89.

2. One example among many is the popular "Frog and Toad" series, by Arnold Lobel (New York: Harper Collins), for children ages 4 to 8.

3. This episode (production code AABF14) was first aired April 4, 1999.

4. For an analysis of the religious elements in *The Simpsons*, see Mark I. Pinsky, *The Gospel According to the Simpsons* (Louisville, Ky.: Westminster John Knox, 2001).

5. Paul Thomas Anderson, *Magnolia: The Shooting Script* (New York: Newmarket Press, 2000), 206–07.

6. These and many other examples are listed at *www.ptanderson.com-Magnolia*.

7. Interview in the Austin American Statesman (1/6/00), available at www.ptanderson.com/articlesandinterviews/austin.htm.
8. Anderson, *Magnolia*, 12. Unless otherwise noted, quotations from the film are from my own transcription.
9. Ibid., 189.
10. Ibid., 189–91.
11. For an interesting study of the convergence of life and film, see Neal Gabler's *Life, the Movie: How Entertainment Conquered Reality* (New York: Albert A. Knopf, 1998).
12. In an on-line article entitled "Magnolia and the Signs of the Times: A Theological Reflection," (*Journal of Religion and Film* 4, no. 2 [2000]: 9), Mario de Giglio-Bellemare argues that the film exposes the "destructive intergenerational effects of the TV industry on people who are seeking liberation from oppressive structures and relationships which are in a state of crisis." This strikes me as overinterpretation, however, as does the criticism that the film underplays the other side of Los Angeles, namely, racial discrimination and poverty in the inner city. The latter elements are hinted at in the presence of the young rapper and in the sequence in which Jim Kurring arrests a woman for murder.
13. The absence of this quotation from the screenplay suggests that it, like the ubiquitous 8s and 2s, was added after Anderson learned about the biblical context of the frog plague.
14. This is not the only allusion to the Ten Commandments, however. Several of the characters are burdened by their offences against the commandment not to commit adultery; others (especially Donnie), by the offence of stealing and coveting; and Frank and Claudia by their complex relationships with their parents. The latter are violated by their parents but also violate them, hence violating the fifth commandment.
15. See Leslie Dick, "Review of *Magnolia*," *Sight and Sound* 10 (April 2000): 56–57.
16. Stephen Hunter ("Miraculous Magnolia," *Washington Post* [Jan 23, 2000]: G 2) views the intercession of a divine intelligence in the very fact that these random patterns make sense and views the small rapper child as the presence of God who "wanders through the landscape issuing small grace and tender mercies to a big miracle."
17. Anderson, *Magnolia*, 67.
18. Ibid., 194.

Chapter 3: *Dead Man Walking* (Leviticus)

1. This concept is the converse of the golden rule. Whereas the golden rule urges us to do unto others as we would have them do unto us, *lex talionis* warns that when it comes to acts of violence, as we have done unto others, so shall it be done unto us. Leviticus 19:17–18, 34 forms the biblical basis for the golden rule.
2. For religious perspectives on capital punishment, see Glen H. Stassen, *Capital Punishment: A Reader* (Cleveland: Pilgrim Press, 1998); Gardner C. Hanks, *Against the Death Penalty: Christian and Secular Arguments against Capital Punishment* (Scottdale, Pa.: Herald Press, 1997); Mark Lewis Taylor, *The Executed God: The Way of the Cross in Lockdown* (Minneapolis: Fortress Press, 2001).
3. Helen Prejean, *Dead Man Walking: An Eyewitness Account of the Death Penalty in the United States* (New York: Vintage Books, 1994).

4. Matthew is a composite of several men for whom the real Helen Prejean acted as spiritual advisor.

5. Unless otherwise noted, movie quotations are taken from my own transcriptions.

6. Tim Robbins, *Dead Man Walking: The Shooting Script* (New York: Newmarket Press, 1996), 55.

7. Roy Grundmann and Cynthia Lucia, "Between Ethics and Politics: An Interview with Tim Robbins," *Cineaste* 22 (1996): 6.

8. The amusing element of this scene is that the same actor who plays the state trooper, Clancy Brown, plays a sadistic prison guard in the film *The Shawshank Redemption*, whose IRS trouble sparked a major scam that is a crucial part of the plot line. Tim Robbins, who directed *Dead Man Walking* and is married to Susan Sarandon (Sister Helen), is the actor who played the male lead in *The Shawshank Redemption*.

9. Paul Lauritzen ("The Knowing Heart: Moral Argument and the Appeal to Experience," *Soundings* 81 [1998]: 228) suggests that the film illustrates the idea that moral theory may be subject to refutation by experience; in his view, watching a man being executed will alter one's views of capital punishment irrespective of the theory that one espouses.

10. This verse is also used in the pro-death-penalty lobby. See Jacob J. Vellenga, "Christianity and the Death Penalty," in *The Death Penalty In America*, 2d ed., ed. Hugo Adam Bedau (Chicago: Aldine Publishing Company, 1968), 124.

11. This argument, while perhaps effective in its cinematic context, is also alarming insofar as it implies a contrast between the stereotypical Old Testament God of vengeance and the New Testament God of grace and love, thereby grossly oversimplifying the complex theologies of both Jewish and Christian scriptures.

12. For an analysis of the prison film genre, see Bruce Crowther, *Captured on Film: The Prison Movie* (London: B. T. Batsford Ltd., 1989).

13. In the shooting script, Sister Helen's line reads, "I will be the face of Christ for you," reinforcing her identification of Christ in relationship to Matthew. See Robbins, *Dead Man Walking*, 129.

Chapter 4: *Fried Green Tomatoes* (Ruth)

1. For interesting analyses of the book of Ruth, see Edward L. Greenstein, "Reading Strategies and the Story of Ruth," in *Women in the Hebrew Bible*, ed. Alice Bach, 211–31 (New York: Routledge, 1999); Danna Nolan Fewell and David M. Gunn, "'A Son is Born to Naomi!' Literary Allusions and Interpretation in the Book of Ruth," in *Women in the Hebrew Bible*, ed. Alice Bach (New York: Routledge, 1999), 233–39.

2. New York: Random House, 1987.

3. Some have argued that the film does not deal honestly with racial issues. According to Lu Vickers ("*Fried Green Tomatoes:* Excuse me, did we see the same movie?" *Jumpcut* 39 [1996]:25–26), the film attempts to appeal to whites' attitudes about blacks as well as to straight people's attitudes about same-sex partnerships. It also carries out Hollywood's trend of depicting blacks as good Negroes—loyal, devoted, and harmless—and denies the horrors of being black in the South in the early part of the twentieth century. Similar views are expressed by Christine Holmlund ("Cruisin' for a Bruisin': Hollywood's Deadly [Lesbian] Dolls," *Cinema Journal* 34 [1994]: 32, 40); and Jeff Berglund ("The Secret's in the Sauce: Dismembering Normativity in *Fried Green Toma-*

toes," Camera Obscura—A Journal of Feminism and Film Theory 42 [1999]). On the possible lesbian elements of the relationship between Ruth and Idgie, see pp. 63–65. With respect to the depiction of blacks, there is some truth to this critique, though the scenes of the Ku Klux Klan do at least hint at the ongoing racism and violence experienced by blacks in this period.

4. Since this issue is not germane to the film's use of the Bible, or, indeed, to its main themes, I also will remain silent and urge readers to view the film for themselves if they have not yet done so.

5. Cf. *The Apostle* and *Dead Man Walking*.

6. Psalm 23 appears frequently in films. Contrast the use of this psalm in *The Apostle* (frequently in his own words and in his preaching) and in *Pale Rider*, in which it is also used in a funeral context. (See chapter 11.)

7. All film quotations are taken from my own transcription.

8. Here, as in *Pale Rider*, looking out through windows is important for focalizing the action.

9. For discussion of this verse, see Tod Linafelt, *Ruth* (Berit Olam; Collegeville, Md.: Liturgical Press, 1999), 78–79.

10. Mrs. Otis does not appear on screen. Initially Ninny's insistence that she is going home as soon as Mrs. Otis is better seems like a delusion. Yet when Mrs. Otis dies, Ninny does leave Rose Hill.

11. Rebecca Alpert, "Finding Our Past: A Lesbian Interpretation of the Book of Ruth," in *Reading Ruth: Contemporary Women Reclaim a Sacred Story* (New York: Ballantine Books, 1994), 92–93.

12. Most commentators believe Ruth to be a fictional "novella." See Edward F. Campbell, Jr., *Ruth* ([Anchor Bible Commentary 7; Garden City, N.Y.: Doubleday, 1975], 3–4).

13. Vickers, "Fried Green Tomatoes," 27.

14. Vicky L. Eaklor ("'Seeing' Lesbians in Film and History," *Historical Reflections* 20 [1994]: 325) comments on the "straight" gaze, according to which gay and straight film historians and critics alike demand proof of sexual intimacy before labeling two people homosexual.

15. Recent examples include *Kissing Jessica Stein* (2001) and *The Hours* (2002). For detailed studies of lesbians in film, see Andrea Weiss, *Vampires and Violents: Lesbians in Film* (New York: Penguin, 1993); and Daniela Sobek, *Lexikon lesbischer Frauen im Film* (Munich: Belleville, 2000).

Chapter 5: *Cape Fear* (Job)

1. For an overview of the biblical concept of Satan, see Victor P. Hamilton, "Satan," *Anchor Bible Dictionary*, vol. 5, ed. David Noel Freedman et al. (New York: Doubleday, 1992), 989.

2. For an introduction to Wisdom literature, see Stuart Weeks, *Early Israelite Wisdom* (Oxford: Clarendon Press, 1994); Roland E. Murphy, *The Tree of Life: An Exploration of Biblical Wisdom Literature* (New York: Doubleday, 1990); and Joseph Blenkinsopp, *Wisdom and Law in the Old Testament: The Ordering of Life in Israel and Early Judaism* (New York: Oxford University Press, 1995).

3. Les Keyser (*Martin Scorsese* [New York: Maxwell Macmillan, 1992], 218) suggests that Cady is competing with Sam for his wife and daughter, whom he lost due to his conviction and imprisonment. The two men are therefore "acting out Freud's primal dream." Rose Capp and Gabrielle Murray ("Two Views of the Martin Scorsese Film *Cape Fear*," *Metro* [6 January 1992]: 4–11) take this

psychoanalytic approach one step further to argue that one of the main themes is incestuous desire. Because his imprisonment deprived Cady of his own daughter, Cady seeks to seduce Bowden's daughter, thereby acting out the unacknowledged incestuous desires of a man whom he sees as his counterpart.

4. In the 1962 version of the film, there is no such moral ambiguity; Bowden has no secrets and no flaws, and Cady has little psychological complexity.

5. David Ansen (Review of *Cape Fear*, *Newsweek* [25 November 1991]: 56) refers to De Niro's character as a "Nietzschean superman disguised as a cigar-smoking Pentacostal sleazebucket."

6. For a hilarious send-up of Scorsese's *Cape Fear*, see *The Simpsons*' episode, "Cape Feare," (9F22, originally aired 7 October 1993), which plays upon the film's ominous music and some of its most striking images, such as Cady's clinging to the chassis of the Bowdens' car.

7. Capp and Murray ("Two Views," 5) note that while the opening frames set Danielle up as the one through whose perspective the narrative will proceed, this position does not remain stable; her perspective is quickly collapsed, and she is positioned as the one who is seen rather than the one who sees.

8. Peter Travers ("Through a Lens Darkly," *Rolling Stone* 618 [28 November 1991]: 101–103) suggests that Cady's desecration of the cinema is the first sacrilege in the film.

9. All film quotations are taken from my own transcriptions.

10. In an ironic move, Cady's lawyer is played by Gregory Peck, the actor who played Sam Bowden in the 1962 film.

11. Max is not the only cinematic "bad guy" to quote the Bible. Other examples include Jules in *Pulp Fiction* and the "Reverend" Harry Powell in Charles Laughton's *The Night of the Hunter* (1955).

12. This phrase is included in the King James Version of Luke 23:34, but later translations, based on a critical comparison of the Greek manuscripts, tend to omit this phrase, which is absent from many of the manuscripts.

13. Ansen, *Cape Fear*, 56.

14. Cady is here quoting from *Der Cherubinische Wandersmann* (The Cherubic Wanderer).

15. Terrence Rafferty, "Mud," *New Yorker* (2 December 1991): 158.

16. Christopher Deacy, *Screen Christologies: Redemption and the Medium of Film* (Cardiff: University of Wales Press, 2001), 135.

17. Some critics have commented that the film is anti-Christian and intends to portray evangelicals and the South in a negative way. See S. Klawards, Review of *Cape Fear*, *Nation* 253 (23 December 1991): 826–28; James D. Davis, "So how did evangelicals become the bad guys in movies?" *Toronto Star*, reprinted from Fort Lauderdale Sun-Sentinel (2 January 1992): F3; John Freed, "Violence and Southern films." *Films in Review* 43 (September/October 1992): 307–9.

18. Keyser, *Martin Scorsese*, 215–16.

19. Ansen (*Cape Fear*, 56) refers to Cady as a Pentecostal, but this may be inaccurate. Although Cady uses biblical language and quotation in a way that is similar to the cinematic portrayal of some Pentecostal preachers (e.g., Sonny in *The Apostle*), he is completely unconnected to any community, Christian or otherwise.

Chapter 6: *The Sixth Sense* (Psalms)

1. Psalm 130 is generally classified as a lament psalm, though it shares features of the thanksgiving psalm genre as well. See C. S. Rodd, "Psalms" in *The Oxford*

Bible Commentary, ed. John Barton and John Muddiman (Oxford: Oxford University Press, 2001), 400.

2. Mitchell Dahood describes Psalm 130 as the lament of an individual, who "pleas for deliverance from sin that has plunged him into a spiritual abyss which he likens to the depths of the netherworld." For a detailed commentary on the Psalm, see Mitchell Dahood, *Psalms 101–150* ([Anchor Bible Commentary 17A; Garden City, N.Y.: Doubleday, 1970], 234–37).

3. The funeral service in the *Anglican Book of Common Prayer* is the source of the famous phrase "ashes to ashes, dust to dust," based on Genesis 3:19.

4. On death and the afterlife, see Rodd, "Psalms," 363, and, at greater length, Colleen McDannell and Bernhard Lang, *Heaven: A History* (New Haven, Conn.: Yale University Press, 1988).

5. Unless otherwise indicated, film quotations are taken from my own transcriptions.

6. The filmmakers seem to have been concerned that even then we might not "get it." After Malcolm's secret has been revealed, the film scrolls quickly through a number of the scenes where the trick was played most skillfully. Among them is the restaurant anniversary scene. What initially looked like Anna's anger at Malcolm's tardiness is now clearly a profoundly sad occasion that she marks on her own by going to the restaurant where he had proposed marriage to her. We now notice more carefully both the solo meal and the table set for one, both in the restaurant and at home. The inclusion of these scenes is a guide to the viewer, to be sure, but, like the explanation of a joke, is both unnecessary and also detracts, if only slightly, from the pleasure at being "had."

7. Cf., for example, the materials at the following Web site www.petersnet.net/research/retrieve.cfm?RecNum=1230#prayers.

8. One example is the 2000 film *Frequency*, in which a son, played by Jim Caviezel, communicates with his dead father (Dennis Quaid) through a ham radio.

Chapter 7: *Pulp Fiction* (Ezekiel)

1. J. Galambush, "Ezekiel," *The Oxford Bible Commentary*, ed. John Barton and John Muddimann (Oxford: Oxford University Press, 2001), 534.

2. For discussion of this theme, see Wayne T. Pitard, "Vengeance," in *The Anchor Bible Dictionary*, vol. 6 (New York: Doubleday, 1992), 786–87.

3. See Susan Niditch, *War in the Hebrew Bible: A Study in the Ethics of Violence* (New York: Oxford University Press, 1993), 4–5.

4. J. Galambush, "Ezekiel," 552.

5. Pitard, "Vengeance," 786.

6. Anthony Lane, "Degrees of Cool," *New Yorker* (10 October 1994): 95–97.

7. The visual reference to the fictional "Red Apple" cigarettes may be a spoof of product placement.

8. For a discussion of the chronology and time in film, see Seymour Chatman, *Story and Discourse: Narrative Structure in Fiction and Film* (Ithaca, N.Y.: Cornell University Press, 1978), 62–95.

9. This is noted by Dana Polan, *Pulp Fiction* (London: British Film Institute, 2000), 24.

10. Unless otherwise noted, movie quotations are taken from my own transcriptions.

11. John Simon ("From Pulp to Pap," *National Review* [21 November 1994]:70) states that this sequence is a nod to the Bible-spouting killer in Charles Laughton's *Night of the Hunter* (1955). Tarantino himself says that the speech was inspired by Sonny Chiba, whose characters in the *Shadow Warriors* television

series always denounced the tyranny of evil before putting a sword through the heart of the "bad guy" at the end of each episode (Jami Bernard, *Quentin Tarantino: The Man and his Movies* [New York: HarperPerennial, 1995], 203).

12. The HPL Tarantino FAQ Page (home.earthlink.net/~hidprod/qtfaq.html) lists eleven possibilities for the contents of the briefcase, including the satchel of diamonds from *Reservoir Dogs*; a cache of gold bricks; Marsellus's soul; and an Oscar, which would make sense of Pumpkin's question, "Is that what I think it is?"

13. The visitor is played by Christopher Walken, who here parodies his famous role as a Vietnam veteran in *The Deer Hunter* (James Naremore, *More Than Night: Film Noir In Its Contexts* [Berkeley: University of California Press, 1998], 217).

14. Butch's opponent is called Willis in the screenplay, but Wilson on the screen. All of these names play on the actor's name, Bruce Willis. See Quentin Tarantino, *Pulp Fiction* (New York: Hyperion, 1994), 88.

15. It is interesting to note that Honey Bunny's tough speech as reiterated here differs slightly from the opening scene of the film. Initially she said, "Any of you fuckin' pricks move and I'll execute every motherfuckin' last one of you!" When the scene is replayed she says, "Any of you fuckin' pricks move and I'll execute every one of you motherfuckers! Got that?!" Woods (*King Pulp*, 105) believes that this difference is intentional, intended to keep the viewer off balance. This feature (no doubt co-incidentally) parallels a similar pattern in the Hebrew Bible, according to which a repeated speech is never identical to its initial iteration. For a detailed study, see George Savran's *Telling and Retelling: Quotation in Biblical Narrative* (Bloomington: Indiana University Press, 1988).

16. This has been noticed on at least some of the *Pulp Fiction* fan pages on the internet, but not, interestingly enough, in many of the publications that discuss this film. See, for example, Woods (*King of Pulp*, 95), who accepts the quotation at face value.

17. Irwin Mark ("Pulp & The Pulpit: The Films of Quentin Tarantino and Robert Rodriguez," *Literature & Theology* 12 [March 1998], note 12), identifies (in my view, mistakenly) this phrase as an allusion to Ezekiel 34. While it is true that shepherds figure prominently in that chapter, they are not divine but the human, faulty leadership of Israel, and they are castigated for failing to lead their flock properly.

18. See Woods, *King Pulp*, passim, for sources.

19. Films (such as *The Godfather* and sequels) and television series (such as *The Sopranos*) have accustomed us to see Italian characters involved with organized crime. Similarly, many films (e.g., the *Lethal Weapon* series) have black characters in violent roles. See Norman K. Kenzin, *Reading Race: Hollywood and the Cinema of Racial Violence* (London: SAGE, 2002).

20. It is possible, however, that Vince is motivated primarily by fear of Marsellus—perhaps fear that Marsellus would punish Vince as he had punished Antwan—rather than loyalty.

21. In the hit television series *The Sopranos*, the main characters, mafia men, all wear crosses around their necks and profess some level of adherence to Catholicism.

22. Bernard, *Quentin Tarantino*, 201.

23. Tarantino, *Pulp Fiction*, 142.

24. Polan, *Pulp Fiction*, 30. For a detailed discussion of the bathroom and the attendant themes of soiling and cleansing, see Sharon Willis, "The Boy's Room," *Camera Obscura—A Journal of Feminism and Film Theory* 41 (1993): 1–37.

Chapter 8: *The Apostle* (John)

1. John 21 is commonly considered to be an epilogue. See Raymond E. Brown, *The Gospel According to John XII–XXI* (AB 29A; Garden City, N.Y.: Doubleday & Co., 1970), 1077–82.
2. Edith L. Blumhofer, *Aimee Semple McPherson: Everybody's Sister* (Grand Rapids: Wm. B. Eerdmans Publishing Co., 1993), 190.
3. Carl Greiner ("The Apostle: A Psychiatric Appraisal," *Journal of Religion and Film* 3 [1999]: 1–9) argues that the Apostle may have a psychiatric disorder. The sense of his complexity may come from his disorder. There is an interplay between psychiatric disorders and religious claims that may be seen in the Apostle's characterization as narcissistic, with a tendency toward grandiosity, arrogance, limited empathy, violence, and gift for oratory.
4. Film quotations are taken from my own transcription.
5. The undisputed letters of Paul are Romans, 1 and 2 Corinthians, Galatians, 1 Thessalonians, Philippians, and Philemon. For an introduction to Paul's letters, see Bo Reicke, *Re-Examining Paul's Letters: The History of the Pauline Correspondence* (Harrisburg, Pa.: Trinity Press International, 2001).
6. For a discussion of the historicity of Acts, see Gerd Luedemann, *Paul, Apostle to the Gentiles: Studies in Chronology* (Philadelphia: Fortress Press, 1984).
7. On the development of early Christian preaching, see C. H. Dodd, *The Apostolic Preaching and its Developments* (Grand Rapids: Baker Book House, 1980 [originally published 1936]).
8. Cf. Charles H. Barfoot and Gerald T. Sheppard, "Prophetic vs. Priestly Religion: The Changing Role of Women Clergy in Classical Pentecostal Churches." *Review of Religious Research* 22 (September 1980): 2–17.
9. Robert Duvall indicates that this scene is based on Matthew 18:20: "For where two or three are gathered in my name, there am I in the midst of them" (KJV), although this verse is not quoted in the film. See Bill Blizek and Ronald Burke. "The Apostle: An Interview with Robert Duvall," *Journal of Religion and Film* 2 (1998) <http://www.unomaha.edu/~wwwjrf>.
10. Roy Anker, "Preacher Man," *Christianity Today* 4 (March/April 1998): 10. Cf. also Daphne Merkin, "Secret Dreams: Gingerbread Man and *The Apostle*," *New Yorker* (2 February 1998): 81–82. A recent example is *O Brother Where Art Thou?*, which caricatures a Bible salesman. See also the Reverend in *Fried Green Tomatoes*.
11. Conrad Ostwalt, "The Apostle," *Church History* 68 (1999): 666–71.
12. Jerome Larcher, "L'Evangile selon Sonny." *Cahiers du Cinema* 525 (1997): 44.

Chapter 9: *The Shawshank Redemption* (1 Corinthians)

1. On the complex issue of Pauline chronology, see John Knox, *Chapters in a Life of Paul*, rev. ed. (Macon, Ga.: Mercer University Press, 1987).
2. In Stephen King, *Different Seasons* (New York: Signet, 1982).
3. Film quotations are from my own transcription.
4. The biblical quotations in this film are from the King James Version.
5. Birds are used throughout the film as a symbol of freedom. For example, Brooks, the old convict, has a bird named Jake whom he cares for and then releases immediately before he himself is released on parole. During the scene in which Andy plays a recording of a Mozart aria, birds are seen flying above the prison yard. For further discussion, see Robert Jewett, "A Problematic

Hope for the Shamed in *The Shawshank Redemption*," in *Saint Paul Returns to the Movies: Triumph Over Shame* (Grand Rapids: Wm. B. Eerdmans Publishing Co., 1999), 168.

6. For a discussion of the philosophical issues raised by this film, see Luc Bovens, "The Value of Hope," *Philosophy and the Phenomenological Research* 59 (September 1999): 667–681.

7. This is probably an error, however. See *www.movie_mistakes.com/film.php?filmid=1146* for a brief explanation of this and other errors in the film.

8. Andy's escape leaves a big hole, not only in the prison wall but in the lives of the other prisoners. See Stephen Brown, "Optimism, Hope and Feel Good Movies: The Capra Connection," in *Explorations in Theology and Film: Movies and Meaning*, ed. Clive Marsh and Gaye Ortiz (Oxford: Basil Blackwell Publishers, 1997), 226.

9. Jewett, *St. Paul Returns*, 164. Cf. also Michael Medved (Review of *The Shawshank Redemption*, *New York Post* [23 September 1994]: 46), who objects to the association of the Bible with the warden.

10. Jewett, *St. Paul Returns*, 180.

Chapter 10: *Pleasantville* (Revelation)

1. See Jean-Pierre Ruiz, "Revelation," *The New Oxford Annotated Bible*, 3rd ed., ed. Michael D. Coogan, et al. (New York: Oxford University Press, 2001), 421 (New Testament).

2. Susan Niditch, *Chaos to Cosmos: Studies in Biblical Patterns of Creation* (Atlanta: Scholars Press, 1985), 71.

3. This and other quotations are based on the *Pleasantville* shooting script, available at the Web site "Screenplays for you" (www.sfy.iv.ru), but they are modified to correspond to the dialogue in the film itself.

4. See chapter 1 for a brief summary of the creation stories.

5. The TV repairman is played by Don Knotts, an actor who was prominent in a number of 1950s and 1960s situation comedies, such as *The Steve Allen Show* and *The Andy Griffith Show*, and in a number of movies in which he played a military officer (*No Time for Sergeants* [1958], *Wake Me When It's Over* [1960]). His connection to the sitcom genre adds a comic edge to his TV repairman role, and his military film persona is alluded to in his imperious behavior with respect to David. On the relationship between *Pleasantville* and the television sitcom, see George Aichele, "Sitcom Mythology," in *Screening Scripture: Intertextual Connections between Scripture and Film*, ed. George Aichele and Richard Walsh (Harrisburg, Pa.: Trinity Press International, 2002), 100–119.

6. Linda A. Mercadante, "The God Behind the Screen: *Pleasantville* and *The Truman Show*," *Journal of Religion and Film* 5 (October 2001): 5.

7. On *Pleasantville* as a social critique of suburbia, see Douglas Muzzio and Thomas Halper, "Pleasantville? The Suburb and Its Representation in American Movies," *Urban Affairs Review* 37 (2002): 543–574.

Chapter 11: *Pale Rider, Nell*

1. Film quotations are taken from my own transcriptions.

2. On this issue generally, see the classic works by R. D. Laing, *Self and Others* (London: Tavistock Press, 1961) and *The Politics of Experience* (New York: Ballantine, 1967).

3. According to the DSM IV (299.80), Asperger's Syndrome or Asperger's Disorder "is a neurobiological disorder." Those who have the disorder typically have normal intelligence and language development but also exhibit some autistic-like behaviors as well as deficiencies in social and communication skills. They show two of the following: "marked impairments in the use of multiple nonverbal behavior such as eye-to-eye gaze, failure to develop peer relationships appropriate to developmental level, lack of spontaneous seeking to share enjoyment, interests or achievement, and a lack of social or emotional reciprocity." Nell does not seem to fit this description, as she has eye contact, not only with Paula and Jerry but also with Mary, the Sheriff's wife, and she seems very interested in communication. The party she hosts at the end of the film suggests that she has developed appropriate social relationships.

4. Terrence Rafferty, "Woman on Top," *New Yorker* 70, no. 42 (19 December, 1994): 107–108.

5. Joseph Natali, "The Call of the Crank: Being Captivated by Nell," in *Speeding to the Millenium: Film and Culture 1993–95* (Albany, N.Y.: SUNY Press, 1998), 388.

6. See David Desser and Garth S. Jowett, ed., *Hollywood Goes Shopping* (Minneapolis: University of Minnesota Press, 2000).

Bibliography

Aichele, George, and Richard Walsh. *Screening Scripture: Intertextual Connections between Scripture and Film*. Harrisburg, Pa.: Trinity Press International, 2002.

Alleva, Richard. "Beaten to a Pulp: Tarantino's 'Fiction.'" *The Catholic Journal* (18 November 1994): 30–31.

Alpert, Rebecca. "Finding Our Past: A Lesbian Interpretation of the Book of Ruth." In *Reading Ruth: Contemporary Women Reclaim a Sacred Story*, edited by Judith A. Kates and Gail Twersky Reimer, 91–96. New York: Ballantine Books, 1994.

Anderson, Paul Thomas. *Magnolia: The Shooting Script*. New York: Newmarket Press, 2000.

Anker, Roy M. "Lights, Camera, Jesus: Hollywood looks at itself in the mirror of the Messiah." *Christianity Today* 44:6 (22 May 2000): 58–63.

———. "Preacher Man." *Christianity Today* 4 (March/April 1998): 10.

Ansen, David. Review of *Pulp Fiction*. *Newsweek* (10 October 1994): 71.

———. Review of *Cape Fear*. *Newsweek* (25 November 1991): 56.

Bal, Mieke. *Lethal Love: Feminist Literary Readings of Biblical Love Stories*. Bloomington: Indiana University Press, 1987.

Banks, Robert. "The Drama of Salvation in George Stevens's *Shane*." In *Explorations in Theology and Film: Movies and Meaning*, edited by Clive Marsh and Gaye Ortiz, 59–71. Oxford: Basil Blackwell Publishers, 1997.

Barfoot, Charles H. and Gerald T. Sheppard. "Prophetic Vs. Priestly Religion: The Changing Role of Women Clergy in Classical Pentecostal Churches." *Review of Religious Research* 22 (September 1980): 2–17.

Barton, John, and John Muddiman. *The Oxford Bible Commentary*. New York: Oxford University Press, 2001.

Bedau, Hugo Adam, ed. *The Death Penalty in America*. Chicago: Aldine Publishing Company, 1964.

Berglund, Jeff. "The Secret's in the Sauce: Dismembering Normativity in *Fried Green Tomatoes*." *Camera Obscura—A Journal of Feminism and Film Theory* 42 (1999): 3–11.

Bernard, Jami. *Quentin Tarantino: The Man and his Movies*. New York: HarperPerennial, 1995.

Bingham, Dennis. *Acting Male: Masculinities in the Films of James Stewart, Jack Nicholson, and Clint Eastwood*. New Brunswick, N. J: Rutgers University Press, 1994.

Bishop, Ronald. "Good Afternoon, Good Evening, and Good Night: *The Truman Show* as Media Criticism." *Journal of Communication Inquiry* 24 (January 2000): 6–18.

Blake, Richard A. "Redeemed in Blood: The Sacramental Universe of Martin Scorsese." *Journal of Popular Film and Television* 24 (spring 1996): 2–9.

Blenkinsopp, Joseph. *Wisdom and Law in the Old Testament: The Ordering of Life in Israel and Early Judaism.* New York: Oxford University Press,1995.

Blizek, Bill, and Ronald Burke. "The Apostle: An Interview with Robert Duvall." *Journal of Religion and Film* 2 (1998).

Blumhofer, Edith L. *Aimee Semple McPherson: Everybody's Sister.* Grand Rapids: Wm. B. Eerdmans Publishing Co., 1993.

Bondi, Roberta. "Glimpses of Goodness." *Christian Century* 117 (15 March 2000): 314.

Botting, Fred, and Scott Wilson. "By Accident: The Tarantinian Ethics." *Theory, Culture & Society* 15 (1998): 89–113.

Bovens, Luc. "The Value of Hope." *Philosophy and Phenomenological Research* 59 (September 1999): 667–681.

Brooker, Peter, and Will Brooker, ed. *Postmodern After-Images: A Reader in Film, Television and Video.* London: Arnold, 1997.

Brown, Raymond E. *The Gospel According to John XII–XXI.* AB 29A. Garden City: Doubleday, 1970, 1077–82.

Brown, Stephen. "Optimism, Hope and Feel-good Movies: The Capra Connection." In *Explorations in Theology and Film: Movies and Meaning,* edited by Clive Marsh and Gaye Ortiz, 219–232. Oxford: Basil Blackwell Publishers, 1997.

Campbell, Edward F. Jr. *Ruth.* Anchor Bible Commentary 7. Garden City, N.Y.: Doubleday, 1975.

Canby, Vincent. Review of *Cape Fear. New York Times* (13 November 1991): C17, C22.

Capp, Rose, and Gabrielle Murray. "Two Views of the Martin Scorsese Film *Cape Fear.*" *Metro* (6 January 1992): 4–11.

Castellitto, George P. "Imagism and Martin Scorsese: Images Suspended and Extended." *Literature/Film Quarterly* 26 (1998): 23–29.

Chatman, Seymour. *Story and Discourse: Narrative Structure in Fiction and Film.* Ithaca,N.Y.: Cornell University Press, 1978.

Chattaway, Peter. "Exit from Eden and a False Messiah: *The Truman Show* is full of ambiguous, possible anti-Christian religious references." *British Columbia Report* 9 (July 1998): 60.

Chattaway, Peter. "*The Truman Show*: Echoes of Gnosticism." *BC Christian News* 18 (July 1998).

Chavez, Linda. "Faith and the Movies." *Jewish World Review* (4 February 1998).

Chumo, Peter N. "The Next Best Thing To A Time Machine: Quentin Tarantino's *Pulp Fiction*" *Post Script* 15 (Summer 1996): 16–28.

Coogan, Michael D., et al, eds. *The New Oxford Annotated Bible,* 3rd ed. New York: Oxford University Press, 2001.

Corliss, Richard. "Divine Inspiration." *Time* (Canadian ed.) (26 January 1998): 52–54.

———. Review of *Cape Fear. Time* 138 (11 November 1991): 84–85.

Corliss, Richard. "Smile: Your Life's On TV!" *Time* 151:21 (1 June 1998):76–79.

———. "Wild Child or Wise Woman?" *Time.* (12 December 1994): 92.

Coursodon, Jean-Pierre. "Magnolia: One Froggy Evening" *L'Actualite* 469 (2002): 13–19.

Cronin, Victor. *The View From Planet Earth.* New York: William Morrow, 1981.

Crowther, Bruce. *Captured on Film: The Prison Movie.* London: B. T. Batsford Ltd., 1989.

Dahood, Mitchell. *Psalms 101–150.* Anchor Bible Commentary 17A. Garden City, N.Y.: Doubleday & Co., 1970.

Dargis, Manohla. "Quentin Tarantino on *Pulp Fiction*." In *Quentin Tarantino: Interviews*, edited by Gerald Peary, 66–69. Jackson, Miss.: University Press of Mississippi, 1998.

Davis, James D. "So how did evangelicals become the bad guys in movies?" *Toronto Star*, reprinted from *Fort Lauderdale Sun-Sentinel* (2 January 1992): F3.

Davis, Todd F. and Kenneth Womack. "Shepherding the Weak: The Ethics of Redemption in Quentin Tarantino's *Pulp Fiction*." *Literature Film Quarterly* 26 (1998): 60–66.

Dayton, Donald W. *Theological Roots of Pentecostalism*. Studies in Evangelicalism No. 5. Metuchen, N.J.: Scarecrow Press, Inc., 1987.

Deacy, Christopher. *Screen Christologies: Redemption and the Medium of Film*. Cardiff: University of Wales Press, 2001.

DeGiglio-Bellemare, Mario. "Magnolia and the Signs of the Times: A Theological Reflection." *Journal of Religion and Film* 4, no. 2 (October 2000).

Denby, David. "Pulp Fiction." In *Flesh and Blood: The National Society of Film Critics on Sex, Violence, and Censorship*, edited by Peter Keough, 227–231. San Francisco: Mercury House, 1995.

———. Review of *Magnolia*. *New Yorker* (20 December 1999): 102–3.

———. "The Spook Doctor." *New Yorker* (23/30 August 1999): 200–202.

Dennis Hopper/Quentin Tarantino. "Blood Lust Snicker Snicker in Wide Screen." *Grand Street* 49 (1994): 11–22.

Denzin, Norman K. *Reading Race: Hollywood and the Cinema of Racial Violence*. London: SAGE, 2002.

Dick, Leslie. Review of *Magnolia*. *Sight and Sound* 10 (April 2000): 56–57.

Dodd, C.H. *The Apostolic Preaching and its Developments*. Grand Rapids: Baker Book House, 1980 (originally published 1936).

Dowd, Maureen. "Clint Eastwood sees *Pale Rider* as a basic conflict between good and evil." *New York Times* (21 July 1985): B1, B25.

Dowell, Pat and John Fried. "Pulp Friction: Two Shots at Quentin Tarantino's Pulp Fiction." *Cineaste* 21 (1995): 4–7.

Duvall, Robert. *The Apostle: A Screenplay by Robert Duvall*. New York: October Books, 1997.

Eaklor, Vicki L. "'Seeing' Lesbians in Film and History." *Historical Reflections* 20 (1994): 321–333.

Ebert, Robert. Review of *Pleasantville*. www.suntimes.com/ebert/ebert_reviews/1998/10/102302.html (5 July 2002).

Ebert, Roger. Review of *Cape Fear*. *Chicago Sun Times* (11 November 1991).

———. Review of *Dead Man Walking*. www.suntimes.com/ebert/ebert_reviews/1996/01/1015393.html.

Eby, Lloyd. "Is Hollywood Hostile to Religion?" *The World & I* 13 (4 January 1998): 92.

Fewell, Danna Nolan, and David M. Gunn, "'A Son is Born to Naomi!' Literary Allusions and Interpretation in the Book of Ruth." In *Women in the Hebrew Bible*. Edited by Alice Bach, 233–39. New York: Routledge & Kegan Paul, 1999.

Fitzmyer, Joseph A. *The Gospel According to Luke X–XXIV*, Anchor Bible Commentary 28A. Garden City, N.Y.: Doubleday & Co., 1985.

Freed, John. "Violence and Southern films." *Films in Review* 43 (September/October 92): 307–9.

Freedman, David Noel, et al, eds. *The Anchor Bible Dictionary*. 2 Vols. New York: Doubleday, 1992.

Friedman, Richard E. *Who Wrote the Bible?* New York: Summit Books, 1987.

Gabler, Neil. *Life, The Movie: How Entertainment Conquered Reality.* New York: Alfred A. Knopf, 1998.

Gallafent, Edward. *Clint Eastwood: Filmmaker and Star.* New York: Continuum, 1994.

Garcia, Maria. Review of *Cape Fear. Films in Review* 43 (January/February 92): 43–44.

Gerstel, Judy. "The New Oz: Pleasantville." *Toronto Star* (23 October 1998): D1–D2.

Giroux, Henry A. "Pulp Fiction and the Culture of Violence." *Harvard Educational Review* 65 (summer 1995): 299–314.

Gliatto, Tom. "Nell." *People Weekly* 21 (12 December 1994): 42.

Graham, David John. "Redeeming Violence in the Films of Martin Scorsese." In *Explorations in Theology and Film: Movies and Meaning,* edited by Clive Marsh and Gaye Ortiz. Oxford: Basil Blackwell Publishers, 1997.

Greenstein, Edward L. "Reading Strategies and the Story of Ruth." In *Women in the Hebrew Bible.* Edited by Alice Bach, 211–31. New York: Routledge & Kegan Paul, 1999.

Greiner, Carl. "The Apostle: A Psychiatric Appraisal." *Journal of Religion and Film* 3 (1999): 1–9.

Groen, Rick. "A Splash of colour in a black-and-white world." *Globe and Mail* (23 October 1998): D1–D2.

Grundmann, Roy and Cynthia Lucia. "Between Ethics and Politics: An Interview with Tim Robbins." *Cineaste* 22 (1996): 4–9.

Guerif, Francois. *Clint Eastwood.* Translated by Lisa Nesselson. New York: St. Martin's Press, 1986.

Gunther, Marc. "Now Starring in *Party of Five*—Dr Pepper." *Fortune* 141, no. 8 (17 April 2000): 88–90.

Hamilton, Victor. *The Book of Genesis, Chapters 1–17.* Grand Rapids: Wm. B. Eerdmans Publishing Co., 1990.

Hansen, Miriam. "Chameleon and Catalyst: The cinema as an alternative public sphere." In *The Film Cultures Reader,* edited by Graeme Turner, 391–419. London: Routledge & Kegan Paul.

Hanks, Gardner C. *Against the Death Penalty: Christian and Secular Arguments against Capital Punishment.* Scottdale, Pa.: Herald Press, 1997.

Hinson, Hal. "A Tale of Giving the Devil His Due." *Washingtonpost.com,* 12 January 1995.

Howe, Desson. Review of *Pulp Fiction. Washingtonpost.com,* 14 October 1994.

———. Review of *Dead Man Walking. Washingtonpost.com,* 12 January 1995.

Hunter, Stephen. "Miraculous Magnolia." *Washington Post,* 23 January 2000, G1–7.

Holmlund, Chris. "Cruisin' for a Bruisin': Hollywood's Deadly (Lesbian) Dolls." *Cinema Journal* 34 (fall 1994): 31–51.

Irwin, Mark. "Pulp & The Pulpit: The Films of Quentin Tarantino and Robert Rodriguez." *Literature & Theology* 12 (March 1998):70–81.

Jewett, Robert. *Saint Paul at the Movies: The Apostle's Dialogue with American Culture.* Louisville, Ky.: Westminster/John Knox Press, 1993.

———. *Saint Paul Returns to the Movies: Triumph Over Shame.* Grand Rapids: Wm. B. Eerdmans Publishing Co., 1999.

Kauffmann, Stanley. "Alabama and Elsewhere." *New Republic* (3 February 1992): 28–29.

———. "Shooting Up." *New Republic* (14 November 1994): 26–27.

———. "Southern Discomfort." *New Republic* 205, no. 24 (9 December 1991): 28–29.

Kempley, Rita. "Truman: The Camera Never Sleeps." *Washington Post,* 5 June 1998, F1.

————. "Pulp Fiction." *Washingtonpost.com*, 14 October 1994.

Kenzin, Norman K. *Reading Race: Hollywood and the Cinema of Racial Violence*. London: SAGE, 2002.

Keyser, Les. *Martin Scorsese*. New York: Maxwell Macmillan, 1992.

Kille, D. Andrew. *Psychological Biblical Criticism*. Minneapolis: Fortress Press, 2001.

King, Stephen. *Different Seasons*. New York: Signet, 1982.

Klawans, S. Review of *Cape Fear*. *Nation* 253 (23 December 1991): 826–28.

Knapp, Laurence F. *Directed By Clint Eastwood: Eighteen Films Analyzed*. Jefferson, N.C.: McFarland & Co., Publishers, 1996.

Knox, John. *Chapters in a Life of Paul*, rev. ed. Macon, Ga.: Mercer University Press, 1987.

Kolker, Robert Phillip. *A Cinema of Loneliness: Penn, Stone, Kubrick, Scorsese, Spielberg, Altman*. 3rd ed. Oxford: Oxford University Press, 2000.

Kraps, John M. "The Gospel According to Eastwood." *The Christian Century* 102 (August 1985): 740.

Kroll, Jack. "Stephen King's Jailhouse Rock" *Newsweek* 24, no. 13 (26 September 1994): 64.

Kuntz, Mary. "The New Hucksterism." *Business Week* 3482 (1 July 1996): 76–84.

Laing, R. D. *Self and Others*. London: Tavistock Press, 1961.

————. *The Politics of Experience*. New York: Ballantine, 1967.

Landy, Marcia. *Italian Film*. Cambridge: Cambridge University Press, 2000.

Lane, Anthony. "In The Big House." *New Yorker* 70, no. 30 (26 September 1994):108–110.

————. "Degrees of Cool." *New Yorker* 70, no. 32, (20 October 1994): 95–97.

Larcher, Jerome. "L'Evangile selon Sonny." *Cahiers du Cinema* 525 (1997): 43–51.

Lauritzen, Paul. "The Knowing Heart: Moral Argument and the Appeal to Experience" *Soundings* 81, nos. 1–2 (spring/summer 1998): 213–234.

Linafelt, Tod. *Ruth*. Berit Olam. Collegeville, Md.: Liturgical Press, 1999.

Luedemann, Gerd. *Paul, Apostle to the Gentiles: Studies in Chronology*. Philadelphia: Fortress Press, 1984.

Lyden, John. "To Commend or To Critique? The Question of Religion and Film Studies." *Journal of Religion and Film* 1 (1997): 1–9.

Maslin, Janet. "Prison Tale by Stephen King Told Gently, Believe It or Not." *New York Times*, 23 September 1994, C3.

Maslin, Janet. "Condemned to Repeat the Joy of the Past: Pleasantville." *New York Times*, 23 October 1998, E23.

Maslin, Janet. "A Woman Within a Wild Child, As Revealed by Jodie Foster." *New York Times*, 14 December 1994, C2, C20.

Matties, Gordon. "Religion & Film: Capturing the Imagination." *Journal of Religion and Film* 2 (1998): 1–4.

McAlister, Linda Lopez. "Nell." *The Women's Show—WMNF-FM (88.5)*, 14 January 1995.

————. Review of *Fried Green Tomatoes*. www.inform.umd.edu./EdRes/Topic/WomensStudies/FilmReviews/fried-tomatoes-mcalister.

McDannell, Colleen, and Bernhard Lang. *Heaven: A History*. New Haven, Conn.: Yale University Press, 1988.

McEver, Matthew. "The Messianic Figure in Film Christology Beyond the Biblical Epic." *Journal of Religion and Film* 2, no. 12 (October 1998): 1–9.

Medved, Michael. *Hollywood vs. America: Popular Culture and the War on Traditional Values*. New York: HarperCollins, 1992.

Mercadante, Linda A. "The God Behind the Screen: *Pleasantville* & *The Truman Show.*" *Journal of Religion and Film* 5, no. 2 (October 2001): 1–7.

Merkin, Daphne. "Secret Dreams: Gingerbread Man and *The Apostle.*" *New Yorker* (2 February 1998): 81–82.

Meyers, Carol. *Discovering Eve: Ancient Israelite Women in Context.* New York: Oxford University Press, 1988.

Miller, Toby, Nitin Govil, John McMurria, and Richard Maxwell. *Global Hollywood.* London: BFI, 2001.

Morgan, David. Movie Review "Back to Cape Fear." *LA Times Calendar* (17 February 1991): 7.

Murphy, Roland E. *The Tree of Life: An Exploration of Biblical Wisdom Literature.* New York: Doubleday, 1990.

Muzzio, Douglas and Thomas Halper. "Pleasantville? The Suburb and Its Representation in American Movies." *Urban Affairs Review*, 37, no. 4 (March 2002): 543–574.

Naremore, James. *More Than Night: Film Noir in Its Contexts.* Berkeley: University of California Press, 1998.

Natoli, Joseph, ed. *Speeding to the Millennium: Film & Culture 1993–1995.* Albany: SUNY Press, 1998.

Neely, Kent. "Praxis: Editorial Statement" *Journal of Dramatic Theory and Criticism* 13, no. 1 (fall 1998): 157–160.

Neil, Vidmar and Phoebe C. Ellsworth. "A Christian Perspective." In *The Death Penalty in America*, 3d ed., ed. Hugo Adam Bedau, 370–375. New York: Oxford University Press, 1982.

Niccol, Andrew. *The Truman Show: The Shooting Script.* New York: Newmarket Press, 1998.

Niditch, Susan. *Chaos to Cosmos: Studies in Biblical Patterns of Creation* (Atlanta: Scholars Press, 1985).

———. *War in the Hebrew Bible: A Study in the Ethics of Violence.* New York: Oxford University Press, 1993.

Nolan, Steve. "The Books of the Films: Trends in Religious Film-Analysis." *Literature and Theology* 12 (1 March 1998): 1–15.

Olsen, Mark. "Singing in the Rain." [Magnolia] *Sight and Sound* 10 (March 2000): 26–28.

O'Sullivan, Michael. "Truman: A Surreally Big Show." *Washingtonpost.com*, 5 June 1998.

Ostwalt Jr., Conrad E. "The Apostle." *Church History* 68 (September 1999): 666–673.

———. "Hollywood and Armageddon: Apocalyptic Themes in Recent Cinematic Presentation." In *Screening the Sacred: Religion, Myth, and Ideology in Popular American Film*, ed. Joel W. Martin and Conrad E. Oswalt Jr., 55–63. Boulder: Westview Press, 1995.

———. "Religion & Popular Movies." *Journal of Religion and Film* 2 (1998): 1–5.

Pagels, Elaine. *Adam, Eve, and the Serpent.* New York: Random House, 1988.

Pakaluk, Michael. "Christians Can Morally Support the Death Penalty." In *The Death Penalty: Opposing Viewpoints*, ed. Carol Wekesser, 67–81. San Diego: Greenhaven Press, 1991.

Peterson, Margaret Kim. "What Else is On? Augustine, Pelagius, and *The Truman Show.*" *Opinion, Pro Ecclesia* 8 (1999): 268–273.

Pevere, Geoff. "Using cliches with conviction." *Globe and Mail*, 23 September 1994, C12.

Pinsky, Mark I. *The Gospel According to the Simpsons.* Louisville, Ky.: Westminster John Knox Press, 2001.

Plate, S. Brent. "Religion/Literature/Film: Toward a Religious Visuality of Film." *Literature and Theology* 12 (1998): 16–38.

Polan, Dana. *Pulp Fiction*. London: British Film Institute, 2000.

Prejean, Helen. *Dead Man Walking: An Eyewitness Account of the Death Penalty in the United States*. New York: Vintage Books, 1994.

Rafferty, Terrence. "Mud." *New Yorker*, (2 December 1991): 156–159.

———. "Woman on Top." *New Yorker* 70, no. 42 (19 December 1994): 107–108.

Rapping, E. "Yuppie Horror Films." *Progressive* 56 (June 92): 34–36.

Reicke, Bo. *Re-Examining Paul's Letters: The History of the Pauline Correspondence*. Harrisburg, Pa.: Trinity Press International, 2001.

Reinhartz, Adele. *"Why Ask My Name?" Anonymity and Identity in Biblical Narrative*. New York: Oxford University Press, 1998.

Reinhartz, Adele, ed. *God the Father in the Gospel of John*. Semeia 85. Atlanta: Society of Biblical Literature, 1999 (appeared 2001).

Riggs, Larry W., and Paula Willoquet-Maricondi. "A Wild Child Goes Shopping: Naturalizing Commodities and Commodifying Nature in Nell." In *Hollywood Goes Shopping*, ed. David Desser and Garth S. Jowett, 330–353. Minneapolis: University of Minnesota Press, 2000.

Robbins, Tim. *Dead Man Walking: The Shooting Script*. New York: Newmarket Press, 1996.

Romney, Jonathan. "The New Paranoia: Games Pixels Play." *Film Comment* 34, no. 6 (November/December 1998): 39–43.

Rothwell, Kenneth S. *A History of Shakespeare on Screen: A Century of Film and Television*. Cambridge: Cambridge University Press, 1999.

Russell, Steve and Michael J. Gilbert. "Truman's revenge: Social Control and Corporate Crime." *Crime, Law & Social Change* 32 (1999): 59–82.

Savran, George. *Telling and Retelling: Quotation in Biblical Narrative*. Bloomington: Indiana University Press, 1988.

Schickel, Richard. "Eastwood plays God, or maybe Death." *Time* (1 July 1985): 62.

Seger, Dr. Linda. "Making the Script Work: Thinking about *Nell*." http://screenwriters.com/hn/writing/swls/columns/nell.html. (5 July 2002).

Sharrett, C. Review of *Cape Fear*. *USA Today Magazine* 120 (March 1992): 69.

Shelley, Marshall. "The Death Penalty: Two Sides of a Growing Issue." In *Capital Punishment*, edited by Thomas Draper, 96–110. New York: H.W. Wilson Company, 1985 (reprinted from Shelley, Marshall. "The Death Penalty: Two Sides of a Growing Issue." *Christianity Today* 28 (1984): 14–19).

Simon, John. "From Pulp to Pap." *National Review* (21 November 1994): 70–71.

———. "Stick Figures in Depth." *National Review* 43 (16 December 1991): 56–58.

Smith, Paul. *Clint Eastwood: A Cultural Production*. Minneapolis: University of Minnesota Press, 1993.

Smith, Gavin. "Robert Duvall." *Film Comment* 23 (1997): 30–40.

Smith, Gavin. "When you know you're in good hands: Quentin Tarantino." *Film Comment* 30 (30 April 1994): 32–36.

Sobek, Daniela. *Lexikon lesbischer Frauen im Film*. Munich: Belleville, 2000.

Stassen, Glen H. *Capital Punishment: A Reader*. Cleveland: Pilgrim Press, 1998.

Stern, Lesley. *The Scorsese Connection*. Bloomington, Ind.: Indiana University Press, 1995.

Stoddart, Helen. "'I Don't Know Whether To Look At Him Or Read Him': *Cape Fear* and Male Satisfaction." In *Me Jane: Masculinity, Movies and Women*, edited by Pat Kirkham and Janet Thumim, 194–202. New York: St. Martin's Press, 1995.

Stone, Bryan P. "Religion and Violence in Popular Film." *Journal of Religion and Film* 3 (April 1999):1–11.

Tarantino, Quentin. *Pulp Fiction: A Quentin Tarantino Screenplay*. New York: Hyperion, 1994.

Taylor, Mark Lewis. *The Executed God: The Way of the Cross in Lockdown*. Minneapolis: Fortress Press, 2001.

Taylor, Simon J. "'A Searching Experience': Salvation in the film *Dead Man Walking* and R.C. Moberly." *Theology* 101 (March/April 1998): 104–111.

Tesson, Charles. "Les demons de la fiction." *Cahiers du Cinema* (February 2001): 44–46.

Travers, Peter. "Through a Lens Daily." *Rolling Stone 618* (28 November 1991): 101–103.

Trible, Phyllis. *God and the Rhetoric of Sexuality*. Philadelphia: Fortress Press, 1978.

Turan, Kenneth. Movie Review: "Pleasantville: In 'Pleasantville,' Life in the 50's Pales by Comparison." *Los Angeles Times*, 23 October 1998, 1.

Turan, Kenneth. Movie Review: "Duvall's 'Apostle': Blessed by Its Creator." *LA Times Calendar*, 17 December 1997, 1.

Turan, Kenneth. Movie Review: "Prayers for the Victims, Victimizer." *LA Times Calendar*, 29 December 1995, 1.

Turan, Kenneth. Movie Review: "His Show of Shows." *LA Times Calendar*, 5 June 1998, 1.

Turner, Graeme ed. *The Film Cultures Reader*. New York: Routledge & Kegan Paul, 2002.

Vickers, Lu. "*Fried Green Tomatoes:* Excuse Me, Did We See the Same Movie?" *Jump Cut* 39 (1996): 25–30.

Wasko, Janet, Mark Phillips, and Chris Purdie. "Hollywood meets Madison Avenue: the commercialization of US films." *Media, Culture, and Society* 15 (1993): 271–293.

Watkins, Greg. Book Review: "Screening the Sacred: Religion, Myth, and Ideology in Popular American Film." *Journal of Religion and Film*: 1–4: http://www.unonaha.edu/~wwwjrf/BR_sacred.htm

Weeks, Stuart. *Early Israelite Wisdom*. Oxford: Clarendon Press, 1994.

Weiss, Andrea. *Vampires and Violets: Lesbians in Film*. New York: Penguin, 1993.

Willis, Sharon. "The Boy's Room." *Camera Obscura—A Journal of Feminism and Film Theory* 41 (September 1993): 1–37.

Wilson, Robert Rawdon. "Graffiti Become Terror: The Idea of Resistance." *Canadian Review of Comparative Literature* 22 (June 1995): 267–285.

Woods, Paul A. *King Pulp: The Wild World of Quentin Tarantino*. London: Plexus, 1998. www.magnoliamovie.com/MAGinfoPROD.html.

Yacowar, Maurice. "Thirteen Ways of Looking at *The Truman Show*" *Queen's Quarterly* 105, no. 3 (fall 1998): 423–433.

Zmijewsky, Boris, and Lee Pfeiffer. *The Films of Clint Eastwood*. Secaucus, N. J.: Carol Publishing Group, 1993.

Index of Scriptural Citations

Index of Modern Authors

Index of Subjects